Critical Perspectives on Hazing in Colleges and Universities

This important resource explores the political, cultural, and historical context of hazing at colleges and universities, and also highlights the diverse settings where hazing occurs on campus. Grounded in empirical practice and research, chapter authors discuss current hazing policies and implications to student success while challenging dangerous and harmful hazing habits. Unpacking common myths, this volume helps higher education and student affairs practitioners understand the implications of policy while providing best practices and practical tools for fostering safe and productive organizations on campus. *Critical Perspectives on Hazing in Colleges and Universities* helps readers continue to educate themselves in prevention while advocating for the lives of people affected by or vulnerable to hazing.

Cristóbal Salinas Jr. is an assistant professor in the educational leadership and research methodology department at Florida Atlantic University, USA.

Michelle L. Boettcher is an assistant professor in the College of Education at Clemson University, USA.

Critical Perspectives on Hazing in Colleges and Universities

A Guide to Disrupting Hazing Culture

Edited by
Cristóbal Salinas Jr. and
Michelle L. Boettcher

Routledge
Taylor & Francis Group
NEW YORK AND LONDON

First published 2018
by Routledge
711 Third Avenue, New York, NY 10017

and by Routledge
2 Park Square, Milton Park, Abingdon, Oxon, OX14 4RN

Routledge is an imprint of the Taylor & Francis Group, an informa business

© 2018 Taylor & Francis

The right of Cristóbal Salinas Jr. and Michelle L. Boettcher to be identified as the authors of the editorial material, and of the authors for their individual chapters, has been asserted in accordance with sections 77 and 78 of the Copyright, Designs and Patents Act 1988.

All rights reserved. No part of this book may be reprinted or reproduced or utilised in any form or by any electronic, mechanical, or other means, now known or hereafter invented, including photocopying and recording, or in any information storage or retrieval system, without permission in writing from the publishers.

Trademark notice: Product or corporate names may be trademarks or registered trademarks, and are used only for identification and explanation without intent to infringe.

Library of Congress Cataloging-in-Publication Data
A catalog record for this book has been requested

ISBN: 978-1-138-03851-6 (hbk)
ISBN: 978-1-138-03852-3 (pbk)
ISBN: 978-1-315-17731-1 (ebk)

Typeset in Perpetua and Bell Gothic
by Apex CoVantage, LLC

Contents

Preface   xi

Part 1
Hazing in Context: History and Personal Experiences   1

1   History and Definition of Hazing   3
     Cristóbal Salinas Jr. and Michelle L. Boettcher

        Hazing as Habit   3
        Hazing Defined   5
        History of Hazing   7
        Hazing Examples   8
        Conclusion   9
        Moving Forward   9

2   Testimonies: Hazing Firsthand   14
     Michelle L. Boettcher and Cristóbal Salinas Jr.

        Testimony 1: Band Hazing   15
        Testimony 2: Fraternal Organization Hazing   16
        Testimony 3: Athletics Hazing   17
        Testimony 4: Fraternity Hazing   19
        Discussion   20
        Testimony 5: Residential Life Hazing—Michelle L.
           Boettcher   21
        Testimony 6: Fraternal Organization Hazing—Cristóbal
           Salinas Jr.   22
        Conclusion   23

CONTENTS

Part 2
The Role of Hazing in Organizations 25

3 Hazing in Intercollegiate Athletics 27
   Ethan Swingle and Cristóbal Salinas Jr.

   Hazing and Intercollegiate Athletics *28*
   Hazing Events: How Likely Are They? *29*
   Proactive Education and Training Hazing Response
      and Accountability *32*
   Administrator, Coach, and Student-Athlete Roles *33*
   Conclusion *35*
   Case Studies *36*

4 Tradition or Torment: Examining Hazing in the College
   Marching Band 40
   Jason M. Silveira

   Marching Bands and Hazing *41*
   An Overview of the Literature *43*
   Future Research and Practice Recommendations *45*
   Case Studies *47*
   Conclusion *49*

5 Fraternity and Sorority Hazing 52
   S. Brian Joyce and Jenny Nirh

   History of Fraternities and Sororities *52*
   Hazing as an Ongoing Issue *54*
   What Is Tradition Really About in the Fraternity/Sorority
      Experience? *55*
   Hazing and Moral Disengagement *56*
   Current Trends *57*
   Challenges and Opportunities in Fraternity
      and Sorority Organizations *58*
   Case Studies *59*
   Conclusion *61*

6 An Overview of Military Hazing in University Programs 65
   Shawn Knight and Michelle L. Boettcher

   The Military and Higher Education *65*
   Definition of Hazing in the Military *66*
   Military Hazing *67*

Military-Related Hazing Cases *68*
Further Research Opportunities *71*
Case Studies *71*
Conclusion *73*

Part 3
Hazing Policies 75

**7 Lessons Learned About Hazing From an Executive Director of
National Organizations**   **77**
Mary Peterson

    Mary's Background *78*
    Hazing *79*
    Organizational Change *80*
    Leadership *81*
    Educational Training and Prevention *82*
    Reflection Questions *84*
    Conclusion *85*

8 Policy and Hazing at the Federal and State Levels   **86**
*Cristóbal Salinas Jr., Michelle L. Boettcher,
and Jennifer Plagman-Galvin*

    Public Policy on Hazing *86*
    State Definitions *86*
    Lack of Federal Guidance *87*
    Organizational Hazing Practices *88*
    A Special Case: The Obligation of Educational Institutions
       in Regard to Hazing *91*
    Disrupting Hazing Practices *92*
    Implications for Practice and Future Research *94*
    Conclusion *96*
    Hazing T-Chart Activity *97*

**9 Preventive or Reactionary? Emerging Policies on Hazing in
Postsecondary Education**   **101**
Cameron C. Beatty

    Reactionary Campus Policies *102*
    Key Considerations for Developing Hazing Prevention
       Policies *104*
    Organizational Reflection Questions *107*
    Conclusion *107*

Part 4
Hazing Prevention, Awareness, and Education 109

10 The Psychological Shadow of Hazing: Mental Health Issues
    and Counseling 111
    Raquel Botello and Natalie Carlos Cruz

   Differentiating Hazing From Bullying *111*
   Hazing Obedience and Conformity *113*
   Belonging and Group Membership *114*
   Psychological Consequences *115*
   Traumatic Hazing *116*
   Factors Increasing Vulnerability to Hazing *116*
   Assessment, Crisis Intervention, and Treatment *117*
   Implications for Research *119*
   Implications for Practitioners *120*
   Reflection Questions *121*
   Conclusion *121*

11 An Appreciative Approach to Hazing Prevention 126
    Jennifer L. Bloom and Amanda E. Propst Cuevas

   What Is Hazing? *126*
   An Appreciative Approach *130*
   Conclusion *134*

12 Preventing Hazing: Promising Practices for College and University
    Administrators and Professionals 137
    Michelle L. Boettcher, Cristina J. Perez, and Cristóbal Salinas Jr.

   Considerations *137*
   Efforts to Reduce and Eliminate Hazing *141*
   Reflection Questions *148*
   Conclusion *149*

13 Closing Discussion: Disrupting Hazing Myths as a Strategy to
    Changing Culture 152
    *Leslie Schacht Drey, Natalie Rooney, Michelle L. Boettcher,
    and Cristóbal Salinas Jr.*

   Myth 1: Everything Can Be Considered Hazing (Chapter 1) *152*
   Myth 2: Hazing Exists Only in Fraternities and Sororities
      (Chapters 4, 5, 6, 7, 12) *154*
   Myth 3: Women Are Not Hazed (Chapter 11) *154*

Myth 4: Only Physical Hazing Is Harmful (Chapters 11, 12, 13)   *155*
Myth 5: Hazing Builds Unity Among New Members
    (Preface, Chapters 3, 11, 12)   *156*
Myth 6: New Members *Want* to Be Hazed (Chapters 3, 11, 12)   *156*
Myth 7: If You Do Not Have the Same Experience as Those Before
    You, Then Your Membership Is Not Valid (Chapter 12)   *157*
Conclusion   *157*

Author Biographies 161
Index 165

Preface

Abuse. Alcohol. Affirmation. Blindfolds. Branding. Belonging. Criticism. Control. Community. Hazing is a set of habits that members claim create a sense of belonging among the group. These patterns of behavior have the potential to infiltrate every organization on a college campus. The cost of belonging, however, is sometimes higher than anyone expects. This text explores the issues related to hazing cultures and hazing habits in an attempt to preserve the values of affirmation, belonging, and community so essential to student success while disrupting notions of humiliation and exercises in physical, mental, and emotional pain that so many groups seem to value as a part of the belonging process.

Critical Perspectives on Hazing in Colleges and Universities: A Guide to Disrupting Hazing Culture is a critical analysis of the history, definition, culture, policy, and implications of hazing. Through empirical research and practice, the authors provide meaningful dialogue around hazing in each chapter by reflecting on the diverse contexts and complexities of hazing habits.

WHY WRITE THIS BOOK?

Often, when we engage in conversations with people about hazing, we receive one of two responses: (1) people do not know what hazing is, or (2) people avoid talking about hazing altogether. People often begin conversations by stating, "My organization is a non-hazing organization," and "I have never been hazed." Although this is true for many organizations, we also know that without a clear understanding of what hazing entails, people will—intentionally or not—default to hazing habits. In order to disrupt hazing, we must first define and understand it.

Hazing is still taboo in our communities and schools. It is taboo in the sense that we know we should not participate and engage in hazing but also taboo in the sense that we know (and organizational cultures reinforce) that we should not ever talk about hazing. With this text and the work of our coauthors, we seek to disrupt these notions and to bring the conversation into the open.

PREFACE

The overarching purpose of this book is to intentionally center the conversation of hazing at colleges and universities. In the process, we provide an overview of the history and different definitions of hazing and hazing culture, explore existing policy related to hazing, challenge the myths around hazing, and explore the implications for hazing on our campuses. This book calls for critical considerations of athletics, marching bands, fraternity and sorority life, and military hazing from both historical and contemporary perspectives. As such, this book will (1) provide a historical understanding of the role of hazing in colleges and universities with a focus on hazing myths and personal experiences, (2) highlight hazing policies and practices on our college campuses, (3) examine the role of hazing in different organizational contexts, and (4) provide promising practices for college and university administrators and student affairs practitioners.

Although this text is meant to be a resource for use across organizational types and across institutions, it is not intended to be an impersonal template. Rather, this is a highly personal and highly emotional work for those engaging with students and student organizations. There are real people whose lives have ended as a result of hazing—Tim Piazza, Raheel Sidiqui, Trevor Duffy, Chu Hsien Deng, Robert Champion, Max Gruver, Andrew Coffey, Matthew Ellis, and more—so do not mistake this work for mere abstraction or as a set of what-if questions. This work is very much focused on what is happening today and is driven by the question "What *now?*"

Hazing continues to be institutionalized at different organizational levels. Every year young people are physically, emotionally, and/or mentally injured, or students die due to a hazing-related activities. Although hazing experiences differ and institutions have different definitions and policies for hazing, we cannot use these distinctions as excuses to ignore, deny, or enable hazing.

Through the power and narrative experience of professionals and students, we aim to increase hazing awareness and to provide an understanding of the student experience as it relates to hazing. This text includes topics about the implications of hazing activities and university policies for student success while challenging dangerous and harmful hazing habits. To reform culture, we must first immerse ourselves in that culture. This knowledge is important on paper in the form of policies, but it is even more important in person through the education of students and organizations and effective enforcement of institutional hazing policies with an ultimate goal of developing healthy, transformative, and productive student experiences.

We hope that you, the readers, continue not only to educate yourselves but also to advocate for the lives of people affected by or vulnerable to hazing. We must continue to educate and train in hazing prevention and inspire our students to prevent hazing and stop historically and organizationally established hazing habits. No one should be humiliated, degraded, or intimidated in order to find a sense of belonging and to be validated on campus. Our hope is that this book builds on the powerful work already being done on this topic and encourages individuals and communities to become agents of change.

Critical Perspectives on Hazing in Colleges and Universities: A Guide to Disrupting Hazing Culture is a book intended for student affairs practitioners, graduate programs, and scholars researching hazing. This book can be useful to practitioners in fraternity and sorority life, student conduct, leadership programming, staff in student activities, organizational advisers, and other professionals working with student groups and student policies. For student affairs practitioners and graduate programs, the book provides a comprehensive view of hazing on campus, and the chapters are useful to individuals developing and implementing membership education and leadership orientation/training for fraternity and sorority life, marching band programs, athletics, military services programs, and other student organizations with hazing habits. For faculty and scholars focused on higher education and student affairs, this book is a valuable resource for examining the history of higher education, current events, student engagement, higher education policy, and crisis management and response.

Additionally, this book is useful to students themselves. As students assume positions of leadership and power within organizations and other higher education settings, it is important for them to know what hazing looks like and what the potential impact of hazing practices might be. The text is intentionally designed to be approachable and useful to this wide variety of groups in order to reach as many audiences as possible.

HOW THIS BOOK IS ORGANIZED

Each book chapter provides practical takeaways and promising practices for student affairs practitioners, graduate programs, and scholars engaged in hazing prevention and awareness programming or research. Additionally, case studies, discussion questions, and/or activities throughout the text can be used to further engage readers to think and talk about the hazing context and its implications.

This book is divided into four parts focused on key aspects of hazing—history, hazing in organizations, policy, and best practices. Beginning with Part 1: Hazing in Context: History and Personal Experiences, Salinas and Boettcher provide definitions and a foundational understanding related to hazing in higher education.

In Part 2: The Role of Hazing in Organizations, Swingle and Salinas open with an examination of hazing in athletics, Silveira looks at hazing in marching band culture, Joyce and Nirh explore hazing in the context of fraternity and sorority life, and Knight and Boettcher look at hazing in military cultures. This section moves beyond stereotypical narratives of hazing being simply a fraternity issue and examines how hazing practices and behaviors surface in other contexts.

In Part 3: Hazing Policies, the authors explore the complexity of hazing and the lack of a centralized policy or oversight agency. Peterson examines hazing policy through the lens of national fraternity organizations; Salinas, Boettcher, and Plagman-Galvin look at federal- and state-level hazing legislation; and Beatty examines emerging higher education hazing policies.

Although the first parts of the book shine a light on the hidden aspects of hazing, the last part offers strategies for transforming organizational practices in higher education. In Part 4: Hazing Prevention, Awareness, and Education, Botello and Cruz examine hazing from a counseling and mental health perspective. Next, Bloom and Cuevas explore the potential effect of cross-organizational advising and appreciative advising practices on hazing. Boettcher, Perez, and Salinas take a look to the future and focus on cultural transformation, discussing what has been done effectively in the past, lessons learned by former conduct and fraternity and student life administrators, and how to anticipate and proactively address hazing-related behaviors in the future. Additionally, this chapter provides reflective questions to guide professionals and organizations as they seek to foster student involvement in safe and community-focused ways. The book's final chapter is designed to build on the case studies throughout the text. In addition to organization- and topic-specific case studies, in order to truly transform culture related to hazing on campus, we must look at hazing more broadly. In the final chapter, Schacht Drey, Rooney, Boettcher, and Salinas present a series of hazing myths in the form of case studies.

Our goal was to produce a comprehensive resource that examines hazing in a variety of contexts. We know that ours contributes to the existing literature, and not everything related to hazing culture is in this—or any—single text. For example, the specific role of race, gender, and other identities is not thoroughly examined here (see Parks, Jones, Ray, & Hughes, 2015).

Similarly, this text does not thoroughly unpack the unique issues facing chapters today related to alcohol or Title IX/sexual misconduct. What this text does do, however, is to provide a more holistic view of hazing cultures across organizations in higher education. Here we attempt to disrupt the myth or underlying narrative that hazing happens in fraternities and nowhere else. We also provide case studies, resources, and approaches to hazing education as well as strategies for disrupting hazing habits and histories in organizations.

Our Positionalities

Just as we have invited other authors and we encourage readers to reflect on their own experiences with hazing, we must also reflect on our experiences as well. As we engaged in this project, we have learned to speak out, ask difficult questions, and bring ourselves to this work. We come to this project with different perspectives. As editors and authors of this book, we have been members of organizations where hazing-related behaviors have taken place. We have engaged in research and educational programming related to hazing. We have developed and enacted

PREFACE

policy and education on this topic, have been student organization advisers, have advised national fraternity and sorority headquarters, and have presented on this topic at various colleges and universities. In an attempt to be even more transparent, here are statements about who we are as authors, scholars, and professionals in this work.

Cristóbal

I am a brother of Sigma Lambda Beta International Fraternity. I currently work as a faculty member at Florida Atlantic University, where I teach courses in higher education leadership. Throughout my educational career, I have been interested in understanding the impact of hazing on college students. Since my undergraduate career at the University of Nebraska at Kearney until now, I have challenged many members of fraternities and sororities in conversations on hazing.

In the past, I have worked in the anti-hazing education members' committee for Sigma Lambda Beta International Fraternity, and I coauthor and colead their national leadership institute, where men and masculinities and hazing were the focus themes of the institute curriculum. I have engaged with student organizations throughout the country by sharing my personal story in relationship to hazing and by providing tools to prevent, avoid, and stop hazing. I am called to do this work because I know hazing can take away life. We cannot allow individuals, families, and communities of people to be victims of hazing.

Michelle

My background is primarily in housing and residence life at Iowa State University, Ohio University, the University of Cincinnati, and the University of Arkansas. Just prior to taking my assistant professor position at Clemson University, I worked for 7 years as assistant dean of students and director of judicial affairs at Iowa State University. In that role, my work focused on policy, education, training, and enforcement. Working in judicial affairs, we were responsible for student organization violations, including hazing violations. Our office collaborated with fraternity and sorority life staff on hazing education, including partnering with fraternity and sorority life judicial board members. That said, we rarely received reports directly from people who had been hazed in these or other organizations. Sometimes chapters contacted us to share things they had seen other chapters doing, and sometimes we got reports from friends who were concerned about people being hazed. At least one time, our staff witnessed hazing activity firsthand right outside the windows of our offices.

As a result of my work in student affairs and my lived experiences in higher education, I have been hazed, I have hazed others, I have educated in order to prevent hazing habits, and I have held people responsible for hazing habits. All these things inform who I am today as an educator, a scholar, and an individual. All these things have also inspired me to take on this project with Cristóbal.

Testimonies

Finally, in an effort to continue our work to be transparent, we each provide a testimony in Chapter 3. At first, we had planned on including those here, but we realized they serve a greater purpose as a part of the testimonials others have been so generous and brave in sharing. We hope that those parts of our stories can add to the work of others and serve as ways to help pull back the curtain on hazing habits, foster further conversation around hazing, and help to transform organizations in higher education. We seek to support students and organizations in developing healthy senses of belonging for members in place of the abuse and humiliation of hazing habits.

CONCLUSION: FINDING LANGUAGE

Blindfolding, handcuffing, kidnapping, scavenger hunts, mandatory road trips, excessive exercise, forced alcohol consumption, forced drug use, personal servitude, inequitable duties, obligatory labor, the exercise of power by senior members over new members, deception, demeaning new members—in short, any type of physical, verbal, emotional, or mental abuse. These are just a few examples of hazing practices implemented on college campuses across the country. This book critically examines membership and community practices in order to disrupt the role pain and humiliation play in many organizational cultures. Each chapter will engage readers in critical reflection and conversations on hazing. In addition to providing hazing scenarios, the book offers information on how to prevent hazing and how to report it.

We hope you enjoy this book and find the authors' passion and expertise useful in your work and learning. Our goal is that you have additional resources and knowledge by the end of each chapter to share with students, organizations, and institutions related to hazing. Ultimately, our goal is that you find yourselves inspired to disrupt, stand against, and stop hazing. Hazing is not an abstraction; it is not innocent. Hazing hurts people. Hazing kills people.

We cannot be silent bystanders. We cannot be complicit in violence and fear perpetuated every year on our campuses. We must disrupt. We must discuss. We must find language to talk about hazing.

Pocos Pero Locos/A Few Crazy Fools

It is with the idea of lacking language and failing to talk about hazing that we conclude with the following poem. Throughout the process of working on this book, we learned that there is no direct translation of hazing for many languages. In cases

PREFACE

where there is some form of the word, just as in U.S. culture, the term is often not used, is misused, or is misunderstood, as hazing is taboo in many cultures.

Although there are not always direct translations of the term *hazing*, some countries have adopted language to recognize that violent events occur in the development of organizations. Hazing in Spanish roughly translates to *novatadas* (which means more literally a practical joke—not the same as hazing), and in French it is *bizutage* (sometimes defined as education or initiation but often including references to abuse in some form). In Brazil, *trote* (prank) is used, and in Chile, *el mechoneo* is used to refer to the verbal, physical, and mental abuse that is used to "welcome" first-year university students. In Venezuela, *el bautizo* (baptism) is used as the metaphor for baptizing new students through hazing events at educational institutions.

In order to emphasize the lack of clarity around language related to hazing (unclear definitions, an unwillingness to talk about the topic) and to reach beyond the campus cultures in this country and to create awareness more globally, we decided to end our introduction with the poem *Pocos pero Locos*. Cristóbal Salinas (2012) wrote this poem in 2012. The poem uses key terms that represent the secretive hazing experiences of individuals.

The poem also represents and validates the trauma that some fraternity men have faced related to secrecy and silence when hazing occurs. Although the poem was first written in Spanish and with the purpose to educate Spanish-speaking communities of people, we must be clear that hazing happens in all communities of people.

We have provided an English translation of the poem, but we recognize that it loses some meaning and significance in translation from Spanish. As Salinas (2017) asserted, we hope that this poem in Spanish "inspires readers to write and promote the Spanish language as a method of healing and to fight a system that has erased history, stories, knowledge, emotions, and many lived experiences" (p. 755). We believe that just as talking is essential, writing (whether through a book like this or a poem like the one that follows) about hazing can help document the lived hazing experiences that are often dismissed, and it can create awareness of hazing among all communities of people.

Pocos pero Locos	A Few Crazy Fools
Bienvenidos al reto.	*Welcome to the challenge*
No entiendo, estoy perdido, y no me respetan,	*I do not understand, I am lost, and they don't respect me,*
Me gritan, me insultan, me mandan, y me ignoran.	*They shout at me, they insult me, they tell me what to do, and they ignore me.*
La Pinta, la Niña, y la Santa María,	*La Pinta, La Niña, y La Santa María,*
Venimos con estrés,	*We come with stress,*
Vivimos entre locos pero pocos,	*We live among a few crazy fools*
Es un hecho, que al caso no lo vez.	*It's a fact; don't you see it?*
Vivimos con historia,	*We live in history,*

(*Continued*)

(Continued)

Pocos pero Locos	A Few Crazy Fools
Paciencia requerida para soportar,	*Patience is required to endure,*
Vivimos confundidos y perdidos,	*We live confused and lost,*
Y ellos siguen sin respetar.	*And they continue to disrespect us.*
Ya estoy cansado de llevar rocas en el bolsillo,	*I am tired of carrying rocks in my pockets,*
Ya no soporto los gritos y los insultos,	*I cannot stand the shouting and insults,*
No les gusta mi trabajo que se sienten a mi lado,	*If you don't like my work, you should come and sit next to me.*
Mi gente es siempre firme,	*My people are always firm,*
Acaso no lo has notado.	*Perhaps you have not noticed.*
Son clases poderosas,	*They are powerful classes,*
Niños que quieren educar,	*Children who want to educate*
Pero en vez de dar clase,	*But instead of teaching,*
Nos ayudan a sofocar.	*They help us to be suffocated.*
Echarle ganas, y mejor que sobresalgas,	*Continue to work hard and you better excel,*
Si te vas no regresaras,	*If you go away, you will not return,*
Todos somos como las estrellas fugases.	*We are all like the shooting stars.*
Nos quieren sacar los ojos,	*They want to take our eyes out,*
Somos causa de su enojo.	*We are the cause of their anger.*
Cero drogas, Cero compasión,	*Zero drugs, zero compassion,*
Pero al final hay mucha tentación.	*But in the end, there is a lot of temptation.*
Hace un año éramos desconocidos,	*A year ago, we were strangers,*
Este año somos reconocidos,	*This year, we are recognized,*
Nos perdimos entre gritos e insultos,	*We got lost between shouts and insults,*
Pero nos hayamos entre los morados.	*But we have found ourselves among the Purple nation/individuals.*
El secreto es que es una obra,	*The secret is that everything is a play,*
Que tiembla y tiembla.	*That shakes and shakes.*
Vivimos entre locos pero pocos,	*We live among a few crazy fools,*
Es un hecho, que si nos equivocamos	*It's a fact, if we make a mistake,*
El poso no perdona.	*The grave will not forgive us.*
Tiene precio.	*It has a price.*
Aunque suene tan sencillo,	*Although it sounds so simple,*
Llevo todos los ladrillos,	*I carry all the bricks,*
Hasta que se cansen los niños,	*Until the children get tired,*
Y de gritar los grillos.	*And the crickets of shouting.*
Todo es como un tornillo,	*Everything is like a screw,*
Hipócritas	*Hypocrites.*
Buscan como humillar,	*They seek how to humiliate*
Pero al final todo es un amar.	*But in the end everything is love.*
Nos pisaron como ratas,	*They step on us like rats,*
Son pocos pero locos,	*They are a few crazy fools,*
Pero todos nos amamos.	*But we love each other.*
No es tan fácil,	*It is not so easy,*
Aunque suene tan sencillo,	*Although it sounds so simple,*
Pintare cada ladrillo,	*I will paint each brick*
De nuestro Castillo.	*Of our castle.*
Mis talentos con ellos no están de sobra,	*My talents with them are well utilized,*
Nos unimos los mejores porque solo estos sobreviven,	*We unite the best because the best only survive,*
Nada tememos, nos unimos, y lo dudo cabrones que nos deriven.	*We fear nothing, we unite, And I doubt those bastards will derive us.*

Thank you for taking the time to engage in this dialogue, this communication, this language, and this work.

—Cristóbal and Michelle

REFERENCES

Parks, G. S., Jones, S. E., Shayne, E., Ray, R., & Hughey, M. W. (2015). White boys drink, Black girls yell: A racialized and gendered analysis of violent hazing and the law. *Journal of Gender, Race, and Justice, 18*(1), 93–158.

Salinas, C. (2012, February 1). Locos Pero Pocos. *Blogging La Voz: NASPA Latino Knowledge Community blog.* NASPA-Student Affairs Administrators in Higher Education; Latino Knowledge Community. Washington, DC. Retrieved from http://latinoakc.blogspot.com/2012/02/locos-pero-pocos.html

Salinas, C. (2017). Transforming academia and theorizing spaces for Latinx in higher education: *Voces perdidas, Voces de poder. International Journal of Qualitative Studies in Education, 30*(3), 747–758. doi:10.1080/09518398.2017.1350295

Part 1
Hazing in Context
History and Personal Experiences

Chapter 1
History and Definition of Hazing

Cristóbal Salinas Jr. and Michelle L. Boettcher

Discussing contemporary hazing practices and future implications without the historical context of the topic is impossible, and even trying to do so is irresponsible. That said, it does not mean that this is an easy task. The dialogue around hazing is limited by the secrecy of organizations, fear of retaliation, and an unhealthy construction of loyalty and community. Additionally, our hazing conversations are limited by our vocabulary (or lack thereof) related to the topic. Before exploring hazing, before examining current events, and before looking at future practices, training, and education, it is important to establish a common understanding of the terms related to hazing and the history of hazing practices.

Hazing is a term with a broad definition that encompasses a variety of activities, rituals, and rites of passage to which individuals are subjected in order to gain organization, group, or team membership (McGlone, 2010). Although hazing practices are present in many organizational settings in the United States—military organizations, athletic teams, marching bands, and honor societies, as well as fraternity and sorority life organizations—this chapter is focused on providing foundational definitions and context upon which to build a larger dialogue. Our approach has been to examine documents in order to critically examine hazing definitions, laws, and policies at the state and national levels. This approach provides us with a systemic perspective about hazing—where we are as a country and in higher education in defining hazing behaviors.

HAZING AS HABIT

Throughout this chapter, we refer to hazing activities as habits instead of traditions. Although the word *tradition* is steeped in history, pride, and organizational backstories, we seek to disrupt this idea when it comes to the role of hazing in the experiences of organizational members. We utilize habits because many of the hazing practices in place are not directly related to pride or healthy community development but are practices implemented without critical thought. Covey (1998) wrote that habits are simply actions, practices, and behaviors done repeatedly: We become what we repeatedly do. There are good habits, such as planning ahead or showing respect, bad habits, like blaming or hazing peers, and neutral habits, including eating French fries with ranch dressing or reading a book from back to front.

In contrast, traditions are the inherited and established customs, beliefs, and values that have been passed from generation to generation. Traditions are important in identifying barriers and obstacles in order to successfully create organizational and institutional change (Kezar, 2003). Therefore, we argue against the notion of hazing as tradition and challenge individuals who practice habits of hazing to reflect on how hazing is experiential learning *without reflection or intention*. Habits are simple replication, while traditions are intentionally developed and established foundations of organizations. Traditions serve to build a sense of connection, healthy bonds among members, and a strong community based on common goals, interests, beliefs, and values.

We further challenge group members, faculty, staff, administrators, and those outside of higher education to think about how hazing reflects (or fails to reflect) the core values of organizations. Having a full understanding of organizational and institutional values can serve to further disrupt hazing practices by bringing to light inconsistencies between what organizations stand for philosophically and what behaviors organizations are unwilling to tolerate.

Throughout this first chapter, we bring together a diversity of experiences and perspectives that highlight the context and complexity of hazing within military organizations, on athletic teams, among marching band members, and in the context of fraternity and sorority life (FSL) organizations. This is intentional, as much of the focus on hazing behaviors centers solely on FSL and even more specifically on fraternity behaviors. We acknowledge that hazing takes place in a variety of organizational contexts. We also acknowledge that the four areas highlighted here are not the only organizations where we might explore hazing. Our hope is to begin the dialogue with these examples and to provide information that is transferable across other organizational contexts.

To advance the development and growth of organizations and institutions as well as the safety of members, anti-hazing education is essential, strong policies are required, and hazing habits must be effectively disrupted. No one should be humiliated, degraded, demeaned, or intimidated in order to feel a sense of belonging. In fact, we argue that those who put potential or new members in positions to be hazed are not leaders of organizations but perpetrators of violence. With that in mind, we intentionally use the term *perpetrator*—as a person who carries out a harmful, illegal, or immoral act—to refer to an individual who humiliates, degrades, abuses, or endangers others through hazing.

HAZING DEFINED

Hazing activities have occurred and been acknowledged for centuries, yet there is no universally accepted definition of hazing (McGlone, 2010). Although hazing is illegal in 44 states (Allan & Madden, 2008; Bailey & Hughey, 2013; StopHazing. org, 2018), the term *hazing* has various definitions and can be perceived differently by individuals, organizations, and institutions. As a result, in order to define hazing, multiple viewpoints must be considered. For example, a perpetrator might have a different definition than the individual being hazed. An administrator may define hazing differently than a coach. Or a college or university policy might define hazing differently from state law. Additionally, some definitions may consider only physical (nonsexual) activities as hazing while others include mental and physical (including sexual) acts (McGlone, 2010).

Allan and Madden (2008) defined hazing as "any activity expected of someone joining or participating in a group that humiliates, degrades, abuses, or endangers them regardless of a person's willingness to participate" (p. 2). Lipkins (2006) defined hazing as

> a process, based on a tradition [habit] that is used by groups to discipline and to maintain a hierarchy (i.e., a pecking order). Regardless of consent, the rituals require individuals to engage in activities that are physically and psychologically stressful.
>
> (p. 13)

Similarly, Finkel (2002) defined hazing as "committing acts against an individual or forcing an individual into committing an act that creates a risk for harm in order for the individual to be initiated into or affiliated with an organization" (p. 228). Cholbi (2009) defined hazing as

> Any method of initiation into a student organization, or any pastime or amusement engaged in with regard to such an organization that causes, or is likely to cause bodily danger or physical or emotional harm to any member of the campus community.
>
> (p. 144)

According to McGlone (2010), hazing activities can be organized into two main categories: physical and mental. Physical hazing may include beatings, branding, paddling, excessive exercises, drinking alcohol or other substances, using drugs, and sexual activities. Sexual assaults are included here because simulated sex acts, sodomy, and forced kissing are sometimes included in hazing processes. In essence, all sexual acts are physical assaults, but physical assaults in the hazing process can include things other than sexual assaults.

Mental hazing is often overlooked or goes undetected, but it can be as serious and dangerous as physical hazing. Mental hazing can be harder to report because not only are there are no physical marks but also expressing mental or emotional distress can be very difficult. Types of mental hazing may include verbal abuse, being blindfolded, being restrained, and being locked in confined spaces.

There is overlap between these types of hazing. Both physical and mental hazing activities may include but are not limited to alcohol consumption, sexual activities, paddling, physical and psychological shocks, fatigue, scavenger hunts, blindfolding, being locked in a confined space, involuntary road trips, and any other behaviors that are inconsistent with the organizational, institutional, or state policies and laws (Keim, 2000). The results of these hazing activities can be exhausting, humiliating, degrading, demeaning, and intimidating, with significant physical and emotional discomfort (Lipkins, 2006). The effect of the stress of these activities required for joining a group—despite their common practice and the ongoing use of these habits for community building—are negative. Researchers have found that individuals at colleges and universities "perceive hazing as harmful" (Campo, Poulos, & Sipple, 2005, p. 146).

Hazing activities can have negative physical and mental effects on the short and long-term well-being of individuals. Researchers found that although the severity of initiation increased the attractiveness of a group, it also generated feelings of frustration, loneliness, and depression for those being hazed (Finkel, 2002; Hollmann, 2002; Lipkins, 2006). In other words, the more challenging the hazing process for an organization, the more people who aspire to be members and the more those members experience isolation and other mental and emotional distress throughout the process. Moreover, severe feelings of shame, self-blame, and posttraumatic stress can be experienced by victims of hazing practices, along with adverse effects on students' academic performance (Maxwell, 2011). Hazing has been defined in multiple ways, which can create misunderstanding and conflict in regard to recognizing when hazing occurs. As a result of misunderstanding and lack of awareness of hazing, there have been various myths that have come to fruition.

Hazing has been defined in multiple ways, which can create misunderstanding, foster a lack of awareness, and generate conflict in recognizing when hazing occurs. As a result, myths have emerged, and they are explored in this book. As referenced earlier, hazing involves forcing potential members to engage in harmful and degrading activities in order to become members of an organization (Allan & Madden, 2008; Cholbi, 2009; Finkel, 2002; Holmes, 2013; Lipkins, 2006). Hazing habits include behaviors that play upon power and hierarchy. Throughout this book, the hazing definitions compiled here provide language to identify hazing habits based on scholarly research and applied in the contexts of athletics, fraternity and sorority life, military, and marching bands.

HISTORY OF HAZING

Understanding the complexity of hazing is challenging, as the history of these habits goes back centuries. In ancient Greece and Rome, rituals for educating and mentoring boys were done through hazing practices (Finkel, 2002; Lipkins, 2006; Nuwer, 2001). Lipkins (2006) found that those activities included kidnapping, requiring sexual favors, and slavery. During the Middle Ages (1000–1399), European college students were systematically hazed as a part of the transition into and membership within higher education. For example, new college students drank urine and endured such physical torture as scraping skin off their ears. Lipkins (2006) wrote that school administrations believed beating, humiliation, and servitude were good ways to teach obedience in educational settings. In the 16th century, Martin Luther claimed that hazing "strengthened the student and prepared him for the obstacles of adulthood" (Lipkins, 2006, p. 3).

In the 1660s, Oxford University students who came to Harvard University introduced beating, humiliation, servitude, and other hazing practices (e.g., wearing special clothes, running personal errands) as ways to teach obedience to their peers. These practices were adapted, published by Harvard sophomores, and distributed to first-year students. In 1781, Harvard's Phi Beta Kappa fraternity began using hazing practices and activities, which are still present in the fraternity and sorority life system (Lipkins, 2006; Shirley, 2014). Since the 1660s, hazing has been reported and has spread to other colleges and universities across the United States.

Hazing practices have become a problem of epidemic proportions in higher education (Bauer Raposo et al., 2015). The practice of hazing was initially a requirement in order to graduate from school and was originally referred to by the term *pennalism*. It was believed that the students who were graduating needed to be properly groomed (Finkel, 2002). Hazing practices were abolished in the 1700s as a result of serious injuries and deaths but were revived in the 18th and 19th centuries (Finkel, 2002). In the late 1800s, hazing practices were documented in the realm of higher education, including the incidents of "fagging," the practice in which upperclassmen students forced underclassmen to act as their servants (Finkel, 2002). Hazing in the late 1800s was a product of the class system, whereby students who entered at the same time were considered members of a single class throughout their college courses (Solberg, 1998).

Since the resurgence of hazing in the 18th and 19th centuries, hazing practices have spread far beyond academic classes. Current hazing has taken root in such areas as the military, marching bands, and fraternity and sorority life, resulting in a surge in student deaths related to these practices. According to Hollmann (2002), hazing practices yielded 35 deaths in more than 100 years between 1838 and 1969, whereas in the decade of the 1970s, 31 students died due to hazing practices. From the years 1980 to 1989, the death toll due to hazing increased to

55 and nearly doubled to 95 deaths during the 1990s (Hollmann, 2002). Since 1990, more deaths have occurred on college and university campuses as a result of hazing, pledging, initiation accidents, and fraternity alcohol-related incidents than all other hazing incidents in recorded history (Hollmann, 2002). As stated earlier, hazing practices have been around and are expected to continue in our society, and we all must make a conscious effort to address and eradicate these habits.

HAZING EXAMPLES

Compared to the past, hazing today is "more frequent, more demanding, more violent, and much more sexual" (Lipkins, 2006, p. 4). Hazing is frequent and relevant in today's society; it continues to occur in student organizations (fraternities, sororities, cheerleading, band, choir, speech, debate, athletic teams, honor societies) and even in church groups. Examples of more recent hazing incidents include the following:

- In the fall of 2011 at Florida A&M University, Robert Champion was hazed and killed during the Marching 100 band trip to the Florida Classic at the Orland Citrus Bowl. Robert Champion was pummeled with fists and bass drum mallets and died with multiple blunt trauma blows to his body within an hour after being hazed (Gast & Levs, 2011; Grasgreen, 2011). More of this hazing accident can be found in Chapter 4.
- In September 2012, Maine West High School soccer coaches were accused of sanctioning the sexual assault of three soccer players in a hazing ritual. The coaches, who ordered the team do a "campus run," which was code for hazing activity, sanctioned the hazing. The three boys were shoved to the ground and beaten by the older senior soccer players (Huffington Post, 2012; Silverberg, 2012).
- In September 2012, the University of Iowa received complaints of hazing and sexual assault allegations in 2008 and 2009 against Sigma Alpha Epsilon, Iowa Beta Chapter. The chapter was closed and removed from the university, and more than 60 members were suspended (Hennigan, 2012).
- On November 2, 2012, David Bogenberger was found dead at Pi Kappa Alpha fraternity house at Northern Illinois University. Alcohol poisoning and cardiac arrhythmia were found to be the causes of death. Twenty-two Pi Kappa Alpha members were arrested and charged with the felony hazing (NBC Chicago, 2012).
- In the fall of 2013 at Pennsylvania State University, Phi Sigma Kappa fraternity was found guilty of hazing its pledges. A pledge committed suicide the semester after he joined the fraternity, and it was alleged that the cause was related to hazing incidents. Pledges were forced to binge drink, endure sleep deprivation of 89 hours, and fight each other (Logue, 2016).

Although the incidents outlined here are devastating, these represent only those cases that become public. That said, it is impossible to collect and track every hazing experience. There currently exists no centralized clearinghouse to report, sort, collect, and maintain records on hazing activities across the country. Although we can reference incidents from recent media accounts, the roots of hazing are much deeper, and the shadow of hazing habits is much larger than those cases we actually hear about.

Therefore, even if a database of hazing incidents did exist, reports of hazing are limited. Among students who witness hazing, 36% said they would not report it because they do not know whom to tell, and 27% would not report hazing because students are not sure how to handle hazing and the reporting process correctly (Alfred University, 2000). Additionally, themes of membership, belonging, and loyalty become blurred around hazing, as keeping organizational secrets is a point of pride for members and an obstacle to transparency when it comes to hazing reform.

CONCLUSION

Hazing has been documented since the Middle Ages (1000–1399). In this chapter we have drawn from definitions of a variety of scholars and ultimately defined hazing as the use of power and hierarchy to force new or potential members to engage in humiliating activities in order to become members of an organization. However, understanding the history and definitions of hazing is a small but important first step in the process of eliminating hazing habits from student organizations and across higher education (and beyond). Having this foundation is important, but research, education, and outreach must continue in order to connect with communities about hazing and to take those important next steps to replacing hazing habits with healthy team- and community-building practices.

Although this book focuses primarily on hazing in college and university settings (athletics, fraternity and sorority life, marching bands, and military organizations), we must recognize and acknowledge that hazing is not only historically but also institutionally and culturally embedded. Hazing is prevalent in all our cultural institutions, including schools, religion, business, and government. Although there are rites and rituals based on organizational traditions, there are also abusive hazing practices that infiltrate our most trusted and necessary social institutions.

MOVING FORWARD

In order to provide a starting point for this work, our first chapter does not wrap up with a tidy conclusion. There is much work to be done, so rather than bringing closure to this chapter, we instead provide three next steps. To prepare readers for maximizing the use of this book, we first offer a series of reflection questions and then present two activities to set the stage for the disruptive work of dismantling hazing habits.

The following questions are designed for use at the individual (leader/adviser/administrator) and organizational levels. Before looking at what else is out there, we encourage readers to examine their own organizations and behaviors.

Reflection

- What is your definition of hazing?
- What actions, behaviors, or activities do you consider hazing practices?
- Have you experience hazing? If so, what were those hazing behaviors? How did you respond at the time?
- If you experienced hazing or saw it being done to someone else, what steps (if any) would you take to stop it? Would you report it? If so, where? If not, why not?

The Hazing Box

We introduce the hazing box activity (see Figures 1.1 and 1.2) to help others understand and engage in critical thinking and reflection about hazing habits. All participants should get two copies of the hazing box activity (Figure 1.1). The activity's purpose is to help individuals create their own definitions of hazing and what hazing looks like to them. First, inside the box, individuals should answer the questions: What is your definition of hazing? What is hazing? And why do people haze? The left side of the box is labeled "Physical Abuse," and the right side of the box is labeled "Mental Abuse." The physical and mental abuse sides are for individuals to describe what hazing looks like physically and mentally. Figure 1.2 is an example of a completed hazing box.

Hazing Box Activity

| Physical Abuse | What is your definition of hazing?
What is hazing?
Why do people haze? | Mental Abuse |
|---|---|---|//

FIGURE 1.1 Hazing Box Activity

Physical Abuse	Need to secure their place/membership	Mental Abuse
Beating	To develop respect	Verbal abuse
Branding	To build leadership and strength	Being blindfolded
Paddling	Rite of passage	Being captured and locked in small places
Excessive exercises	Discipline	
Drinking alcohol or abusing other substances	Maintain hierarchy	
	Maintain "culture and tradition"	

FIGURE 1.2 Example of a Hazing Box Activity

Why Activities?

The preceding prompts and activities are examples of how to start the conversation about hazing. The point is that the dialogue must happen, organizations and individuals must engage in reflective practice, and education is essential in order to disrupt hazing habits. Whether using these activities and questions or others specific to organizational or institutional contexts, the key is to no longer choose silence but to shed light on the hazing habits that hurt those who are hazed, the perpetrators of hazing, organizations, and our larger culture. We can no longer afford to be silent and secretive. The costs are too high.

REFERENCES

Alfred University. (2000). *Initiation rites in American high schools: A national survey*. Retrieved from www.alfred.edu/hs_hazing/

Allan, E. J., & Madden, M. (2008). *Hazing in view: College students at risk*. Retrieved from www.stophazing.org/wp-content/uploads/2014/06/hazing_in_view_web1.pdf

Bailey, H. E., & Hughey, A. H. (2013, January 16). A realistic, pro-active approach to eradicating hazing for Greek organization. *Diverse Issues in Higher Education*. Retrieved from http://diverseeducation.com/article/50714/#

Bauer Raposo, B.Y., Nunes, C. S., Martins, M. J. D., Mendes, M., Pinho, B. S., & Silva, O. (2015). About hazing in higher education. *European Scientific Journal*, August 2015 (special edition), 1–17.

Campo, S., Poulos, G., & Sipple, J. W. (2005). Prevalence and profiling: Hazing among college students and points of intervention. *American Journal of Health Behavior*, 29(2), 137–149.

Cholbi, M. (2009). On hazing. *Public Affairs Quarterly*, 23(2), 143–160.

Covey, S. (1998). *The 7 habits of highly effective teens*. New York, NY: Fireside.

Finkel, M. A. (2002). Traumatic injuries caused by hazing practices. *American Journal of Emergency Medicine, 20*(3), 228–233.

Gast, P., & Levs, J. (2011, December 14). For many in FAMU band, pain a part of admission process. *CNN Justice*. Retrieved from www.cnn.com/2011/12/13/justice/florida-hazing-charges

Grasgreen, A. (2011, December 23). Hazing beyond the frat house. *Inside Higher Ed*. Retrieved from www.insidehighered.com/news/2011/12/23/florida-am-death-illuminates-prevalence-non-greek-hazing

Hennigan, G. (2012, September 25). University of Iowa fraternity suspended; hazing alleged. *The Gazette*. Retrieved from www.thegazette.com/2012/09/25/university-of-iowa-fraternity-suspended-for-hazing

Hollmann, B. B. (2002). Hazing: Hidden campus crime. *New Directions for Student Services, 99*, 11–23.

Holmes, R. W. (2013). *How to eradicate hazing*. Bloomington, IN: AuthorHouse.

Huffington Post. (2012, November 11). West Maine High School hazing: Another incident involving coach Michael DiVincenzo reported. *Huffington Post Education*. Retrieved from www.huffingtonpost.com/2012/11/26/another-hazing-incident-i_n_2193287.html

Keim, W. (2000). *The power of caring*. Retrieved from www.stophazing.org/definition

Kezar, A. (2003). Achieving student success: Strategies for creating partnerships between academic and student affairs. *NASPA Journal, 41*(1), 1–22.

Lipkins, S. (2006). *Preventing hazing: How parents, teachers and coaches can stop the violence, harassment and humiliation*. San Francisco, CA: Jossey-Bass.

Logue, J. (2016, March). Restroom unrest. *Inside Higher Ed*. Retrieved from www.insidehighered.com/news/2016/03/28/north-carolina-bathroom-law-could-change-practices-public-colleges-and-universities

Maxwell, T. (2011). *The hidden harm of hazing: Shame*. Retrieved from www.hazingprevention.org

McGlone, C. A. (2010). Hazy viewpoints: Administrators' perceptions of hazing. *International Journal of Sport Management and Marketing, 7*, 119–131.

NBC Chicago. (2012, December 17). 22 arrest warrants issued after alleged fraternity hazing death at Northern Illinois. *NBC News*. Retrieved from http://usnews.nbcnews.com/_news/2012/12/17/15976992-22-arrest-warrants-issued-after-alleged-fraternity-hazing-death-at-northern-illinois?lite

Nuwer, H. (2001). *Wrongs of passage: Fraternities, sororities, hazing, and binge drinking*. Bloomington: Indiana University Press.

Shirley, Z. E. (2014). *Declining participation in fraternity and sorority life: A comparison of perceptions of Greek-lettered organizations between affiliated and non-affiliated students* (Unpublished dissertation). University of North Texas, Denton.

Silverberg, M. (2012, November 25). District says 2008 Maine West hazing case similar to 2012 allegations. *Daily Herald*. Retrieved from www.dailyherald.com/article/20121125/news/711259764/

Solberg, W. (1998). Harmless pranks or brutal practices? Hazing at the University of Illinois, 1868–1913. *Journal of Illinois State Historical Society*, 91(4), 233–259.

StopHazing.org. (2018). *States with anti-hazing laws*. Retrieved from www.stophazing.org/states-with-anti-hazing-laws/

Chapter 2

Testimonies
Hazing Firsthand

Michelle L. Boettcher and Cristóbal Salinas Jr.

Throughout the development of this book and in our scholarship, we discussed the importance of the firsthand account. For those who have been a part of the organizations highlighted in this text, what have their experiences with hazing been? How has hazing played a role in their senses of belonging and joining of groups or organizations? With questions like these in mind, we asked individuals for short (500 words or less) perspectives related to hazing. The stories shared by others are presented to you here. To maintain each individual's privacy, they all agreed to be listed as anonymous. We respect and honor their trust for sharing their stories and perspectives with us.

Part of the rationale for sharing testimonies comes from a desire to understand these experiences beyond the abstraction of research articles or quantitative data. In hearing some individual stories, we are able to develop an understanding of the larger context in organizations. The individual becomes a translation of the group. As Crotty (1998) wrote,

> When we describe something, we are, in the normal course of events, reporting how something is seen and reacted to, and thereby meaningfully constructed within a given community or set of communities. When we narrate something, even in telling our very own story, it is . . . the voice of our culture—its many voices, in fact—that is heard in what we say.
>
> (p. 64)

Another way of understanding and valuing the individual voice in the context of social issues is to move the insights beyond critique and into action. As Bloom (2002) noted, "Studies of narratives, when used to construct social critique, also help us construct social action at both personal and collective levels" (p. 312).

In his book *Black Haze*, Jones (2015) wrote about black fraternity and sorority hazing. He hypothesized that "hazing in BGFs [black Greek fraternities] is more physically violent than that found in similar organizations" (Jones, 2015, p. 3).

Through his work, Jones provides a historical context for the purpose of black fraternities and sororities, how they were founded, and examples and cases of how hazing is rooted in these organizations. As you read his work, as well as some of the testimonies provided in this chapter, you might think that hazing happens only in fraternities and sororities and that it is more physical and violent in multicultural fraternities and sororities. We argue that hazing is not a black problem; hazing is a human problem. Therefore, this chapter highlights the hazing perspectives of people from different organization affiliations, race/ethnicity, and gender to challenge the idea that hazing happens only in black fraternities and sororities and mainly in men's organizations.

We offer each of the following as additional perspectives in the dialogue related to hazing that we are seeking to inform through this text. Although the experiences described here are not the experiences of all band members, fraternity members, or organizational members, they provide insights into how we understand the hazing victim's perspective. Rather than concluding this chapter with a set of case studies, these narratives are followed by questions that could prompt engagement with each of these testimonials as case studies by themselves.

One additional epiphany we had when preparing this text was that it is incumbent upon us as authors to lead the way in pulling back the curtain and fostering a more open dialogue around hazing. With that in mind, this chapter includes anonymous narratives about personal hazing experiences and our own experiences. As the editors, we both are drawn to this work not only through our jobs but also through our lived experiences. As such, we close this set of testimonials with one by each of us—attributed. It is our hope that this will encourage others to tell their stories in the work to disrupt hazing and to transform the higher educational and organizational experiences of students.

TESTIMONY 1: BAND HAZING

During the 1988 and 1989 college football seasons, I was part of the trombone section in the marching band at a large public university in the Midwest. At that time, the marching band consisted of more than 200 instrumentalists and flag corps members. I was fairly typical in the sense that I was not a music major but had participated in marching band in high school.

Although I never considered hazing to be a part of my marching band experience, there were certainly things that, looking back, seem inappropriate for a university-sanctioned organization. I found many of these things funny at the time, but I have to believe that they must have made many new band members uncomfortable. None of these things was required for marching band membership, but they were integral components to fitting into the culture of the group.

As with many college groups, alcohol was a major part of band culture. In the trombone section, we met every Friday afternoon before rehearsal and tapped a keg, then met with members from the rest of the band on Friday nights before home games for beer band, which consisted of marching to different bars to play the fight song in exchange for free beer. On road trips, band members would store their hats in their suitcases because our hatboxes were the perfect size to hold a gallon ice cream pail full of frozen margaritas.

The oral history of the band included several revised lyrics to various fight songs. For our own fight song, words were changed to convert a song about the football team's athletic prowess into one about the band's ability to drink itself into a stupor. Altered fight songs for other schools ranged from silly to profane. One song was so obscene that when my daughters learned of its existence without actually hearing any of the words, I told them I would sing it to them only after they turned 18. Again, no one was ever forced to sing any of the altered songs as far as I know, but it's easy to see how many of them could have made the overall band experience uncomfortable for many students.

Questions to Consider

1. What are the behaviors outlined in this scenario that do or could constitute hazing?
2. What are the contributing factors to the potential hazing culture described in this scenario?
3. Do you consider the altered song lyrics examples of hazing or elements of a hazing culture? Why or why not?
4. The author stated, "None of these things was required for marching band membership, but they were integral components to fitting into the culture of the group." How does this concept relate to hazing in student organizations?
5. The author discusses the value of perspective in looking back and seeing behaviors in a different light. Is it possible to achieve this in the moment as events unfold for students?

TESTIMONY 2: FRATERNAL ORGANIZATION HAZING

On a frigid night in early February, six young men stood in a straight line by height: shortest to tallest. They were given numbers to answer to in place of their given names. They were given restrictions: no condiments, no soda, no haircuts, and no girls. No wearing the fraternity's colors. . . . Tell no one about where you go at night.

This was life for the next seven weeks. Every night as the sun went down, the levels of dread and anxiety increased. Hoping that inevitable call from a 'big brother would never come, knowing there was no chance it wouldn't. Verbal and physical abuse became the norm as current brothers shared secrets and knowledge. It became the way of life. It was normal to be hit, pushed, yelled at, and made to do embarrassing things.

These incidents occurred at a large, predominantly white institution in the south. Brothers of a black Greek letter organization were hazing the potential new members.

Looking back on this experience as a new member, it is easily the hardest thing I've ever done—and for many reasons. Late nights turned into longer days in class. Friendships, extracurricular activities—really, anything frivolous—quickly got reprioritized for studying and catching up on sleep.

If I'd known everything that we would be doing when I signed up to pledge, I absolutely would not have done it. The physical challenges aside, the mental exhaustion and simply embarrassing tasks we were made to do would have been enough to make me walk away. We were told throughout our process, "It'll all be worth it when it's over." Bull. Don't get me wrong; I'm thankful to be a member of my organization. It has allowed me to connect with people I work with on a level that wouldn't be possible had I not joined. However, there are days that I can't focus on work because I'm angry for no reason. Older members still treat us like we're pledging. Some days it has been worth it; some days it hasn't.

Questions to Consider

1. Although this narrative does not give specifics, it does provide examples of forms of hazing the author experienced. Do you think the author was aware he was being hazed as it was happening? Do you think most new members are aware of hazing in the moment?
2. What are the pros and cons of the experience the author highlights?
3. The long-term effects of hazing are often overlooked. What are some of the long-term impacts the author describes here? How might we work to educate leaders and organizations about this?
4. The author talks about "embarrassing tasks." What do you think the organizational goals are for embarrassing new members? Are there other ways to achieve those goals?
5. Do you think this student's experience is representative of most fraternity members? Why or why not?

TESTIMONY 3: ATHLETICS HAZING

Hazing is something I heard a lot about as an athlete being recruited to go to Division I schools. I was terrified of being hazed as a freshman going into college. After I chose which school I wanted to go to, I started hearing rumors of the freshman class getting hazed at the beginning of the school year. I had absolutely no interest in this. I was extremely fortunate to have a girl in my freshman class who stood up to the upperclassmen and told them that we refused to be hazed. We were the first class in years not to be "initiated."

My friend who was an upperclassman on the team told me what happened to her when her class had freshman initiation. The night started off by all the freshmen being blindfolded and having pitchers taped to their hands. The upperclassmen filled up the freshmen's pitchers with an absurd amount of liquor, and the freshmen were forced to drink whatever was put in their pitchers throughout the night. Each of the upperclassmen was assigned a freshman, and it was their job to dress up their freshman in trash bags and to write obscene pictures and phrases all over their bodies with permanent markers. I saw some pictures from this night . . . they were absolutely outrageous. I would not have wanted to experience that. My friend said it was funny and was something the class was able to bond over because they all made it through this initiation together. Another one of the girls on the team with whom I am still friends said that this was one of the worst nights of her life, and she is still upset that it happened to her.

Other teams at the university had their own hazing habits. Men's freshmen soccer players were forced to shave their heads. Women's soccer players were forced to take part in a freshman initiation after being taken from their apartments by older teammates and thrown into trunks of cars and taken to the event. One year a girl ended up smashing her face against a brick wall during the initiation after her older teammates told her to run faster while being blindfolded. This girl is no longer playing soccer due to this injury. This event was followed by a very serious lawsuit.

The most recent event happened when I was a staff member. Multiple sports teams were at a surprise birthday party for a freshman soccer player. This girl was surprised at an athlete's apartment where athletes from different teams were there to celebrate with her on her birthday. She was strapped down to a chair so she couldn't move, and a soccer player performed an extremely inappropriate dance around and on her while all the athletes were in the background filming, drinking, and laughing. He was wearing almost no clothing at all.

I don't know if this is considered hazing, but I consider it to be. The best part is that we as a staff got in trouble for trying to hold our athletes accountable for the situation, and administrators told our staff to tell the athletes on our team to delete any pictures and videos they had from their phones. After being questioned, the girl said she was okay with the situation, but even if she wasn't, is she going to say so due to the fact that it would put her team and her university at risk?

Questions to Consider

1. The author here says she was not hazed, but she describes the anxiety she felt about potentially being hazed. How does this fear affect potential or new members' ability to connect with teams or other organizations?
2. How can organizations encourage new (and established) members to speak out when they see hazing habits emerging, as a team member did in this example?
3. What is the responsibility of members of larger organizations (athletics, fraternity and sorority life, etc.) to report hazing by other teams, chapters, or organizations? What obstacles do organizations face in reporting hazing? How can those obstacles be addressed?
4. In the final example at the birthday party, the author writes, "I don't know if this is considered hazing." Is it? Why or why not? Is it something other athletes should have addressed or prevented? Is it something the coaching staff should have addressed? If no, why not? If yes, how?

5. Finally, consider the question asked by the author of this piece: "After being questioned, the girl said she was okay with the situation, but even if she wasn't, is she going to say so due to the fact that it would put her team and her university at risk?"

TESTIMONY 4: FRATERNITY HAZING

It is a November night, and temperatures are dropping into the low 40s. I am blindfolded in a shed with 11 fellow pledge brothers wondering what waits outside the doors. We can hear the water hose running full blast, splashing water into the corners of the rusted shed. One by one, we anxiously wait for our names to be called to learn what fate has in store for us on this cold, windy night.

When I reflect back on how I was hazed as an undergraduate fraternity man, I think of a group of young men seeking to make meaning of those words "sense of belonging" that colleges are always talking about at orientation. What does it mean to belong to a community? Do I have to earn membership into said community, or is it afforded to me based just on my presence? These are the questions that raced through my mind as an 18-year-old emerging adult looking to make meaning of the next 4 years of my college experience. As a first-generation college student moving 6 hours away from the only friends and family I had, I undoubtedly wanted to belong. I wanted to find a community—a home away from home. As a college freshman, I wasn't going to let my fear and anxiety get in the way.

Where has the path changed from becoming yesterday's heroes to tomorrow's villains? When did a fraternity stop becoming a place to connect over shared values and become a place to simply host beer Olympics or the next flannel and handles party? We put young men and women in environments and spaces where they feel pressured to engage in dangerous activities in order to live up to the expectations of their peers.

From the college a cappella group to a local fraternity house, students live in anxiety as they eagerly seeking acceptance and some semblance of a sense of belonging. Unfortunately, some of today's organizations take advantage of that desperate need to belong. Individuals feed off that power, resulting in the development of expectations that one must "earn" the right to belong. When did belonging become about earning instead of being?

As higher education professionals, we must find ways to develop belonging in meaningful and safe ways for our students. If we don't, they will continue to develop them for themselves. My fear is they will continue to involve hard alcohol, a cold night in a shed, and result in still more pointless student deaths.

Questions to Consider

1. In this case study, the author describes his situation. He doesn't go into detail about what happens with the water or what happens when potential members are taken out of the shed. Given the description here of what has happened, what hazing habits have already taken place regardless of what happens next?

2. Do you agree that having a sense of belonging is a critical element of the collegiate experience for most students? Why or why not?
3. What is your sense of belonging? How did it develop for you? Were any of the ways that you gained membership to your organization(s) hazing habits? Provide examples and discuss how each experience fostered a sense of belonging for you.
4. Does someone have to earn membership to belong to an organization? To all organizations? Why or why not?
5. The author concludes from the perspective of someone working in student affairs (potentially student activities, fraternity and sorority life, etc.). What is your expectation of staff in those roles when it comes to hazing habits on your campus? Who are the key people affiliated with your organizations who help leaders develop traditions and rituals for belonging to those groups?

DISCUSSION

The hazing examples in this chapter are very limited, but that is to be expected given the fact that "hazing thrives on secrecy and hierarchy" (Cholbi, 2009, p. 160). The willingness of hazers or those who have been hazed to come forward and share their stories is a complex matter. Not only is there hierarchy in the organizations and potential insider consequences but also fears related to judgment from those outside of student organizations. As Silveira and Hudson (2015) wrote, "Despite students' anonymity and confidentiality, it is also possible that students might not have been entirely forthcoming in their responses, especially if they feared scrutiny from outside entities. Secrecy traditionally has been a necessary component of hazing" (p. 21).

Without more transparency and examples to guide the conversation, we run into obstacles in addressing hazing culture. We sought here to provide a few examples from which others can draw as practitioners, educators, leaders, students, members, and other constituents connected with organizations vulnerable to hazing traditions. It is our hope that others will continue to contribute to the work of disrupting and dismantling hazing culture by talking more openly about hazing traditions across organizations in and beyond higher education.

With that in mind, we offer two additional testimonials by the editors of this text. In these cases, the authors are transparent in their experiences and authorship of these cases. We fully appreciate and respect the contributions of those who are not identified in the cases presented earlier. Issues of position, power, and privilege influence our ability to be fully transparent in our sharing. We hope that all the examples in this chapter will foster additional dialogue.

TESTIMONY 5: RESIDENTIAL LIFE HAZING—
MICHELLE L. BOETTCHER

There is one example that I experienced consistently across my involvement in working in residence life that I want to highlight here. Although it doesn't involve alcohol, physical abuse, or late-night phone calls requiring new staff to show up at a secret location, it is pervasive and something on which we need to reflect deeply and intentionally. It is a part of the housing culture and needs to be disrupted.

My entire career has been in student affairs. I started as a resident assistant (RA) as an undergraduate student. I worked in housing and residence life programs around the country. At every institution where I worked, there was some version of "behind closed doors." The training exercise—endorsed by, scheduled by, and structured by housing professionals—involved new RAs approaching a room to deal with an issue. The purpose was to give a sense of the kinds of things you might face as a staff member. The issues included roommate conflicts, parties with underage drinking, suicidal ideation, fights, and other examples of policy violations the staff might encounter. My issue my very first year as an RA was a loud room with underage drinking and illegal road signs on the walls. I remember the building I was in. I remember the conversation that I had. I remember the debriefing afterward.

It was not a big deal. I did a pretty good job. I was nervous but not scared and not embarrassed afterward.

And I remember other people's experiences. Specifically, I remember the experience of a student when I was a graduate hall director. She had to confront a party, and the experienced RAs who were the actors pushed and pushed to the point that she was trapped in the room, was triggered by the experience, began to cry, and had to force her way out of the room/scenario. I remember people telling her what she did wrong after the fact. I remember her saying she needed to get a drink of water and then sobbing uncontrollably by the water fountain afterward. I remember the professional and graduate staff (myself included) standing by and letting this happen.

This was on-the-job training. It was required in order to become a staff member. It was also an activity outsiders had to go through in order to become insiders. It was hazing.

Questions to Consider

1. Do you think the incident described here constitutes hazing? Why or why not?
2. What is the difference between training and hazing? Can training become hazing? Why or why not?
3. Does this experience help to foster community or sense of belonging? If no, why not? If yes, in what ways?

TESTIMONY 6: FRATERNAL ORGANIZATION HAZING—CRISTÓBAL SALINAS JR.

As a brother of Sigma Lambda Beta International fraternity, I had the opportunity to learn and experience firsthand what hazing is. At the time, I did not understand what hazing meant or its effect on individuals. As I write this section, I recognize that my experience is unique to me and different to all other Sigma Lambda Beta brothers as well as the hazing experiences of others. Also, I acknowledge that not all members of Sigma Lambda Beta have experienced hazing. As I share my hazing story, my goal is not to disrespect the members of Sigma Lambda Beta or the organization. Rather, my purpose here is to share my story with the hope of educating others, preventing future incidents, and taking a visible stand against hazing.

I present on this topic, and after each presentation across the country where I share my story, I get multiple e-mails from students sharing their hazing experiences. Yet many of these people are afraid and ashamed to tell their stories. Although I feel honored and privileged to be the person to whom they have chosen to disclose, I also feel responsible for continuing hazing education and prevention in order to advocate for those who are invisible, unheard, and afraid to speak against and report hazing.

During the process of becoming a brother of Sigma Lambda Beta, I was required to attend "educational programming" for 4 months. I would participate in 3-hour meetings two to three times a week. Each time, I was blindfolded and forced to stand in line with other members trying to join the brotherhood. We had assignments prior to each meeting: We were required to remember the history, founding fathers, and values and principles of the fraternity, along with learning the Greek alphabet and additional literature and poems. We were required to recite the information in unison at each meeting. If one of us did not know the information or was too slow or fast, we had to start from the beginning until we got it right. The goal of this process was to create unity, to become "one line" and "one brotherhood."

In addition to being blindfolded and sharing the memorized assignments and information, "big brothers" (senior fraternity members) would ask additional questions or scream at us with loud music in the background. Often the yelling turned to verbal abuse. I fully acknowledge that other members might not have experienced it the same way. This is how I experienced it. The philosophy of the big brothers was that by yelling, they were challenging us, making us stronger, and helping us become men of character.

When I asked senior members why they verbally abused me during the meeting, I was told, "We are breaking you down and then building you up because as Latino men, we have been and continue to be oppressed by society." At this point, let me acknowledge that I do recognize and have experienced racism, oppression, and marginalization, and often I feel I am culturally invisible to some individuals, institutions, or the larger society. That said, I make the argument that breaking people down and then building them up is hazing. I pose the question, "Would my real brothers break me down, then build me up?"

Lastly, I want to recognize that to some my hazing experience may seem "typical" or even "easier" than many others' experiences. However, my hazing experience led me to try to commit suicide. Since then I have been attending counseling and continue to heal from those experiences. *My experience is testament to the fact that much of the damage done—despite what is portrayed in the media—is not physical but affects us on several other levels and does not end when we become members of our organizations.*

Questions to Consider

1. How can we as professionals connect with students and support them when they may be going through extended and secret organizational indoctrination processes?
2. If you were made aware of a situation like this as the result of an attempted suicide, what education or sanctions might you suggest for the organization involved?
3. Knowing that this is one experience, but not an "only" experience, how can you use this case to proactively train and educate student leaders?
4. How might you respond to a student who has attempted suicide if you are made aware of all these other factors? What support and options would you offer?

CONCLUSION

This chapter was designed not as a means of finger-pointing or placing blame but to remove any idea that hazing is an abstract concept that affects only one population of students on campus. The truth is that hazing is incredibly personal and traumatic, with implications for individuals and organizations alike. By surfacing stories across organizational types and from the perspectives of different students, the goal of the contributors here is to make transparent what hazing can look like. In so doing, our hope is to create communal dialogue where all students can participate and find ways to play roles in transforming the culture around hazing in students' search for belonging on college campuses.

REFERENCES

Bloom, L. R. (2002). From self to society: Reflections on the power of narrative inquiry. In S. B. Merriam & Associates (Eds.), *Qualitative research in practice: Examples for discussion and analysis* (pp. 310–313). San Francisco, CA: Jossey-Bass.

Cholbi, M. J. (2009). On hazing. *Public Affairs Quarterly, 23*(2), 160.

Crotty, M. (1998). *The foundations of social research: Meaning and perspective in the research process.* Thousand Oaks, CA: Sage.

Jones, R. L. (2015). *Black haze: Violence, sacrifice, and manhood in black Greek-letter fraternities* (2nd ed.). Albany: State University of New York Press.

Silveira, J. M., & Hudson, M. W. (2015). Hazing in the college marching band. *Journal of Research in Music Education, 63*(1), 5–27.

Part 2

The Role of Hazing in Organizations

Chapter 3

Hazing in Intercollegiate Athletics

Ethan Swingle and Cristóbal Salinas Jr.

Intercollegiate athletics can be a controversial topic as pay for play, commercialization, academic scandals, and hazing dominate the headlines of mainstream media across the country and serve as the focus of scholarship and research in higher education. Although the growth of athletics has blossomed since the first intercollegiate event in 1852, there is a side of athletics few see or hear about: hazing. As stated in Chapter 1 of this book, the definition of hazing is ambiguous and can be interpreted in a multitude of ways; therefore, for this chapter, we define hazing in intercollegiate athletics as "any activity expected of someone joining or participating in a group that humiliates, degrades, abuses, or endangers them regardless of a person's willingness to participate" (Allan & Madden, 2008, p. 2).

This chapter will explore the relationship between hazing and intercollegiate athletics, provide a detailed analysis of hazing events that have occurred in intercollegiate athletics, describe the legal issues related to hazing, and cover hazing prevention techniques for administrators, coaches, and most importantly, student-athletes to ensure hazing does not continue at colleges and universities across the country. Ultimately, the goal of this chapter is to provide resources and insights to disrupt hazing practices in athletics in order to allow student-athletes to thrive as scholars and as athletes in their respective sports.

Rowing was the sport of the first intercollegiate athletic contest and took place in 1852 between Harvard and Yale. The Intercollegiate Athletic Association was created in 1905 and was renamed the National Collegiate Athletic Association (NCAA) in 1910. It now governs sports and provides oversight to 450,000 student-athletes who attend approximately 1,123 institutions in the United States (NCAA, 2017b). Although there are many associations, such as the National Association of Intercollegiate Athletics and the National Junior College Athletic Association, the NCAA focuses on Division I intercollegiate athletics. Intercollegiate athletics have become an integral part of campus life (Chen, Snyder, & Magner, 2010), but further understanding needs to occur with student-athletes and their participation in sports while at college.

HAZING AND INTERCOLLEGIATE ATHLETICS

Both intercollegiate athletics and hazing have evolved since the start of the 20th century. From that first rowing competition, intercollegiate athletics have expanded, and today the NCAA provides oversight for more than 90 sports, and college athletics are a nearly $1 billion business (NCAA, 2017b). Hazing has seen a similar growth. At first, hazing was thought of as a tradition or rite of passage for new members joining an organization. Unfortunately, many of the initiation traditions have become hazing habits that demean, degrade, and demoralize potential and new members. These events often transpire behind closed doors and go unreported because the new members fear the consequences of not being a part of the group (or team) and do not think hazing events are serious until someone is injured and medical assistance is required (McGlone & Schaefer, 2008).

Athletic hazing has forced universities to cancel seasons, fire administrators, coaches, and staff, and face complex legal issues that are difficult to resolve; however, that was not always the case. In 1923, the first reported case of hazing in the intercollegiate setting took place at Hobart College, a small liberal arts institution in New York. In this instance, a first-year football player was beaten by two senior players and then thrown into a lake (Carroll, Connaughton, Spengler, & Zhang, 2009; Sussberg, 2003). From the beginning, hazing in intercollegiate athletics involved violence and upper-division students hurting and humiliating newer students or team members.

It took more than 60 years from the first reported case of hazing and nearly 150 years from the first intercollegiate athletic event before an NCAA hazing investigation was conducted. The first report of intercollegiate athletic hazing was titled *Initiation Rites and Athletics for NCAA Sports Teams* (Hoover, 1999). This document reported the findings from surveys of more than 1,000 universities involving 325,000 student-athletes, making it the largest survey related to athletic hazing to date. To briefly summarize the results, over 250,000 student-athletes experienced hazing, alcohol consumption was the primary form of hazing, hazing was involved with more female than male student-athletes, football players were the most at risk for hazing, and universities located in the southern and Midwest regions of the United States were more likely to encounter hazing (Hoover, 1999).

Since this study, much more research about hazing in athletics has been conducted by scholars and practitioners. Waldron and Kowalski (2009) found that student-athletes believed hazing was fun for both the hazee and the hazed and that certain student-athletes were more prone to being hazed. In a follow up study, Waldron and Kowalski (2010) found that some coaches allowed hazing to occur if it was "under control" or no one got injured, while others had a zero-tolerance policy related to hazing. Additionally, this study found that some student-athletes believed hazing should be allowed because they perceived it to enhance team cohesion and success.

Kerr, Jewett, MacPherson, and Stirling, (2016) found that hazing was more likely to occur in the form of relational aggression or social manipulation than physical aggression, and the influence of power among teammates played an important role in who hazes and who gets hazed. This study also found that athletics provided a social context where hazing is perceived as normal and tolerable behavior. Additionally, studies have been conducted on athletic hazing and masculinity (Allen & DeAngelis, 2004; Chen, Snyder, & Magner, 2010; Fields, Collins, & Comstock, 2010), institutional liability for hazing in athletics (Crown & Rosner, 2002; Hekmat, 2001; McGlone & Schaefer, 2008; Somers, 2006), and hazing prevention in athletics (Crow, Ammon, & Phillips, 2004; Crow & Macintosh, 2009; Etzel, Watson, Visek, & Maniar, 2006). Since the Hoover (1999) study, the dialogue around hazing in athletics has grown and continues to evolve.

HAZING EVENTS: HOW LIKELY ARE THEY?

Hoover's (1999) study was thorough, but it is dated, and a more recent study by Allan and Madden (2008) provided a clearer overview of the hazing trends in intercollegiate athletics. Results of this study indicated that 47% of students entering college experienced some form of hazing, and approximately 54% of college athletics incidents involved alcohol. Additionally, Allan and Madden (2008) found that hazing occurred on both club and intramural teams as well as university-sponsored teams with student-athletes on full scholarships.

Past Hazing Cases in Athletics

Because many cases of hazing go undetected and do not enter the court system, there is no way to determine the total number of hazing incidents in intercollegiate athletics. Just as in other contexts, athletics hazing statistics are neither federally nor centrally collected. However, there are cases that can inform the conversation in the context of collegiate athletics.

A hazing case took place in 1990 at the University of Northern Colorado and involved the university's baseball team. A first-year player broke two bones in his neck and bruised his spinal cord when he slid headfirst into a pool of mud, resulting in paralysis from the waist down (Monaghan, 1990). The event occurred after a canceled practice because of poor field conditions, but the upper-division teammates decided it would be a good time to initiate the new players.

In a case in 1993 at the University of Minnesota, Morris, the wrestling team staged a fake Ku Klux Klan rally to initiate and scare their African American teammates. This event occurred at an off-campus Halloween party, where many of the wrestling team members were dressed as white supremacists (McGlone & Schaefer, 2008). This led to several court cases, and as a result of this incident, an assistant coach was suspended, and the five wrestlers who staged the event were indefinitely suspended. According to Ukura (2014), criminal charges were filed against the players and coach and included assault, making terroristic threats, negligent fires, and two counts of witness tampering. The case resulted in jail time, community service, and fines for the players and the coach (Ukura, 2014).

In 2000, members of the University of Vermont's men's hockey team coerced team recruits into drinking large amounts of alcohol, parading naked while holding one another's genitals, and engaging in other degrading activities (Associated Press, 2000). As a result, a lawsuit was filed, and the university canceled the remainder of the season (Gardiner, 2001).

Another hazing incident involved the women's soccer team at Northwestern University in 2006. This case involved the athletes drinking alcoholic beverages and included the online posting of pictures of the women in just shirts and their underwear or shorts. In some of the more graphic pictures, the student-athletes were blindfolded, had their hands bound behind their backs, and were sitting on the laps of soccer players from the men's team (Sprow, 2006). In light of this incident, the athletic director suspended all team activities indefinitely. Results of this investigation led to members of the men's team being put on probation for an extended period of time, and the head coach resigned.

A final example involved members of the men's lacrosse team at Cornell University in 2013. This case specifically involved upper-class students hazing underclass students by forcing them to drink an entire keg together. Additionally, throughout the academic school year, the upper-class students coerced the underclass students to do tedious tasks. Both of these were seen as serious hazing events after the 2011 death of a student who was forced to drink alcohol and was bound by duct tape (Fox News Sports, 2013). Although the school had created a zero-tolerance policy around hazing and had shut down four fraternities for hazing, the ramifications of this specific event led to the suspension of the team's competitions. Additionally, after an investigation led by the athletic department, the team members were required to participate in anti-hazing educational programming.

Current Athletic Hazing Cases

It is important to keep in mind that hazing events are not things of the past. Hazing in athletics continues today, and this section highlights more recent events. In December 2016, the Dartmouth women's swimming and diving team admitted to a violation of the college's hazing policy. First-year team members were forced to create and present a sexualized PowerPoint presentation for their teammates during their winter break training trip (Brackett, 2017). As a result, the team was placed on a 1-year probation and could not compete in the events scheduled for the upcoming fall semester. The team was also required to attend educational and team development events periodically throughout the remainder of the year.

Another recent case involved the St. Olaf College baseball team. In the winter of 2015, the team was involved in both on- and off-campus activities that violated university hazing policy. Players then attempted to cover up the incidents (Nelson,

2015). This case is different from some others because it was reported on the social media platform YikYak, which allowed anonymous posts. When administrators learned about it, student-athletes began covering up what had transpired. As a result, the college canceled the upcoming season's tournaments and games and disciplined individual students.

In 2016, five football players at Wheaton College were convicted of felony hazing. The incident involved the five players hazing a first-year teammate who was restrained with duct tape, beaten, and left half-naked with two torn shoulders on a baseball field (Gutowski & St. Clair, 2017). The student withdrew from the university, and the administration found out about the incident from coaches and other teammates afterward. As a result of the incident, Wheaton College implemented a process wherein student-athletes must sign an anti-hazing contract.

The most current case presented in this chapter focuses on Drury University. This case involved the swimming team coercing members to drink an excessive amount of alcohol until they vomited or blacked out during an initiation week. Hazing continued throughout the rest of the year and included such incidents as student-athletes being hit by dodge balls while nude and athletes being forced to watch pornographic videos and to judge the female swimmers by their looks (Associated Press, 2017). Furthermore, this case resulted in one student-athlete being treated for conversion disorder and posttraumatic stress disorder (Associated Press, 2017). In response, the institution introduced new hazing education for student-athletes, including penalties for violating the hazing policy that includes a $200 fine and 40 community service hours for a first violation and an increased fine from $100 and 20 hours with another occurrence that also carries the penalty of suspension off the team or expulsion from the university.

The Trends

Recent studies have suggested that 80% of all student-athletes have faced hazing at some point during their college athletic careers (Doyle, 2015). Table 3.1 describes the severity of hazing in the intercollegiate athletic setting from a study conducted by Alfred University (1999). Table 3.2 examines alcohol-related events.

TABLE 3.1 Distribution of Athletes by the Severity of Collegiate Athletic Initiation

Grouping of Athletes Involved in Alcohol-Related Initiation		
Activities	%	Estimated *N*
Alcohol on recruitment	42%	136,160 athletes nationally
Drinking contests	49%	158,823 athletes nationally

Adapted from Alfred University (1999).

TABLE 3.2 Grouping of Athletes Involved in Alcohol-Related Initiation

Distribution of Athletes by the Severity of Collegiate Athletic Initiation

Activities	%	Estimated N
Acceptable initiation activities only	19%	61,888 athletes nationally
Questionable initiation rites; no unacceptable activities	19%	61,342 athletes nationally
Alcohol-related initiation; no other unacceptable activities	39%	126,254 athletes nationally
Unacceptable initiation activities other than alcohol related	21%	68,041 athletes nationally
Hazed (total of questionable, alcohol, and other unacceptable)	79%	255,637 athletes nationally

Adapted from Alfred University (1999).

Although the trends in intercollegiate athletics are difficult to track, alcohol-related events have increased in the last decade (Alfred University, 1999). Even though more universities have conducted educational training sessions for their student-athletes and administrators and some universities have developed zero-tolerance policies regarding hazing, incidents continue to occur.

PROACTIVE EDUCATION AND TRAINING HAZING RESPONSE AND ACCOUNTABILITY

What can be done to prevent hazing incidents from taking place in the context of college athletics? The NCAA and other organizations, such as HazingPrevention.org, provide guidance related to education, training, and orientation for new students and student-athletes to prevent hazing. Because hazing is so complex, creating a multifaceted approach to prevent hazing and educating about hazing is required (Etzel, Watson, Visek, & Maniar, 2006). It is worth noting that the tools and strategies highlighted here can be useful at any level of athletics across and beyond higher education. Although there is no federal or centralized law related to hazing or standardized proactive measures to ensure hazing will never occur on campus, the following provides examples of what some universities are doing to prevent hazing.

For many universities, the first types of proactive education they give to their student-athletes are mandatory presentations during the preseason, the season, and the post-season (Crow, Ammon, & Phillips, 2004). In many instances, these presentations—often provided to student organizations across campus as well as athletic teams—define and describe hazing policies.

Additionally, the Massachusetts Institute of Technology has developed an Education and Hazing Committee program that serves as a model for several institutions. This program made its debut in 2013 and has seen significant campus and community growth and involvement to prevent and further educate constituents about hazing. Another exemplar program that involves opportunities for universities to educate all constituents about hazing is the Hazing Education Initiative at Florida State University. This program has resources for students, student-athletes, organizations, parents, and fraternities and sororities to create a true hazing-free community and university. Finally, the NCAA's website and HazingPrevention.org provide more detailed information related to hazing prevention in and beyond NCAA athletics (National Collegiate Athletic Association, 2017a).

ADMINISTRATOR, COACH, AND STUDENT-ATHLETE ROLES

Although policies and accountability are key aspects of hazing prevention, ultimately it is the people who are involved who have the power to transform the culture of athletics. This final section provides an overview of techniques and tips administrators, coaches, and student-athletes can utilize to prevent hazing. Although this is not an exhaustive list, the goal is to provide some additional techniques to build on anti-hazing strategies already in use in programs across the country.

Administrators

At least one athletics administrator should be designated to address hazing. For example, many universities use their director of student-athlete development as the liaison for these events with the coordinator. Student-athletes must know exactly who to go to if they witness or experience hazing. Similarly, athletics staff will also have clear lines of reporting and information sharing around hazing or potential hazing incidents.

Next, the athletic department should invite the appropriate staff, offices, trainers, or facilitators to teach their athletes about hazing. Some individuals or offices that may do this work on campuses include the Title IX coordinator, the office of student conduct, national organizations that provide training, and others on campus who can give educational presentations on hazing. By doing this, student-athletes can more fully understand what hazing is, how frequently hazing occurs in this specific setting, where they can go if they witness or experience hazing, and what the potential ramifications are for hazing habits as a part of team activities.

Furthermore, each athletic director and other top administrators needs to develop, implement, and be prepared to enforce hazing policies. This may include the development of an anti-hazing contract that all student-athletes must sign before participating in their sports. Fordham University, the University of Florida, and Bates College have examples of this on their websites (see also Bates College, 2017; Fordham, 2017; University of Florida, 2017).

Lastly, universities should have specific protocols and policies in place if a hazing event does occur on campus. Strategies for education are essential, policies and processes are critical, and all of that depends on the strategies institutions have in place for reporting, investigating, charging, and sanctioning hazing allegations. Crow, Ammon, and Phillips (2004) stress that institutions must first recognize that every hazing offense is a serious offense, thorough investigations involving athletics and student affairs are central to hazing cases, appropriate sanctions are necessary, and support of hazing victims is essential. By following this guidance, athletic departments and other university administrators can be prepared for hazing events that may occur on campus.

Coaches

Coaches are some of the most important people in the lives of student-athletes, and it is through the actions of coaches that athletic hazing cultures can be disrupted. That said, coaches do not get into athletics because they are hazing experts. Coaches need ongoing training and education related to hazing and the potential effects of hazing habits on their athletes as individuals and as teams.

Additionally, coaches need to conduct team activities throughout the year to build team cohesion that do not involve drinking or bullying. Many programs around the nation generate team bonding by going to other university games and events on campus, engaging in community service activities, and ensuring the team captains provide the right type of leadership to new team members. These events develop positive traditions that are meaningful to everyone on the team and can reduce the likelihood of other incidents that involve hazing as a means of team bonding (NCAA, 2017a). Finally, all coaches should document and report any type of hazing experience they hear about, see, or know of as soon as possible.

Student-Athletes

Student-athletes are the most important part of the university's athletic department, and their physical and mental well-being must be the top priority of all staff. In order to prevent hazing among teammates, prospective student-athletes should be able to meet with and ask questions of current students during a recruiting visit to really gain their perspectives and to see if it would be a good fit. By doing this, the prospective student-athlete could ask such questions as "What team traditions are currently in place?" and "Has anyone ever heard about or seen hazing on this campus by any team?"

Additionally, student-athletes should have peer mentors on the team or different teams that meet weekly or biweekly to discuss their experiences so far, and the upper-class students could provide guidance if an underclass student is troubled. The upper-class students would need to be trained by the compliance office and the director of student services so that hazing is not perpetuated. For guidelines and current practices used by universities, please see the references with links to California State University, Long Beach (2017), and Northwestern University (2017).

By transforming the culture of unhealthy programs, space can be fostered for student-athletes to have open dialogue with one another around such uncomfortable topics as hazing. Student-athlete advisory committees are a great way for these conversations to occur and have student-athletes involved in enhancing their experience. Student-athletes are the reason intercollegiate athletics are even possible; therefore, their opinions need to be heard and heeded.

CONCLUSION

Intercollegiate athletics is often central to the student experience and institutional culture in higher education. We are obligated to create safe environments for everyone—including student-athletes. Although hazing has historically been conceptualized as a way to build team unity and as a rite of passage for new athletes, it is essential to disrupt that narrative and replace hazing habits with more powerful and safer team-building experiences. It is important for us to understand the history of hazing in athletics and how it informs the athletics landscape today. Similarly, coaching and athletics staff members need to be aware of current athletics hazing cases, as those incidents are opportunities for learning and doing better in the experiences of student-athletes.

Although there is some research on hazing in the intercollegiate athletic setting, it is still very misunderstood, and much of it is outdated. There are many implications for future research on this topic, including research around safe and successful non-hazing team-bonding experiences, lessons learned from teams where hazing has taken place, and a more current examination of the extent to which we find hazing throughout college athletics. Additionally, examining hazing through the lenses of gender, sexual orientation, race, and other politicized identities will give more insight into the topic.

Finally, coaches, staff, administrators, and athletes themselves need to be supported in disrupting hazing cultures in athletics. Clear lines of communication should be outlined for reporting hazing. Well-written and transparent policies must be developed and enforced in order to hold hazing perpetrators accountable. Whether on the field, the court, or the track and whether running, swimming, throwing, or jumping, our athletes need to be safe in order to excel.

CASE STUDIES

Hazing habits vary among organizations, institutions, and athletic teams. For the purposes of the case studies presented in this chapter, no specific sports teams are identified, but the cases reveal hazing practices that could potentially have implications for a variety of different teams. The goal is to provide a set of general ideas that all athletic teams can adapt to fit their sports. For each of the cases, respond to the following questions:

1. Is this an example of hazing?
    a. If yes, what makes this hazing, and how could this hazing event be stopped and prevented?
    b. If no, why is it not hazing, and what additional elements could potentially make this a hazing incident?
2. Should coaches be informed of the incident? Why or why not? How would you notify a coach?
3. If this is a hazing incident, are teams responsible? Individual athletes? Coaching and athletics staff? Others?
4. What other factors need to be considered in each scenario?

Case Study 1

As a way of building community across sport teams at Champion University, upper-level students have historically hosted a party for new team members. The party is not required, but incoming members have been told, "You won't want to miss it," "Everyone will be there," and "It is where the real student-athlete experience starts here at Champion." New members are told to brush up on team statistics and information about senior players on their teams.

When all student-athletes arrive at the party, the men and women are separated into two different rooms. In each room are several bottles of hard alcohol. The older teammates say, "You know what you need to do. We'll be back in 30 minutes." The new members assume they are supposed to consume the alcohol during the 30 minutes as stated by the senior teammates.

After 30 minutes, the older teammates return to the rooms and bring all the new members blindfolded to one room. Men and women are paired off (both blindfolded) and instructed to figure out each other's sport without talking or removing their blindfolds. Most pairs simply spell the names of their sports in the palms of the other students' hands, but one pair feels each other's arms and legs to try to identify the sport. After guessing, blindfolds are removed, and the party continues without any other required interactions among the new team members.

Case Study 2

In preparing to travel via bus to an athletic event out of state, nonstarter athletes are told to arrive before starter athletes on the team and that they are expected to help load luggage and athletic equipment. The institution is not large enough and athletics is not well-resourced economically to have staff or student managers available to do this form of work.

Two of the nonstarting team members, both first-year students, arrive late and do not help load the luggage and equipment as a result. The coach tells them they will have to come early to practice for the next two weeks (until the next game out of state) to run as a punishment for not following through on their duties. Additionally, teammates refer to the players as "bag hags" rather than using their names for the next two weeks.

REFERENCES

Alfred University. (1999). *National survey of sports teams: How many athletes are hazed?* Retrieved from www.alfred.edu/sports_hazing/howmanystudents.cfm?

Allan, E. J., & DeAngelis, G. (2004). Hazing, masculinity, and collision sports: (Un)Becoming heroes. In J. Johnson & M. Holman (Eds.), *Making the team: Inside the world of sport initiations and hazing* (pp. 61–82). Toronto, Ontario: Canadian Scholars.

Allan, E. J., & Madden, M. D. (2008). *Hazing in view: College students at risk*. Retrieved from www.stophazing.org/wp-content/uploads/2014/06/hazing_in_view_web1.pdf

Associated Press. (2000, January 15). Hockey: Vermont cancels season in player hazing scandal. *New York Times*. Retrieved from www.nytimes.com/2000/01/15/sports/hockey-vermont-cancels-season-in-player-hazing-scandal.html

Associated Press. (2017, January 17). Ex-Drury University swimmer says hazing ended her athletic career. *ESPN*. Retrieved from www.espn.com/college-sports/story/_/id/18496251/hazing-ended-athletic-career

Bates College. (2017). *Hazing and team initiation activities policy*. Retrieved from http://athletics.bates.edu/hazinginitiations

Brackett, C. (2017, December). *Women's swimming and diving team sanctioned for hazing*. Retrieved from www.dartmouthsports.com/ViewArticle.dbml?DB_OEM_ID=11600&ATCLID=211650412

California State University, Long Beach. (2017). *Student-athlete peer mentors*. Retrieved from www.web.csulb.edu/divisions/aa/undergrad/bac/support/mentors.html

Carroll, M., Connaughton, D., Spengler, J., & Zhang, J. (2009). Case law analysis regarding high school and collegiate liability for hazing. *European Sport Management Quarterly*, 9(4), 389–410.

Chen, S., Snyder, S., & Magner, M. (2010). The effects of sport participation on student-athletes' and non-athlete students' social life and identity. *Journal of Issues in Intercollegiate Athletics*, 3(1), 176–193.

Crow, B., Ammon, R., & Phillips, D. (2004). Anti-hazing strategies for coaches and administrators. *Strategies: A Journal for Physical and Sport Educators*, *17*(4), 13–15.

Crow, R., & MacIntosh, E. W. (2009). Conceptualizing a meaningful definition of hazing in sport. *European Sport Management Quarterly*, *9*(4), 433–451.

Crow, R. B., & Rosner, S. R. (2002). Institutional and organizational liability for hazing in intercollegiate and professional team sports. *St. John's Law Review*, *76*, 87–115.

Doyle, C. (2015, December 28). Hazing still common in collegiate and youth sports. *Huffington Post*. Retrieved from www.huffingtonpost.com/entry/hazing-youth-college-sports_us_56814d6de4b06fa688809254

Etzel, E. F., Watson, J., Visek, A., & Maniar, S. (2006). Understanding and promoting college student-athlete health: Essential issues for student affairs professionals. *NASPA Journal*, *43*(3), 518–546.

Fields, S. K., Collins, C. L., & Comstock, R. D. (2010). Violence in youth sports: Hazing, brawling, and foul play. *British Journal of Sports Medicine*, *44*(1), 32–37.

Fordham University. (2017). *Anti-hazing policy*. Retrieved from www.grfx.cstv.com/photos/schools/ford/genrel/auto_pdf/ford-compliance-hazing-polic.pdf

Fox News Sports. (2013, September 23). Cornell details hazing incident that led to men's lacrosse team suspension. *Fox News Sports*. Retrieved from www.foxnews.com/sports/2013/09/23/cornell-details-hazing-incident-that-led-to-lacrosse-team-suspension.html

Gardiner, A. (2001, February 4). Vermont hockey wounds heal after hazing scandal. *USA Today*. Retrieved from https://usatoday30.usatoday.com/sports/hockey/shc/2001-02-04-vthazing.htm

Gutowski, C., & St. Clair, S. (2017, September 19). 5 Wheaton College football players face felony charges in hazing incident. *Chicago Tribune*. Retrieved from www.chicagotribune.com/news/local/breaking/ct-wheaton-college-football-hazing-met-20170918-story,amp.html

Hekmat, R. R. (2001). Malpractice during practice: Should NCAA coaches be liable for negligence? *Loyola of Los Angeles Entertainment Law Review*, *22*, 613–642.

Hoover, N. C. (1999). *National survey: Initiation rites and athletics for NCAA sporting teams*. Retrieved from www.alfred.edu/sports_hazing/docs/hazing.pdf

Kerr, G., Jewett, R., MacPherson, E., & Stirling, S. (2016). Student-athletes' experiences of bullying on intercollegiate teams. *Journal for the Study of Sports and Athletes in Education*, *10*(2), 132–149.

McGlone, C., & Schaefer, G. R. (2008). After the haze: Legal aspects of hazing. *Entertainment and Sports Law Journal*, *6*(1), 1–14.

Monaghan, P. (1990, November 14). University of Northern Colorado athlete paralyzed in hazing incident. *The Chronicle of Higher Education*. Retrieved from www.chronicle.com/article/U-of-Northern-Colorado/89880

National Collegiate Athletic Association. (2017a). *Building new traditions: Hazing prevention in college athletics*. Retrieved from www.ncaa.org/sites/default/files/hazing%20prevention%20handbook%2057315.pdf

National Collegiate Athletic Association. (2017b). *What is the NCAA?* Retrieved from www.ncaa.org/about/resources/media-center/ncaa-101/what-ncaa

Nelson, E. (2015, March 28). St. Olaf cancels baseball season after hazing investigation. *Star Tribune.* Retrieved from www.startribune.com/st-olaf-cancels-baseball-season-after-hazing-investigation/297841441/

Northwestern University. (2017). *Peers urging responsible practices through leadership and education.* Retrieved from www.nusports.com/sports/2015/3/18/GEN_2014010135.aspx?path=wten

Somers, N. (2006). College and university liability for the dangerous yet time-honored tradition of hazing in fraternities and student athletics. *Journal of College and University Law, 33*(3), 653–680.

Sprow, C. (2006, May 16). Northwestern women's soccer team suspended after hazing. *The New York Times.* Retrieved from www.nytimes.com/2006/05/16/sports/soccer/16hazing.html

Sussberg, J. A. (2003). Shattered dreams: Hazing in college athletics. *Cardozo Law Review, 24*(3), 1421–1491.

Ukura, K. (2014, February 16). What happened to the perpetrators Michael Johnson describes? *The CAPs Times.* Retrieved from http://host.madison.com/ct/news/local/what-happened-to-the-perpetrators-michael-johnson-describes/article_c29b5b1e-95c1-11e3-804d-001a4bcf887a.html

University of Florida. (2017). *UAA hazing policy.* Retrieved from www.dso.ufl.edu/documents/sccr/uaa-hazing-policy.pdf

Waldron, J. J., & Kowalski, C. L. (2009). Crossing the line: Rites of passage, team aspects, and the ambiguity of hazing. *Research Quarterly for Exercise and Sport, 80*, 291–302.

Waldron, J. J., & Kowalski, C. L. (2010). Looking the other way: Athletes' perceptions of coaches' responses to hazing. *International Journal of Sports Science & Coaching, 5*, 87–100.

Chapter 4

Tradition or Torment
Examining Hazing in the College Marching Band

Jason M. Silveira

On the evening of November 19, 2011, Robert Champion, the drum major of the Florida A&M University's Marching 100 band, left his hotel room and approached one of the charter buses transporting the band to the annual Florida Classic. He was about to endure a hazing ritual known as Crossing Bus C, which consisted of walking shirtless from the front of the bus to the back of the bus backward while a bus full of band members beat him with punches, kicks, bass drum mallets, and drum sticks. The following is an excerpt from the 911 call made that evening by fellow Marching 100 band member Henry Nesbitt:

911 Operator: Hi, I need to know what's going on.
Caller: We have a band member right here on the bus, and he's not breathing.
911 Operator: He's not breathing?
Caller: We're at the Rosen Plaza.
911 Operator: OK, I know. Are you with him right now?
Caller: Yes, I'm with him, ma'am. He's not breathing. I tried to give him CPR; he started to vomit.
911 Operator: OK, I want you to lay him on the floor. Is he on the floor?
Caller: OK. Yes, ma'am, he's on the floor.
911 Operator: OK, is there anything under him?
Caller: No. No, ma'am, there's nothing under him.
911 Operator: OK, is there an AED [*automated external defibrillator*] available?
Caller: I just sent somebody in to try and get one inside the hotel.
911 Operator: OK, like I told them already, we do already have help on the way. You're in the back of the hotel on a bus, correct?
Caller: Yes, ma'am.
911 Operator: OK, and you're right by him now?
Caller: He's on my hand, ma'am. He's cold. He's in my hands.
911 Operator: OK, I want you to lay him flat on his back and remove anything from under his head, OK?

Caller:	All right, cool. All right, he's flat. He's flat on his back.
911 Operator:	He is. OK, then I want you to kneel next to him, and I want you to look in his mouth for food or vomit.
Caller:	Yes, it's vomit.
911 Operator:	There is vomit in his mouth?
Caller:	Yes.
911 Operator:	OK, then I want you to turn his head to the side, and I want you to clean out his mouth and his nose. Can you hear me? Sir, can you hear me? *[Talking going on.]*
911 Operator:	Hello? Sir? *[Call ends.]*

Champion would never make it back to his hotel room alive. He died at 10:36 p.m. on the evening of November 19, 2011, due to a fatal hemorrhagic shock caused by blunt force trauma (Alvarez, 2012). This ritual was conducted under the guise of what state Attorney Jeff Ashton called a "dark tradition.... The fact that this is a tradition is not a defense to the people involved" (CBS News, 2014). The death of Robert Champion was an outcome due to, in the words of Champion's parents' lawyer, the "culture of hazing" within the university's Marching 100 (Breen, 2012). Although the investigation surrounding Champion's death led to several convictions, including prison sentences, questions remain regarding the prevalence of hazing within college marching bands and what the higher education community can do to help prevent it in the future. This chapter will share results from the limited number of empirical studies surrounding hazing in college marching bands and provide recommendations for future research and practical implications and suggestions for hazing prevention and reporting.

MARCHING BANDS AND HAZING

The earliest continuously operating college marching band in the United States is at the University of Notre Dame (Wells, 1976). Notre Dame's founder, Rev. Edward Sorin, CSC, decided that the new university needed a band. With modest beginnings, the band played at the first graduation ceremony in 1846. The college marching band is perhaps one of the most visible aspects of any music program, and it has the potential to develop esprit de corps among its members. There are many benefits associated with the college marching band both to students and to the college at large. Administrators have long noted the positive association between a strong marching band program and public relations (Foster, 1978; Schwardon, 1974). Given the high visibility of the college marching band, it is often seen as a useful recruitment tool as well, and it can even influence prospective students' choice of which institution to attend (Dunnigan, 2007; Madsen, Plack, & Dunnigan, 2007). In Cumberledge's (2016) review of the literature, he outlines several benefits of and challenges associated with college marching band participation. Among the student benefits discussed include leadership roles and decision-making skills, social experiences, including a "home away from home" (Kuntz, 2011, p. 26), and possible health benefits. Cumberledge (2016) also broaches the subject of hazing in the college marching band as a challenge facing these ensembles, specifically mentioning the hazing death of Robert Champion and the related litigation and media attention.

As outlined in Chapter 8, 44 states and the District of Columbia currently have anti-hazing statues, although some specifically exclude groups from coverage or limit coverage to certain contexts (e.g., sporting events), time periods (e.g., in connection with initiation), or only to physical harm. In any of these instances, it is conceivable that protection for marching band students may be limited in such states.

Protection under the auspices of the university may also be unclear from institution to institution. University liability has changed over the years from in loco parentis (in place of the parents), where universities were responsible for students' well-being, to the no-duty rule, which stated that universities were responsible for students' education but not for their care. However, courts have now determined that universities have a duty to regulate reasonably foreseeable activities that take place on university property.

Ganellen's (2016) analysis of hazing in university marching bands outlined several instances in which university liability surrounding marching band hazing is unclear and inconsistent: "Although courts have not been willing to say that universities owe a duty of care to students generally, they have been somewhat more receptive to finding a duty to student athletes in certain situations" (p. 2333). A related court ruling in *Kleinknecht v. Gettysburg College* (1992) stated that the university owes student-athletes a duty of care if (1) the student-athlete was actively recruited by the university; (2) the incident occurred while the student-athlete was acting in his or her capacity as an athlete, not just as a student; and (3) the risk of harm was foreseeable by the university. However, at the time of this writing, no similar ruling or interpretation of *Kleinknect v. Gettysburg College* has been applied to encompass marching band members.

Despite the increased media attention on hazing in college marching bands, there are few published research reports that investigate this topic. Much of the published literature regarding hazing has examined fraternity and sorority life (see Chapter 5) and athletics (see Chapter 3). However, when examining how hazing is defined, it is perhaps not surprising that hazing occurs in college marching bands. For example, Bauer and colleagues (2015) broadly defined hazing as a ritual initiation in three phases: separation, marginalization, and aggregation as well as "a complex set of behaviors taking place during the integration process of newcomers in a coalitional group" (p. 2). A coalitional group is one where member generations overlap, have a past, and are expected to engage in cooperative actions for a long period of time. Marching bands certainly meet those requirements, as there is an overlap of members as students graduate and freshmen enter. The very nature of a marching band is cooperative and can last anywhere from 1 to 4 (or more) years. Students are typically first integrated into the group during marching band "camp," which is a highly concentrated period of time usually occurring before the start of the academic year to prepare for the upcoming football season. In the preceding sense, a marching band's culture can mimic the social structure of fraternities and sororities. Nuwer (2012) has stated that although not a fraternity in the strictest sense, many marching bands share a common value system of character, camaraderie, strong social bonds, service to the community, and individual and collective musical, academic, and social growth. It has been suggested that students in these types of organizations continue to haze to preserve group features and to promote cognitive, social, and emotional manifestations of social dependency (Keating et al., 2005).

AN OVERVIEW OF THE LITERATURE

The limited published research reports on hazing in college marching bands have approached the topic from defining hazing to reporting incidents of hazing to documenting the frequency and type of hazing behaviors. What makes the study of hazing in marching bands more difficult is that even among students who have been hazed, many do not necessarily define it as hazing per se (Allan & Madden, 2012). Among the college student population at large, there also appears to be confusion regarding the definition of hazing (Hoover & Pollard, 1999; Kittle, 2012). Additionally, various college groups have different perceptions regarding what activities constitute hazing (Drout & Corsoro, 2003; Ellsworth, 2004; Wegener, 2001).

Although Ellsworth's (2004) work was one of the few studies to specifically include marching band students in the sample, there were some notable limitations. Marching band participants were drawn by recruiting members of Kappa Kappa Psi and Tau Beta Sigma. Both of these organizations are honorary college band-specific fraternities, and both have defined hazing and very specific anti-hazing policies. Additionally, only eight marching band students (a 16% response rate) were included in the study. As a result of these limitations, these marching band students would not constitute a representative sample and thus this study is not generalizable. Carter (2013) investigated the experiences of gay black male marching band members in historically black colleges and universities and also made a tangential reference to hazing:

> All four participants stated that the hazing they experienced was not something they ever discussed, not even with their fellow band members. They each indicated that their hazing was not as severe as what was described in news reports at FAMU [Florida A&M University]. However, each stated that what

they did endure was shameful and embarrassing and not something, even years later, they wished to share with me or anyone else.

(Carter, 2013, p. 39)

In their landmark study, Allan and Madden (2012) investigated several college organizations, including performing arts organizations, but more research was recommended, with specific mention of marching bands. To answer this call, Silveira and Hudson (2015) conducted the first nationwide study specifically investigating hazing in the college marching band. Using a random cluster sampling approach, they sampled 116 NCAA Division I schools, which resulted in 1,215 marching band participants. From the perspective of the one being hazed, they found that of the 23 enumerated hazing behaviors they provided, there were only four in which more than 10% of respondents answered in the affirmative. The four behaviors cited were (1) sing/chant by self or with others in public in a situation that is not related to an event, rehearsal, or performance (20%); (2) being yelled, cursed, or sworn at (19%); (3) associate with specific people and not others (15%); and (4) deprive yourself of sleep (12%) (Silveira & Hudson, 2015).

When asked how often study participants engaged in the 23 hazing behaviors as the one doing the hazing, the majority of participants selected "Never" (Silveira & Hudson, 2015). The two behaviors that elicited the most affirmative responses were "sing/chant by self or with select others in public in a situation that is not related to an event, rehearsal, or performance" (8%) and "endure being yelled, cursed, or sworn at" (5%). Perhaps one of the most alarming findings of the study was that after being given a definition of hazing, 30% of participants reported that they had observed hazing in their marching bands. Furthermore, 12% of respondents reported that members of their marching bands encouraged acts of hazing. The majority of participants who observed hazing behaviors did not report the incidents because of fear of retaliation or being ostracized from the group or because they viewed the hazing behavior as harmless.

Two promising findings emerged. One was that the majority of the marching band participants were informed of their institutions' hazing policies by their band directors, and the second was that, contrary to existing hazing research, the majority of the marching band participants viewed hazing and the outcomes of hazing primarily as detrimental and harmful (Silveira & Hudson, 2015). These could be signs of the effectiveness of hazing education and prevention efforts specifically directed toward marching bands.

In a follow-up study, Hudson and Silveira (2016) asked marching band students to provide their own definitions of hazing, given that previous research has shown that students have differing interpretations of the term. Nine themes emerged from the independently coded data:

1. Hazing is a means of exerting power or control upon another.
2. Hazing is something that is endured for acceptance into the group.
3. Hazing is a ritualistic experience that is used as a means to initiate new members.
4. Hazing is physical, sexual, psychological, or emotional abuse.
5. Hazing is meant to embarrass or humiliate the one being hazed.
6. Hazing is an activity not officially sanctioned by the group.
7. Hazing consists of dangerous behaviors that new group members take part in.
8. Incidents are labeled as hazing based on individuals' moral and legal judgments rather than on institution-specific policies.
9. Hazing can be misconstrued as bullying.

Based on these findings, it appears that marching band students have a variety of different interpretations of what would constitute hazing. However, many of the responses did align with current legal and legislative policies regarding hazing. Some themes of note included numbers two, three, seven, eight, and nine. Themes two, three, and seven specifically relate to new incoming members. However, in the case of Robert Champion, for example, he was already a member in a leadership position within the marching band. Perhaps, as Nuwer (2012) suggested, hazing definitions need to be modified to include current group members who "let down" the group. Themes eight and nine further illustrate confusion surrounding how individuals define, interpret, and recognize hazing.

FUTURE RESEARCH AND PRACTICE RECOMMENDATIONS

Given the preceding research, several suggestions for future research are recommended. The investigation into hazing in college marching bands is growing and has become more visible in the research community. This is a promising direction. However, there has also been an increased prevalence of hazing (in general) in high schools. Future research on hazing in marching bands might investigate the possibility of a culture of hazing in high school marching bands as well. Additionally, based on the research findings presented here, as well as the increased attention on the dangers of hazing, there still appears to be confusion regarding the definition of hazing and identifying and labeling behaviors as hazing. It is suggested that the wording in legislative and judicial policies regarding hazing be adjusted as not to exclude certain groups (e.g., marching bands). It is also suggested that policies be adjusted to acknowledge that hazing can include emotional and psychological trauma (not just physical abuse) and occur at any point during the course of students' affiliations with an organization, not just during initiation (Ganellen,

2016). In addition to continued research and implementing legislative changes, there are several practical implications and suggestions for marching band students and directors for hazing prevention and reporting.

As Matthews (2017) found in her recent study, the potential for a hostile and combative atmosphere in marching bands is greater during the middle of the season. She specifically advised organizations to revisit institutional harassment and hazing policies with students at the midpoint of the marching band season, as tensions tend to increase at this point. She further stated,

> Knowing that there is a potential for a pejorative atmosphere in the middle of the season, directors can plan ways to help students understand their frustrations and provide opportunities for students to develop coping strategies, whether it be team building exercises, social events, or helping students access university resources to help balance academic and personal life outside of the ensemble.
>
> (Matthews, 2017, p. 197)

Additional strategies to combat hazing include supporting student leadership, inviting motivational speakers and professional musicians, and organizing social or service-learning activities.

At the local and department levels, there are several ways marching band directors and marching band students can help prevent and report hazing incidents. For example, Holmes (2013) offers a nine-step ERADICATE model:

1. **E**ducate all stakeholders on policies, procedures, and laws on hazing.
2. **R**eview routinely policies, procedures, and laws on hazing.
3. **A**ddress and ensure all stakeholders are accountable for policies, procedures, and laws on hazing.
4. **D**istinguish hazing myths and truths.
5. **I**mplement activities in the educational setting and community on anti-hazing prevention strategies.
6. **C**ommunicate the impact of hazing on victims and their families as well as solutions to end it.
7. **A**dvertise continuously in the media research-based solutions and best practices on eradicating hazing.
8. **T**each anti-hazing curriculum in education settings and the community.
9. **E**valuate periodically anti-hazing prevention strategies in education settings and the community.

Providing students with resources to identify and (anonymously) report hazing via marching band websites can also be a useful tool to report existing hazing practices and to reduce future instances of hazing. There are also several discussion guides and webinars, along with a documentary offered by the Clery Center

(2017), to help students identify, report, and prevent hazing. The Be a Champion Foundation (2016), created by Robert Champion's family, offers programs and resources designed to "end the senseless violence that ails communities, fragments families, and limits our nation's potential." It is also suggested that marching band directors periodically conduct climate surveys to assess the culture of the marching band, determine if hazing is occurring, and develop strategies to combat it. A hazing climate assessment is available through StopHazing.org (2018b) for a fee. However, directors might choose to modify Silveira and Hudson's (2015) questionnaire to meet the needs of their particular institutions.

At the university and national levels, the following recommendations could prove useful. Silveira and Hudson (2015) suggested the development of an anti-hazing task force within the College Band Directors National Association (CBDNA) to educate students and faculty and to make them aware of potential warning signs. At the time of this writing, there is only one reference to hazing on the association's web page regarding hazing: "The members of the College Band Directors National Association discourage hazing in any form and encourage bands to fully comply with the hazing and student conduct standards of their institutions" (College Band Directors National Association, 2013).

There is no reference to hazing education or prevention in the College and University Athletic Band Guidelines provided by the association's Athletic Band Task Force. Finally, colleges and universities are encouraged to join the Hazing Prevention Consortium organized by StopHazing.org (2018a). This consortium is a multiyear research-to-practice initiative that compiles evidence of hazing and methods of prevention on several college campuses. There is a second cohort of schools being established from fall 2017 through spring 2020.

CASE STUDIES

Although recent events have highlighted serious band-related hazing incidents, there are a variety of situations that can constitute hazing in the context of college and university bands. The following case studies will help surface different practices that could potentially constitute hazing. Each case study is followed by a set of questions for further discussion and reflection.

Case Study 1

The Marching Pride, the band for the Western State University Lions, has a strong reputation at its institution and throughout the marching band community. One of the program's strengths is the high level of investment students make when joining the band. Part of their obligation includes returning to campus three weeks early to begin practice before the first home athletic events.

A third-year member of the band has to leave campus due to a family emergency during the second week of practice. As a result, the band directors have decided that the member is not allowed to march in the first two events of the season. Additionally, the drum major and seniors who are a part of the band have decided the student must "run the gauntlet." Their intention is to have every band member hand the student a card or message of support related to the family emergency, although they do not tell the student that this is their plan.

Other band members report the incident to the band director because the member is afraid of repercussions and possible physical harm as a result of the incident.

1. What should the band director do?
2. What are the potential implications for the junior member, drum major/senior band members, and the band as a whole?
3. Is this hazing? Why or why not?

Case Study 2

At the home game closest to Halloween weekend, band members are told to wear their favorite Halloween costumes for their performance. All upper-division students agree not to show up in costume without telling the first-year band members. The day of the event, the band director is upset about the lack of uniformity among band members. The director admonishes the first-year students and assigns additional duties and practices to them as a result.

1. Is this hazing? Why or why not?
2. What should the upper-division band members do in response to the band director's actions?

Case Study 3

Part of the marching band culture involves singing some common songs ("Row, Row, Row Your Boat"; "Happy Birthday"; "Twinkle, Twinkle Little Star") and replacing the original lyrics with profane and obscene lyrics instead. A songbook is developed and passed down from one class of band members to the next. Band members are expected to learn the new lyrics and to sing them along with upper-division students. When asked to perform the songs, if students (new or upper-division) make a mistake, they must take a shot of alcohol.

One of the new members leaves a copy of the songbook in a biology classroom after class one day. The faculty member gives the songbook to the dean of students and says, "I don't know if this is something that you should follow up on, but I just wanted to make you aware." The faculty member clearly has no expectation of punishment being issued and does not feel a need to be kept posted as the situation moves forward. The dean of students reaches out to the band director and shares the information about the rules and a copy of the songbook.

1. Is the existence and distribution of this book hazing? Why or why not?
2. Is the fact that members are expected to memorize and be able to perform these songs hazing? Why or why not?
3. What should the band director do? What should the dean of students do?
4. What are the potential implications for students' relationships among band members? (Accountability of senior members for distributing; issues for the student who left the book in class; trust among members?)

CONCLUSION

In the words of Robert Champion's parents, "Our loss and pain is no secret. We have faced an unimaginable darkness that no parents are ever prepared for . . . we seek to carry out our commitment to prevent such heinous acts of violence from destroying any other families" (Be a Champion Foundation, 2016). Given the dangers associated with hazing behaviors, it is incumbent upon various stakeholders to educate marching band students and to provide them with resources to report hazing and help prevent future incidents of hazing. Hazing prevention in marching bands is an ongoing process that must occur at various points throughout the year. Researchers have documented that by involving marching band directors and student leadership in the process can help cultivate an anti-hazing culture within the group. It is hoped that this collaboration with researchers and other stakeholders can truly help eradicate hazing.

REFERENCES

Allan, E. J., & Madden, M. (2012). The nature and extent of college student hazing. *International Journal of Adolescent Medicine and Health*, *24*, 83–90. doi:10.1515/IJAMH.2012.012

Alvarez, L. (2012, May 24). Hazing ritual of a band is described in documents. *The New York Times*, p. A16.

Bauer, B. Y. R., Nunes, S. C., Martins, J. D. M., Mendes, M., Pinho, S. B., & Silva, O. (2015). About hazing in higher education. *European Scientific Journal*. Retrieved from http://hdl.handle.net/10400.26/13909

Be a Champion Foundation. (2016). *Home*. Retrieved from www.beingachampion.org

Breen, D. (2012, May 29). FAMU band's hazing culture: How did school officials miss it? *Orlando Sentinel*. Retrieved from www.orlandosentinel.com/news/famu-hazing-band/os-famu-hazing-culture-20120525-story.html

Carter, B. A. (2013). "Nothing better or worse than being black, gay, and in the band": A qualitative examination of gay, undergraduates participating in historically black college or university marching bands. *Journal of Research in Music Education, 61*, 26–43. doi:10.1177/0022429412474470

CBS News. (2014, October 28). Hazing trial begins in death of FAMU drum major Robert Champion. *CBS News*. Retrieved from www.cbsnews.com/news/hazing-trial-begins-in-death-of-famu-drum-major-robert-champion/

Clery Center. (2017). *We don't haze: A Clery Center documentary*. Retrieved from https://clerycenter.org/initiatives/hazing-project/

College Band Directors National Association. (2013). *Athletic bands*. Retrieved from www.cbdna.org/cgi-bin/taskforce_athletic_bands.pl

Cumberledge, J. P. (2016). The benefits of college marching band for students and universities: A review of literature. *Update: Applications of Research in Music Education, 36*(1). doi:10.1177/8755123316682819

Drout, C. E., & Corsoro, C. L. (2003). Attitudes toward fraternity hazing among fraternity members, sorority members, and non-Greek students. *Social Behavior and Personality, 31*, 535–544. doi:10.2224/sbp.2003.31.6.535

Dunnigan, P. (2007). *Marching band techniques* (2nd ed.). Northfield, IL: The Instrumentalist.

Ellsworth, C. W. (2004). *Definitions of hazing: Differences among selected student organizations* (Unpublished master's thesis). University of Maryland, College Park.

Foster, R. E. (1978). *Multiple-option marching band techniques*. Port Washington, NY: Alfred.

Ganellen, B. D. (2016). When marching to the beat of the drum means beating the drummer: An analysis of hazing in university marching bands. *University of Illinois Law Review, 2016*(5), 2309–2346.

Holmes, R. W. (2013). *How to eradicate hazing*. Bloomington, IN: AuthorHouse.

Hoover, N., & Pollard, N. (1999). *Initiation rites and athletics: A national survey of NCAA sports teams*. Alfred, NY: Alfred University and Reidman Insurance.

Hudson, M. W., & Silveira, J. M. (2016). *In their own words: Marching band students' definitions of hazing*. Research poster presented at the 2016 Biennial Meeting of the National Association for Music Education, Atlanta, GA.

Keating, C. F., Pomerantz, J., Pommer, S. D., Ritt, S. J. H., Miller, L. M., & McCormick, J. (2005). Going to college and unpacking hazing: A functional approach to decrypting initiation practices among undergraduates. *Group Dynamics: Theory, Research, and Practice, 9*(2), 104–126. doi:10.1037/1089-2699.9.2.104

Kittle, P. R. (2012). *Assessing the efficacy of analytical definitions in hazing education* (Unpublished doctoral dissertation). Auburn University, Auburn, AL.

Kleinknecht v. Gettysburg College. 786 F. Supp. 449 (1992). Retrieved from http://openjurist.org/989/f2d/1360/kleinknecht-v-gettysburg-college-w-kleinknecht-p-r-w-p

Kuntz, T. L. (2011). High school students' participation in music activities beyond the school day. *Update: Applications of Research in Music Education, 30*(1), 23–31. doi:10.1177/8755123311418478

Madsen, C. K., Plack, D., & Dunnigan, P. (2007). The marching band as a recruiter for the university. *Journal of Band Research, 43*(1), 54–62.

Matthews, W. K. (2017). "Stand by me": A mixed methods study of a collegiate marching band members' intragroup beliefs throughout a performance season. *Journal of Research in Music Education, 65*, 179–202. doi:10.1177/0022429417694875

Nuwer, H. (2012). A band hazing may forever increase the legal consequences for hazing deaths. *Fraternal Law, 119*, 1–3.

Schwardon, T. (1974). Why the marching band? *Music Educators Journal, 32*(9), 30–31.

Silveira, J. M., & Hudson, M. W. (2015). Hazing in the college marching band. *Journal of Research in Music Education, 63*, 5–27. doi:10.1177/0022429415569064

StopHazing.org. (2018a). *Hazing prevention consortium*. Retrieved from www.stophazing.org/hazing-prevention-consortium/

StopHazing.org. (2018b). *Services*. Retrieved from www.stophazing.org/about/services/

Wegener, C. J. (2001). *Perceptions of hazing among Greek and ROTC students at the University of Nebraska-Lincoln* (Unpublished master's thesis). University of Nebraska–Lincoln.

Wells, J. R. (1976). *The marching band in contemporary music education*. New York, NY: Interland.

Chapter 5

Fraternity and Sorority Hazing

S. Brian Joyce and Jenny Nirh

Fraternities and sororities are among the oldest forms of student involvement on college campuses, but they unfortunately have a long and complicated history with hazing. This chapter presents a brief history of fraternities and sororities and the introduction of hazing into organizations, presents actionable ways to combat hazing in fraternities and sororities, and provides case studies for use in discussions about hazing with respect to practical applications for practitioners and scholars.

HISTORY OF FRATERNITIES AND SORORITIES

Fraternities and sororities are unique to North America, existing only in the United States and Canada. The earliest roots of the modern college fraternity date back to Phi Beta Kappa, which was formed in 1776 at the College of William and Mary (Boschini & Thompson, 1998). Today's fraternity and sorority organizations maintain many similarities to Phi Beta Kappa, including names comprised of Greek letters, secret rituals, cultures that are unique to each group, and a badge or pin that is reserved for initiated members only (Whipple & Sullivan, 1998), but Phi Beta Kappa members were chosen based on their grade point averages. The first society originating for mostly social purposes was Kappa Alpha Society, founded by five students at Union College in 1825 (Syrett, 2009). The Kappa Alpha Society branched out to several other colleges to open local chapters, sparking the spread of the modern-day college fraternity.

Kappa Alpha Society was not only the first social fraternity founded on campus but also where the first reported incidents of fraternity or sorority hazing took place. A pledge named Mortimer Leggett was blindfolded and taken into the woods as part of a Kappa Alpha Society initiation at Cornell University in 1873 (Nuwer, 1999). He fell to his death in a gorge while being led by two members of the fraternity. Edward Fairchild Berkeley, another Kappa Alpha Society pledge at Cornell, fell into a canal and drowned in 1899 after being instructed to pin a piece of paper onto a tree (Nuwer, 1999).

Diversification of Fraternities and Sororities

Fraternities and sororities are governed by umbrella organizations, the distinctions of which are helpful to understand in order to develop a complete picture of the history and incongruence of hazing within fraternity and sorority life. Historically, fraternities were founded at a time when the student bodies on college campuses were white, male, and Christian (Boschini & Thompson, 1998). As college and university demographics diversified, so too did the purposes of their social organizations. The North-American Interfraternity Conference was founded in 1909 to "advance its local fraternity community" (North-American Interfraternity Conference, 2018); it now has 75 member organizations, with over 5,500 chapters on more than 800 campuses.

Part of the adaptation to demographic changes in higher education came with the introduction of women's social fraternities. Fraternities for women, eventually known as sororities, were established beginning in the 1850s with the organization that grew to become Alpha Delta Pi and when Pi Beta Phi became the first national women's fraternity in 1867 (Torbensen & Parks, 2009). As the growth of women's fraternities flourished and the groups moved from academic societies to primarily social organizations, alumni members of national organizations called together the Inter-Sorority Council. The group, which later became the National Panhellenic Conference, gathered to address recruitment and pledging and to establish standards for the sorority experience (Turk, 2004). The National Panhellenic Conference "was established in 1902 to assist collegiate and alumnae chapters of the NPC member organizations in cooperating with colleges and universities and to foster interfraternal relationships" (National Panhellenic Conference, n.d., para. 2). Black fraternity and sorority organizations formed at the beginning of the 20th century "in cultural and social opposition to the exclusively white fraternity and sorority organizations that were in existence" (Whaley, 2008, p. 54). The National Pan-Hellenic Council formed in 1930 as an umbrella organization for the nine historically black fraternity and sorority organizations known today as the Divine Nine (Whaley, 2008). The council ended the pledging process in 1990, opting instead for a new member intake process in response to a Morehouse College student who died as a result of hazing (Foster, 2008). This led to hazing going underground and becoming more covert, resulting in a rise in the number of incidents involving violent beatings and branding the skin of new members, primarily in the men's groups (Ruffins, 1997).

Multicultural fraternities and sororities emerged on college campuses in the 1980s and 1990s. The first multicultural sorority, Mu Sigma Upsilon, was founded in 1981. The National Association of Latino Fraternal Organizations was founded in 1998, "uniting the Latino fraternal community" (National Multicultural Greek Council, n.d., para. 6); it became the National Multicultural Greek Council in 1998. Just as in other fraternity and sorority councils, the increase of organizations in the National Multicultural Greek Council came with an increase in the reported instances of hazing, specifically drinking deaths in Asian American fraternities (Hu, 2015). It is important to recognize that hazing has happened in all fraternities and sororities, yet there are few studies that explore hazing and no institutionalized form to report hazing events.

There are often gendered differences in hazing perspectives and habits. According to Nuwer (1999), hazing in sororities is less common and less physical than in men's fraternities, but it was reported to be on the rise for many years (Gerahty, 1997). The National Study of Student Hazing provided specific gendered differences in terms of hazing experiences across different types of student organizations. Men experienced some physical hazing activities, such as forced alcohol consumption or exposure to harsh elements, at significantly higher rates than women (Allan & Madden, 2008). Campo, Poulos, and Sipple (2005) also reported that women are more likely to feel more susceptible to the dangers of hazing and more likely to believe that hazing is harmful.

The diversification and growth of fraternities occurred concurrently with the increase in hazing, including injuries and deaths as a result of hazing (Alvarez, 2015). After the introduction of the GI Bill and the related influx of college students following both World War II and the Vietnam War, hazing behaviors increased. At the same time, organizations became more exclusive because of the increased interest in membership, and hazing became a strategy for ensuring that exclusivity (Alvarez, 2015). Additionally, the increase in military veterans in fraternities and colleges changed the hazing landscape and incorporated more military-related hazing, including calisthenics, lineups, and drills (Nuwer, 1990).

HAZING AS AN ONGOING ISSUE

Although hazing has increased over time—in part due to the growth of fraternities and sororities on college campuses—the number of hazing-related deaths is something that defines the contemporary era of hazing culture in higher education. Nuwer (2018) reported that there has been at least one hazing death per year from 1969 to 2017, while Hollmann (2002) stated that there were more hazing-related deaths between 1990 and 2002 than all previous college and university hazing-related deaths combined. Hazing deaths remain a far too common occurrence in 2017, with the vast majority caused by alcohol poisoning ("Hazing deaths on American," 2017).

Through the National Study of Student Hazing, Allan and Madden (2008) surveyed 11,482 undergraduate students at 53 college campuses across the United States in 2007. Today the study remains the largest research set on hazing behaviors. Allan and Madden (2008) reported that more than half of college students involved in clubs, teams, and/or organizations experienced hazing. Although hazing occurs in a variety of settings, it is most closely associated with social fraternities and sororities on college campuses. With very few exceptions, almost all hazing-related deaths since 1970 have been connected to fraternities and sororities (Nuwer, 2004). Despite the fact that all the umbrella Greek councils and all Greek organizations officially ban hazing, 73% of fraternity and sorority members reported experiencing hazing (Allan & Madden, 2008).

WHAT IS TRADITION REALLY ABOUT IN THE FRATERNITY/SORORITY EXPERIENCE?

Why do hazing practices continue when organizational policies at all levels prohibit them? As stated in Chapter 1, hazing is often confused with tradition in the culture of fraternity and sorority organizations. Fraternities and sororities are grounded in tradition. The purpose of the rituals they perform, many of which go back more than 100 years, should be to create purpose and meaning in the organization. People value rites of passage, rituals, and traditions, and college students are no different (Terenzini, Pascarella, & Blimling, 1996). During college, students are searching for admittance and acceptance into peer groups. Participating in certain rituals or traditions allows new or potential new members to feel more like legitimate group members. In fraternities and sororities, the shared experience is what creates connections to others in the organization.

Recent scholarship also highlights the role of exclusivity in membership. Parks, Jones, Shayne, Ray, and Hughey (2015) wrote about the role of hazing practices in connection with joining exclusive organizations and that over time hazing transitioned from institutional practice to one concentrated in a few exclusive organizations on campus. Although many organizations have removed policy-implemented restrictions on membership based on gender, sexual orientation, race, or religion, these as well as social class and gender expression remain barriers to membership. Additionally, these organizational policy changes "may not reflect campus realities and practices" (Barber, Espino, & Bureau, 2015, p. 244).

Group member transition involves three phases: detachment from one's previous group, the transitional period into the new group, and then full group membership (Elkins, Braxton, & James, 2000; Turner, 1977; Van Gennep, 2004). This transition can be seen in the fraternity and sorority community as students move from potential members, new members, and *neos* through initiation, through their first years in the group, to becoming senior members of the organization. Throughout each of these time periods, traditions and rituals are key factors in helping move students through those phases. According to Turner (1977), not all traditions or ceremonies need to be those *sacred* rituals, like initiation, to have an impact. Participating in ceremonies, traditions, or rituals creates a stronger connection to an organization. It is important to acknowledge, however, that research has failed to determine that harmful traditions create those same connections

(Johnson, 2002; Lodewijkx & Syroit, 1997). In the context of this chapter, harmful traditions are hazing habits designed to humiliate and degrade potential or new organizational members.

The Connections Between Hazing and Tradition

All traditions are not hazing, and not all hazing is (mis)framed in tradition. In the first chapter of this book, the authors refer to hazing as habit instead of tradition. The routines and expectations of fraternity- and sorority-affiliated students are often built around the routines of institutions and thus the lines between hazing habits and organizational traditions become blurred. This lack of clarity combined with institutional and organizational routines can create and perpetuate hazing habits. Academic school years follow the same pattern, with little modification: the year begins, there are midterms, there are finals, and then the semester ends. What events occur between those milestones can be meaningful traditions that add to the college experience when the activities are properly aligned with organizational values, missions, and goals.

Although it may be a tradition to go camping as a chapter each year, prohibiting the pledges/new members from taking sleeping bags or tents is hazing. Camping together can create positive memories for members. However, a camping trip where pledges/new members are not allowed sleeping bags or tents would create further disharmony between older and new members, possibly causing resentment and creating potential health risks for the pledges/new members (Johnson, 2002; Lodewijkx & Syroit, 1997).

Cokley et al. (2001) reported that fraternity and sorority members are more likely to believe that hazing has positive impacts than nonmembers. Although many participants in hazing behaviors perceive hazing will result in positive outcomes and specifically identify team unity and teamwork as justifications of their actions, more than two thirds of respondents fail to list teamwork or unity as an actual outcome of their hazing experiences (Allan & Madden, 2008). Many students assume hazing builds positive team dynamics within their organizations, but the reality is that these benefits are not actual outcomes for the majority of those experiencing hazing (Johnson, 2002; Lodewijkx & Syroit, 1997).

HAZING AND MORAL DISENGAGEMENT

The lack of clarity on the part of student members around the value of hazing is not the only concern about these habits. Hazing in organizations can be compared to domestic violence in terms of the cycle of violence that is perpetuated and then hidden—in this case behind tradition. According to Bandura (1999), individuals are able to justify their own participation in immoral acts or reprehensible conduct through a process called moral disengagement. In moral disengagement theory

(Bandura, 1999), there are key ways in which individuals justify their actions: moral justification, euphemistic labeling, advantageous comparison, displacement of responsibility, diffusion of responsibility disregarding or misrepresenting injurious consequences, dehumanization, and attribution of blame. Throughout this process, individuals are able to hide or justify their activities as organizational tradition. Fraternity and sorority members are able to engage in hazing activities in the name of their organizations while feeling justified in their behavior.

In fraternities and sororities that haze members, students morally disengage and justify hazing under the guise of moral justification and euphemistic labeling, specifically as they refer to tradition (Nirh, 2014). Moral justification of hazing links the specific activities to a higher purpose or value of the organization, while euphemistic labeling is creating a new name or title for a hazing behavior. By simply calling a hazing behavior a tradition or ritual, students are able to disengage from the activity's negative repercussions. In fact, even calling activities hazing is a form of euphemistic labeling, as some hazing behaviors are actually physical and/or sexual assaults (Nirh, 2014).

By linking hazing behaviors to tradition, students become comfortable with the abuse and humiliation of potential and new members. Students can say that the hazing habit is acceptable because "we've always done it this way" or "this is part of what it means to become a [new chapter] man/woman." This, by extension, means that it is acceptable to continue the behavior or that the hazing habit affords members the opportunity to provide retribution to those who follow, perpetuating the cycle of violence (Nirh, 2014). The nature of fraternities and sororities is one of tradition, but when tradition is not grounded in care for members that aligns with the organizational values, it is no longer a tradition but instead becomes a hazing habit. This creates more opportunities for hazing in the name of *tradition*. The rapid turnover of members, moral justification, and euphemistic labeling all make it possible for hazing to grow and continue in organizations.

CURRENT TRENDS

Hazing has been present on college campuses since the earliest institutions were established. Hazing is increasingly dangerous, with a focus on hard alcohol and physical assault (Hollmann, 2002; Lipkins, 2006). Students have died on college campuses due to hazing every year from 1970 to 2017 (Flanagan, 2017; Levenson & Hassan, 2017; Nuwer, 2004).

The visibility of these incidents is a recent component of hazing habits. Students' access to smartphone cameras and increased social media use has resulted in hazing behaviors being documented now more than ever before. This also means that fraternity and sorority hazing incidents are bigger stories that stay in the media for longer than in the past. As a result, organizations face more public scrutiny and outrage when hazing takes place (Lohse, 2012; Reitman, 2012).

The visibility of hazing behaviors has also become more entrenched in contemporary culture. Recently movies like *Goat* (2016) and *Burning Sands* (2017) have shown the violence in fraternities. Whether accurate or dramatically exaggerated, these artifacts inform the environment and student assumptions and dialogue around hazing behavior.

Additionally, individuals are more often charged in hazing-related crimes than in the past. In 2007, administrators and students were initially charged in the death of a fraternity pledge at Rider University (Hu & Miller, 2007), the hazing death of Timothy Piazza resulted in more than 1,000 criminal charges filed against 18 fraternity members of Beta Theta Pi at Penn State (Ganim & Welch, 2017), and four students pled guilty in the Baruch College hazing death of Chun Hsieng Deng (Rojas, 2017).

Risk-related issues in fraternity and sorority organizations, such as hazing and sexual assault, have led colleges and universities to make significant changes. These calls to action have come from administrators, parents, and the public, and as a result, many small, private, liberal arts colleges, including Colby College, Bowdoin College, Middlebury College, and Williams College, have banned fraternity and sorority life on campus (New, 2014).

Private colleges and universities, such as Dartmouth College, Gettysburg College, and Wesleyan University, have discussed at length the idea of abolishing the system due to complaints of alcohol abuse, sexual assault, and hazing (New, 2014). At institutions that enacted dry-campus policies and ended fraternity and sorority life, rogue fraternity chapters have still turned up, often operating in more dangerous ways than before (Ryan, 2014). Colleges and universities have struggled to change the culture of fraternity and sorority hazing, and the path ahead remains unclear. Many institutions feel stuck between campus regulation with liability for potentially dangerous organizational activities and the alternative of unregulated and unmonitored fraternities or sororities.

CHALLENGES AND OPPORTUNITIES IN FRATERNITY AND SORORITY ORGANIZATIONS

As with any issue facing higher education, the hazing culture of fraternities and sororities provides challenges and opportunities. The challenges for staff members working with student organizations or fraternity and sorority life are not theirs alone. Rather, there is work to be done by faculty, students, organizations, alumni, and others vested in the university experience to create transformative change.

Challenges in Fraternity and Sorority Organizations

Hazing prevention efforts continue to be challenging for several reasons. First, many stakeholders (including current undergraduates, alumni, advisers, and parents) might believe hazing activities are fun (Keating et al., 2005; Nirh, 2014).

Members who engage in hazing do not believe it is dangerous; they minimize abuse and see it as harmless (Allan & Madden, 2008; Marcitllach & Freire, 2013; Nirh, 2014). Additionally, members engaged in hazing value tradition, ritual, and earning organizational membership. Finally, members have the perception that they can place blame on the organization rather than take responsibility themselves when incidents occur.

Institutions struggle with hazing in terms of creating policies that align with federal and state hazing policies. Further, establishing structural and institutional processes for individuals to report hazing activities is complex. Overall, having those involved understand the severity of hazing and the extent to which their behavior is a problem is an individual, organizational, and institutional issue.

Opportunities in Fraternity and Sorority Organizations

Despite the challenges facing higher education around hazing prevention, there are also opportunities. In addition to university faculty, staff, and administrators, students (both victims and perpetrators), parents, and alumni can all serve as facilitators of prevention efforts to make the fraternity and sorority experience safe, healthy, and aligned with chapter missions and goals. First, labeling hazing habits as assault and humiliation rather than as tradition and ritual changes the conversation.

Additionally, by holding individuals and organizations accountable, universities and colleges can transform the culture by removing one of the obstacles to accountability—invisibility through membership. If on a college campus the organization as a whole is held accountable but the members who made individual choices to be involved are not, it enforces the idea that members can hide within the organization. Creating different levels of individual responsibility will promote the creation of more engaged and civically responsible students.

Finally, addressing hazing behaviors provides the opportunity to create powerful communities and senses of belonging for students. Rather than driven by fear, toxic masculinity, other problematic gender issues, violence, and degradation, fraternities and sororities have a chance to celebrate successes that embody a positive and enriching undergraduate experience, including opportunities for leadership, academics, service, and belonging, all of which can lead to transformation for the individual member in the organization, at the institution, and in the larger community.

CASE STUDIES

One of the goals of this text is to offer practitioners new and useful ways to respond to hazing. We hope these case studies provide a forum to begin that discussion.

Case Study 1

Scenario: The new member educator for Alpha Beta (AB) fraternity sent out a group text to all new members stating that they were each required to carry a red hat with AB letters on it at all times and to wear a pack around their waists that includes a list of items should their big brothers make a request. The new members were told there would be "extreme consequences" if they did not have these items in their possession. AB's rival fraternity found out about the new member activities, and a group of five of the fraternity brothers cornered an new AB member and stole his hat. When the new member told AB leaders what happened, they decided not to punish him for losing his hat, saying that the punishments were only meant to scare the new members into doing what they said.

Discussion questions: Was this hazing? If so, in what ways? What is concerning about this behavior?

Post-discussion considerations: This activity is a violation of most institutions' hazing policies. The new member educator did not punish the new member, but the act was clearly intended to control and embarrass new members. Additionally, the requirements could have caused psychological harm or other unintended consequences. Furthermore, the activity specifically and only targeted new members. It was implied that the activity was a condition of membership that was required for continued involvement in the group.

Case Study 2

Scenario: All the new members for Delta Iota (DI) sorority were instructed to report to the sorority house for a new member lock-in. Once everyone arrived, the new members were divided into groups of four new members each. The DI members turned off the lights, turned on loud music, and locked each group in a separate room. There were no instructions provided, but each room had a table in the center with one bottle of hard alcohol on it. The new members assumed they had to finish the bottle of alcohol to be able to leave the room, so they took turns drinking from the bottle until it was finished. One new member began vomiting and had to be taken to the hospital, stopping the events for the night.

Discussion questions: Was this hazing? If so, in what ways? What is concerning about this behavior?

Post-discussion considerations: The sisters of Delta Iota never specifically told new members to drink the alcohol in the room, but a reasonable person might assume that the bottle of alcohol was there to be consumed. The implication was that finishing the alcohol was a condition of membership. Some would argue that the new members voluntarily drank the bottle, but voluntary participation is not a factor in whether an activity is considered hazing. This was a dangerous activity that resulted in a health and safety concern for one of the new members. Regardless, alcohol should never be part of new member activities, as this violates national fraternity and sorority regulations as well as college and university policies. Additionally, most new members are under 21. If the Delta Iota members were under 21, the Delta Iota sisters provided alcohol to minors.

The fact that the new Delta Iota members were locked in a room and subjected to loud music is also a concern. This action was meant to intimidate, confuse, and cause undue stress to the new members; therefore, the behavior constitutes harassment hazing.

Case Study 3

Scenario: The brothers of Zeta Omega convened the entire brotherhood to celebrate a flag football intramural championship win over Sigma Alpha. The entire chapter was invited, including the new member class. The brothers ordered a couple of kegs for the evening, used mostly to play drinking games throughout the night. A new member suggested that several of the guys parade the Zeta Omega flag past the Sigma Alpha house to taunt them. Several brothers and new members did so. Once there, they took the prank one step further by entering the Sigma Alpha house and stealing the latest fraternity composite. Campus police responded to the scene.

Discussion questions: Was this hazing? If so, in what ways? What is concerning about this behavior?

Post-discussion considerations: Although the evening's activities were certainly dangerous and concerning, this would probably not be considered hazing. The new members were not singled out for this activity, and participation was not a condition of membership. There were several violations of campus policies, including playing drinking games (which are banned at most institutions and for most fraternities), underage drinking, and the stolen property. Zeta Omega is guilty of poor decision making. Individuals and the organization may be held accountable through university or criminal processes.

CONCLUSION

Hazing has existed on college campuses for hundreds of years and has been present in fraternities and sororities since their creation. Fraternities and sororities are deeply rooted in tradition, and the same rituals and traditions that make the organizations meaningful can aid in the development of hazing habits. A simple call to the adherence of values is not enough to combat or prevent hazing in fraternities and sororities. Both the (inter)national organizations and the local institutions should have more open and frank discussions about hazing and effective strategies that will hold individuals, chapters, and (inter)national organizations accountable.

REFERENCES

Allan, E. J., & Madden, M. (2008). *Hazing in view: College students at risk*. Retrieved from www.stophazing.org/wp-content/uploads/2014/06/hazing_in_view_web1.pdf

Alvarez, D. (2015). Death by hazing: Should there be a federal law against fraternity and sorority hazing? *Journal of Multidisciplinary Research*, 7(2), 43–75.

Bandura, A. (1999). Moral disengagement in the perpetration of inhumanities. *Personality and Social Psychology Review*, 3(3), 193–209.

Barber, J. P., Espino, M. M., & Bureau, D. (2015). Fraternities and sororities: Developing a compelling case for relevance in higher education. In P. A. Sasso & J. L. DeVitis (Eds.), *Todays college students: A reader* (pp. 241–255). New York, NY: Peter Lang.

Boschini, V., & Thompson, C. (1998). The future of the Greek experience: Greeks and diversity. In *New directions for student services* (pp. 19–27). San Francisco, CA: Jossey-Bass.

Campo, S., Poulos, G., & Sipple, J. W. (2005). Prevalence and profiling: Hazing among college students and points of intervention. *American Journal of Health Behavior*, 29(2), 137–149.

Cokley, K., Miller, K., Cunningham, D., Motoike, J., King, A., & Awad, G. (2001). Developing an instrument to assess college students' attitudes toward pledging and hazing in Greek letter organizations. *College Student Journal*, 35(3), 451–457.

Elkins, S., Braxton, J., & James, G. (2000). Tinto's separation stage and its influence on first-semester college student persistence. *Research in Higher Education*, 40(2), 251–268.

Flanagan, C. (2017, November). Death at a Penn State fraternity. *The Atlantic*. Retrieved from www.theatlantic.com/magazine/archive/2017/11/a-death-at-penn-state/540657/

Foster, K. M. (2008). Black Greeks and underground pledging: Public debates and communal concerns. *Transforming Anthropology*, 16(1), 3–19.

Ganim, S., & Welch, C. (2017, May 15). Parents: "Criminal" inaction by Penn State, frat members led to son's death. *CNN*. Retrieved from www.cnn.com/2017/05/15/us/penn-state-fraternity-piazza-family-interview/

Gerahty, M. (1997, June 20). Rise in hazing incidents at sororities alarm colleges. *The Chronicle of Higher Education*. Retrieved from www.chronicle.com/article/Rise-in-Hazing-Incidents-at/77622

Hazing deaths on American college campuses remain far too common. (2017, October 13). *The Economist*. Retrieved from www.economist.com/blogs/graphicdetail/2017/10/daily-chart-8

Hollmann, B. (2002). Hazing: Hidden campus community. In *New directions for student services* (pp. 39–47). San Francisco, CA: Jossey-Bass.

Hu, W. (2015, October 12). Hazing and drinking deaths at Asian-American fraternities raise concerns. *The New York Times*. Retrieved from www.nytimes.com/2015/10/13/

nyregion/hazing-and-drinking-deaths-at-asian-american-fraternities-raise-concerns.html?_r=0

Hu, W., & Miller, J. (2007, August 4). Prosecutors charge five in the death of a student. *The New York Times*. Retrieved from www.nytimes.com/2007/08/04/nyregion/04rider.html

Johnson, J. (2002). Are sisters doing it to themselves? *Canadian Woman Studies*, *21*(3), 125–131.

Keating, C., Pomerantz, J., Pommer, S., Ritt, S., Miller, L., & McCormick, J. (2005). Going to college and unpacking hazing: A functional approach to decrypting initiation practices among undergraduates. *Educational Publishing Foundation*, *9*(2), 104–130.

Levenson, E., & Hassan, C. (2017, November 7). Florida State University suspends all Greek life after pledge dies. *CNN*. Retrieved from www.cnn.com/2017/11/07/us/florida-state-fraternity-greek-suspension/index.html

Lipkins, S. (2006). *Preventing hazing: How parents, teachers, and coaches can stop the violence, harassment and humiliation.* San Francisco, CA: Jossey-Bass.

Lodewijkx, H. F. M., & Syroit, J. E. M. M. (1997). Severity of initiation revisited: Does severity of initiation increase attractiveness in real groups? *European Journal of Social Psychology*, *27*, 275–300.

Lohse, A. (2012, January 1). Lohse: Telling the truth. *The Dartmouth*. Retrieved from www.thedartmouth.com/article/2012/01/lohse-telling-the-truth

Marcitllach, A., & Freire, A. G. (2013). *Novatadas. Comprender para actuar.* Madrid, Spain: Universidad Pontificia Comillas.

National Multicultural Greek Council. (n.d.). About NMGC. Retrieved from http://nationalmgc.org

National Panhellenic Conference. (n.d.). *National Panhellenic Conference.* Retrieved from www.npcwomen.org/about/mission-vision-and-purpose/

New, J. (2014, September 30). Banning frats? *Inside Higher Ed*. Retrieved from www.insidehighered.com/news/2014/09/30/should-colleges-ban-fraternities-and-sororities

Nirh, J. L. F. (2014). *Explanations of college students for engaging in hazing activities* (Unpublished dissertation). University of Arizona, Tucson.

North-American Interfraternity Conference. (2018). *About IFC*. Retrieved from http://nicindy.org/ifc

Nuwer, H. (1990). *Broken pledges*. Atlanta, GA: Longstreet Press.

Nuwer, H. (1999). *Wrongs of passage*. Bloomington: Indiana University Press.

Nuwer, H. (2004). *The hazing reader*. Bloomington: Indiana University Press.

Nuwer, H. (2018). *Hazing deaths*. Retrieved from www.hanknuwer.com/articles/hazing-deaths/

Parks, G. S., Jones, S. E., Shayne, E., Ray, R., & Hughey, M. W. (2015). White boys drink, Black girls yell: A racialized and gendered analysis of violent hazing and the law. *Journal of Gender, Race, and Justice*, *18*(1), 93–158.

Reitman, J. (2012, March 28). Confessions of an Ivy League frat boy: Inside Dartmouth's hazing abuses. *Rolling Stone*. Retrieved from www.rollingstone.com/culture/news/confessions-of-an-ivy-league-frat-boy-inside-dartmouths-hazing-abuses-20120328

Rojas, R. (2017, May 15). 4 plead guilty in Baruch College student's hazing death. *The New York Times*. Retrieved from www.nytimes.com/2017/05/15/nyregion/baruch-college-hazing-death-pi-delta-psi.html?mcubz=1

Ruffins, P. (1997). Frat-ricide: Are African American fraternities beating themselves to death? *Diverse Issues in Higher Education, 14*(8), 18.

Ryan, E. (2014, April 25). The story behind American University's rapey, violent "secret" frat. *Jezebel*. Retrieved from http://jezebel.com/the-story-behind-american-universitys-rapey-violent-se-1566309032

Syrett, N. L. (2009). *The company he keeps: A history of white college fraternities*. Chapel Hill: University of North Carolina Press.

Terenzini, P., Pascarella, E., & Blimling, G. (1996). Student's out-of-class experiences and their influence on learning and cognitive development: A literature review. *Journal of College Student Development, 37*(2), 149–162.

Torbensen, C. L., & Parks, G. (2009). *Brothers and sisters: Diversity in college fraternities and sororities*. Madison, NJ: Fairleigh Dickinson University Press.

Turk, D. (2004). *Bound by a mighty vow: Sisterhood and women's fraternities, 1870–1920*. New York: New York University Press.

Turner, T. (1977). Transformation, hierarchy, and transcendence: A reformulation of Van Gennep's model of the structure of the Rites de Passage. In S. F. Moore & B. G. Myerhoff (Eds.), *Secular ritual* (pp. 53–72). Assen, The Netherlands: Van Gorcum & Comp.

Van Gennep, A. (2004). *The rites of passage* (M. B. Vizedom & G. Caffee, Trans.). London, England: University of Chicago Press. (Original work published 1960)

Whaley, D. (2008). Links, legacies, and letters: A cultural history of Black Greek-letter organizations. In C. L. Torbenson & G. S. Parks, (Eds.), *Brothers and sisters: Diversity in college fraternities and sororities* (pp. 46–82). Madison, NJ: Fairleigh Dickinson University Press.

Whipple, E. G., & Sullivan, E. G. (1998). Greek letter organizations: Communities of learners? In E. G. Whipple (Ed.), *New challenges for Greek letter organizations: Transforming fraternities and sororities into learning communities* (pp. 7–17). San Francisco, CA: Jossey-Bass.

Chapter 6

An Overview of Military Hazing in University Programs

Shawn Knight and Michelle L. Boettcher

The U.S. military has a long history of honor and respect. In order to develop leadership throughout the military, many universities have established Reserve Officers' Training Corps (ROTC) programs. ROTC programs are designed to prepare officers throughout the branches of the military. The structure of these programs is very similar to that of a military unit. Many of the ROTC programs and their associated student organizations are no more immune to hazing than other student organizations. Unfortunately, the impact of hazing is often overlooked as the operation and structure of the military-affiliated organizations are very different from typical student organizations.

In their study of leadership behaviors (broadly defined beyond hazing or military contexts), Murray, Mann, and Mead (2010) identified two key traits for group effectiveness: consideration (developing group trust and respect) and initiating structure (defining individuals' roles). In the context of hazing practices, these two elements can at times be in conflict. Although issues related to trust and respect focus on equity and equality, those related to structure focus on hierarchy, position, title, and power. In fact, the military structure of ROTC programs creates a power dynamic and circumstances that are ideal in leading to hazing of both new and "initiated" members.

This chapter examines the systems, hazing experiences, laws, and policies related to military hazing. It concludes with areas for further research as well as case studies related to hazing in military contexts. A brief examination of the history of military-affiliated programs and institutions and ROTC programs positions this chapter in the higher education context.

THE MILITARY AND HIGHER EDUCATION

Although ROTC programs officially started with the National Defense Act of 1916 (Abrams, 1989), military connections to higher education go back much further. According to Kotakis (2016), in 1783, New York Governor George

Clinton advocated for each state to have a civilian institution that provided military education. The American Literary, Scientific, and Military Academy (now Norwich University) in Norwich, Vermont, was established in 1819 and is largely recognized as the founding institution of the ROTC and the concept of the citizen-soldier (Kotakis, 2016).

Over time, the notion of the citizen-soldier has become a focal point in terms of the value of ROTC and military-affiliated groups and institutions in higher education. The United States has historically sought to support a military large enough to protect itself and its interests. Neiberg (2000) wrote that training citizen-soldiers has "allowed the United States to have a military large and professional enough to protect the nation from without while avoiding the dangers and heightened militarism, which, if unchecked, could destroy the nation from within" (p. 3).

Over the course of time, military education has become less of a requirement but is still present on many college and university campuses. The most common manifestation of that presence is through the ROTC program. The army, navy, and air force all have ROTC programs. Campuses can have multiple different ROTC programs. Today it is possible to enroll in an ROTC program on more than 1,100 college campuses. Not all campuses have ROTC, but many partner with other institutions to enroll their students in nearby programs (U.S. Army). In addition to ROTC, some colleges and universities also offer majors and minors in military science that are available to students. Student organizations exist to further support the military experience and develop camaraderie.

DEFINITION OF HAZING IN THE MILITARY

Given the unique context and history of the military in higher education, an examination of hazing in this culture requires intentional focus as not all generalizations about student organizations apply in the same way to ROTC and other military experiences on campus. Chapter 1 of this book provided a definition of hazing on a college campus. However, it is important to understand that most of those working with students who are involved in a military program are military personnel, not student affairs professionals, nor are many of them civilians (Goldman et al., 1999). The faculty and staff leading ROTC programs have primary experiences and knowledge related to their branches of service and the U.S. Department of Defense. As such, whatever training or understanding these leaders have of hazing is rooted in the government's training on the topic. It is important to understand what that definition is and acknowledge the differences that exist between the view of student affairs professionals and military personnel and how these incidents play out differently in nonservice academy settings as opposed to military institutions or the military itself.

In 1997, the U.S. Department of Defense issued a memorandum defining hazing in the military service organizations.

Hazing is defined as any conduct whereby a military member or members, regardless of service or rank, without proper authority causes another military member or members, regardless of service or rank, to suffer or be exposed to any activity which is cruel, abusive, humiliating, oppressive, demeaning, or harmful. Soliciting or coercing another to perpetuate any such activity is also considered hazing. Hazing need not involve physical contact among or between military members; it can be verbal or psychological in nature. Actual or implied consent to acts of hazing does not eliminate the culpability of the perpetrator.
(Cohen, 1997)

In 2013, the U.S. Department of Defense issued a report to the U.S. Congress that assessed hazing in the armed forces where concern was expressed at the rather broad scope of this definition (Keller et al., 2015). One critical component to note is that hazing can happen to anyone in the military by anyone in the military. Many discussions of hazing highlight the power dynamics between two individuals, such as hierarchies between a pledge and a new member of an organization or a senior member of a team versus a freshman.

A primary critique of the Department of Defense definition of hazing (reiterated in AR 600-20 Army Command Policy) is around the use of the statement "without proper authority." In an organization where authority is paramount, the ability to grant one authority to perpetrate a hazing offense seems to be written into the definition (Keller et al, 2015). This is difficult to disrupt in overtly hierarchical systems, such as those in place in ROTC programs.

After conducting a thorough examination of hazing in the U.S. Armed Forces, Keller et al. (2015) identified the types of hazing that exist in the military, including initiation rituals, newcomer testing, and maintenance of group structure. Although ROTC programs are direct reflections of the experience of active duty soldiers and are run by men and women with military experience, it is expected that ROTC members experience hazing. There are countless examples of hazing that have occurred within active military units, ROTC programs, and military institutions. Many of these incidents violate what may be a more restrictive university policy on hazing, but they also violate hazing law and the U.S. Department of Defense hazing statement that is applicable to ROTC programs.

MILITARY HAZING

A key element of the U.S. military structure is its hierarchy. As Godfrey (2016) wrote, the military is associated with "a high degree of formal rule-based behaviour, adherence to strict levels of discipline, and obedience to hierarchy" (p. 165).

Firestone and Harris (1999) found that hazing plays a (re)socialization role for individuals transitioning from civilian to military life.

Hazing in a military context is a complex issue to navigate. In the service academy setting, there are structures in place to complicate the understanding of hazing. For example, Pershing (2006) wrote of the three Department of Defense service academies:

> A fundamental component of military training at DOD [Department of Defense] service academies is the indoctrination system for fourth classmen (freshmen), which includes traditions and rituals passed down through several generations. Because these systems are primarily student-run by upperclassmen (juniors and seniors), and since the distinction between hazing and legitimate military training has sometimes been ambiguous in the past, the fourth class indoctrination systems are subject to potential abuse.
>
> (p. 471)

This notion of indoctrination goes beyond the military and the service academies to ROTC and military preparation programs in other institutional settings.

In ROTC programs or other military-based organizations, unity and teamwork are essential. Hazing is often used as a means of creating unity for a team or group. However, Keller et al. (2015) noted, "One of the most common justifications for hazing is that it increases . . . commitment to the group" (p. 26). Many hazing rituals in the military occur during the early stages of membership. These rituals create an environment where a person feels the group he or she is joining is more desirable (Keller et al., 2005). Sosis, Kress, and Boster (2007) stated that "individuals pay the costs of ritual performance, but by doing so they demonstrate their commitment and loyalty to the group and can thus achieve a net benefit from successful collective action" (p. 245) This statement helps explain why individuals, including service members, are susceptible to acts of hazing. The rationale that membership and unity are essential to organizations and teams also explains why military-related hazing in higher education is not significantly different from why hazing exists in athletics, among band members, or in the any of the groups examined within this text.

MILITARY-RELATED HAZING CASES

As exemplified in other chapters in this book, it is important to examine hazing culture through the use of examples. The following cases highlight the dangers of hazing in ROTC and at military-affiliated institutions. Although many of these cases are decades old, there are also much more recent incidents, and as such, education, prevention, and dialogue continue to be crucial to the well-being of students involved in these organizations.

St. John's University ROTC, 1976

On Friday, November 5, 1976, Thomas Fitzgerald, a cadet in the St. John's University ROTC, was fatally stabbed in the process of pledging the Pershing Rifles military society. Prior to the incident, Fitzgerald told his mother that pledges "had been directed to hold unloaded pistols to their heads and pull the triggers" (Kihss, 1976, p. 27). The weekend of his death, Fitzgerald was part of 20 members of the ROTC program who "had gone to a South Shore island for what the police called 'a combination war game and form of hazing'" (Kihss, 1976, p. 27). Kihss (1976) went on to report that Fitzgerald was stabbed by an upper-class student during an interrogation role-play. The accused student was later found not guilty of murder and acquitted (Gupte, 1978).

Texas A&M University ROTC, 1984

In 1984, four Texas A&M students were indicted in the hazing death of Bruce Goodrich. Goodrich

> was awakened at 2:30 A.M. on Aug. 30 and forced to run and do pushups and situps for about an hour in hot, humid weather. Officials said he collapsed but was encouraged to keep running as part of the exercises.
> (Associated Press, 1984, para. 2)

In addition to negligent homicide, the students were also charged with violating a state statute against hazing. As a result, ROTC training exercises were halted after the incident (United Press International, 1984).

Norwich University ROTC, 1990

In August 1990, William C. Brueckner Jr. arrived as an incoming student at Norwich University (*Brueckner v. Norwich University*, 1999). Although Brueckner had already served 5 years in the U.S. Navy, "under the authority and training of Norwich and its leadership, certain upperclassmen were appointed by the university to indoctrinate and orient" (*Brueckner v. Norwich University*, 1999) new students. Brueckner attended Norwich for only 16 days during which he was verbally assaulted, prevented from eating and studying, had his academic work destroyed by upperclassmen, and was forced to participate in calisthenics despite having an injured shoulder. According to the case law, "Norwich investigated plaintiff's complaints and, as a result, several cadets were disciplined" (*Brueckner v. Norwich University*, 1999).

The Virginia Military Institute, 1998

The case of George Wade Jr. at the Virginia Military Institute exemplifies a change in thinking about hazing and accountability. According to Wade, he and five other university freshmen were beaten with a belt and coat hangers "about three times a week from Sept. 11 to mid-October, leaving the students with welts and bruises" (Finn, 1998, para. 2). Although today most policies and laws make it clear that students cannot consent to hazing, in this case Wade was told that

> a charge of assault would be hard to sustain because the former cadet could be seen as a willing participant in the events. Wade said he acknowledged to the prosecutor that he made statements such as, "I want to go first to get it over with," and that he repeatedly returned to a dorm room knowing that he was likely to be struck. . . . Wade, who expressed frustration at the decision, said that although he endured the beatings without objection, there was nothing voluntary about it because he felt he had no choice and had no one to turn to for help at VMI [Virginia Military Institute].
> (Finn, 1998, para. 3)

No one was charged as a result of Wade's allegations.

University of New Hampshire ROTC, 2007

In October 2007, university police stopped three students who were leaving a field near campus. Police found that a senior ROTC cadet had been left tied up in the bucket of a utility truck on the field (Sutters, 2007). According to Sutters (2007), "'From what we know at this point, the students thought this was a harmless prank,' said Deputy Police Chief Paul Dean in the release. 'From our point of view, we are investigating this as an alleged hazing incident'" (para. 5). No one was charged as a result of the police investigation.

The Citadel, 2015

One of the more notable recent cases of hazing in college military programs occurred in 2015 at The Citadel, the Military College of South Carolina. The case resulted in 85 allegations of hazing related to upper-division members repeatedly requiring new members to do sit-ups, push-ups, and other physical training behind closed doors and outside of regularly scheduled training activities (Kerr & Pan, 2015). The violations that resulted from the investigation were referred to as training violations against first-year cadets. As a result, 19 cadets were recommended for suspension, dismissal, or expulsion. This is the most recent in a series of hazing incidents at the institution. In 2009 and 2011, instances of physical abuse of first-year cadets were also reported (Kerr & Pan, 2015).

FURTHER RESEARCH OPPORTUNITIES

Overall there is a very limited amount of research about the thousands of students who participate in ROTC programs across the country each year. The lack of information from the media or research from academics highlighting examples of ROTC hazing is worth consideration. Much of the literature related to ROTC experience is focused on diet, wellness, and physical ability. Although these are important aspects of ROTC programs, the developmental aspects—particularly as they relate to leadership development and teamwork—are also important to understanding this experience on campus.

Research is needed to answer questions about the impact of hazing on ROTC cadets. Administrators could benefit from knowing to what degree hazing is occurring, what anti-hazing training is being provided, and how students define and experience hazing in their involvement on campus. Specifically, ROTC and other military-affiliated programs in higher education are potentially more susceptible to hazing because of the indoctrination required in transitioning from civilian to military life. Most ROTC administrators come from a military background and do not have the same perspective on hazing that student affairs professionals do. Research about how to bridge these two areas—military science and student affairs—can provide new and more effective strategies for eliminating hazing in an ROTC context.

CASE STUDIES

In this final section, we provide three case studies to examine the role of hazing in the context of ROTC programs on college campuses. Each scenario is followed by a series of reflective questions. Although these studies focus on ROTC experiences, they can be translated to other student and student organizational contexts.

Campus Swim

You are a graduate student at Southeastern University, a large public institution with an army and air force ROTC program. Your institution commonly touts its military heritage, and you know that ROTC is highly respected on campus. You have never personally worked with an ROTC student or had experience with the military. Beyond knowing that the program prepares students to go into military service, you have no knowledge of training regimens, requirements, or meeting times.

It is a Wednesday evening around 8:45 p.m. Campus is dark, and you are walking to the library, which is near a large shallow pond. As you approach the library, you hear splashing in the distance and see around 20 students standing in the waist-deep water of the pond. Several of them are holding what appear to be batons or drill rifles above their heads.

1. What do you do?
2. What other information might you want to know in deciding what next steps to take?
3. What are possible implications for your actions/failure to act?

Cross-Unit Training

You have just been hired to work at Lutheran University, a small public school in the rural northeast. One of your responsibilities is advising student groups, including fraternities and sororities. When you arrived at the beginning of the summer, your director told you that you will be responsible for developing a comprehensive hazing prevention program that will be offered in the fall semester. Your director also informed you that you will be presenting it not only to fraternities and sororities but also to the ROTC program, athletics, and the band in three large sessions with members from each group present rather than training targeted to the specific needs of individual organizations. Although you have been told that hazing is not rampant on the campus, all these groups have had issues over the last 6 years.

1. Brainstorm ideas for how you would approach this training. Utilize relevant legislation, policy, theory, and best practices to shape your training.
2. What are your learning outcomes for the training? How will you assess whether you have achieved those outcomes?
3. What are the benefits of hazing education in this format? What are the challenges?

Promotion and Partnership

You currently serve as the conduct coordinator at Central College. Central is a midsize regional public institution in the Pacific Northwest with a strong STEM focus. There is also a military heritage on campus, reflected by the presence of army, navy/marines, and air force ROTC units. In your role as the conduct coordinator, you are responsible for student group/organization conduct. As the school year wraps up, you are reviewing your workload over the past year. You realize that all three ROTC programs had cases of physical training hazing reported to your office. You also recall a case with Phi Sigma Delta fraternity where physical training hazing was reported. The students in the fraternity who were leading those hazing efforts were also upper-class ROTC students. Clearly there is an issue with the ROTC students' understanding of hazing, particularly around physical activities. You have decided you want to work with the ROTC staff to implement a proactive program to combat hazing. However, you know they are resistant to the traditional "liberal" college definition of hazing.

1. How might you go about developing a hazing prevention program and partnering with the military science department?
2. Would you hold these sessions individually or not? Why?
3. Are your outcomes the same for the ROTC organizations as for the fraternity? Why or why not?

CONCLUSION

The experiences of ROTC members and military-affiliated organizations differ from many other student groups because of the physical aspects of ROTC and similar groups. Calisthenics, running, and other physical activity make up a part of the goals and outcomes for military-affiliated organizations. Additionally, these groups are built on concepts of honor, integrity, and leadership in ways directly connected with potential future service in and beyond the military.

As a result, the lines between hazing and member effectiveness can be blurred. It is important that military-affiliated and ROTC organizations seek and adhere to guidance from the military and from officers and faculty associated with these programs. Ongoing reflection on activities and expectations is essential to ensuring the safety of individuals and the cohesion of teams. Incidents involving ROTC or similar organizations can have repercussions beyond the organization and beyond the members' experiences as participants in these organizations.

REFERENCES

Abrams, R. (1989). The U.S. military and higher education: A brief history. *American Academy of Political and Social Sciences, 502*(1), 15–28.

Associated Press. (1984, September 28). 4 indicted in hazing death. *The New York Times*. Retrieved from www.nytimes.com/1984/09/29/us/4-indicted-in-hazing-deat.html?mcubz=1

Brueckner v. Norwich University, 97 Ver. S.C. 396. (Ver. S.C., 1999).

Cohen, W. A. (1997). *Hazing memorandum for the secretaries of the military departments*. Washington, DC: U.S. Department of Defense.

Finn, P. (1998, June 24). No charges in alleged VMI hazing. *The Washington Post*. Retrieved from www.washingtonpost.com/archive/local/1998/03/22/no-charges-in-alleged-vmi-hazing/53c6e570-ca07-40f5-9f98-cf3f0b1e7ebe/?utm_term=.a1fecbf7f6ac

Firestone, J. M., & Harris, R. J. (1999). Changes in patterns of sexual harassment in the U.S. military: A comparison of the 1988 and 1995 DOD surveys. *Armed Forces & Society, 25*(1), 613–632.

Godfrey, R. (2016). Soldiering on: Exploring the role of humour as a disciplinary technology in the military. *Organization*, *23*(2), 164–183.

Goldman, C. A., Orvis, B. R., Mattock, M. G., & Smith, D. A. (1999). *Staffing army ROTC at colleges and universities: Alternatives for reducing the use of active-duty soldiers*. Santa Monica, CA: RAND.

Gupte, P. (1978, June 24). L.I. man acquitted in stabbing of fellow cadet during "hazing". *The New York Times*. Retrieved from www.nytimes.com/1978/06/24/archives/li-man-acquitted-in-stabbing-of-fellow-cadet-during-hazing-training.html?mcubz=1

Keller, K. M., Matthews, M., Curry Hall, K., Marcellino, W., Mauro, J. A., & Lim, N. (2015). *Hazing in the U.S. Armed Forces: Recommendations for hazing prevention policy and practice*. Santa Monica, CA: RAND.

Kerr, A., & Pan, D. (2015, 27 April). 19 involved in hazing at the Citadel. *The Post and Courier*. Retrieved from www.postandcourier.com/archives/involved-in-hazing-at-citadel/article_de64b34f-3f1e-5382-b591-092302f30b6b.html

Kihss, P. (1976). R.O.T.C. is investigating reports of hazing at St John's University. *The New York Times*. Retrieved from www.nytimes.com/1976/11/09/archives/rotc-is-investigating-reports-of-haying-at-st-johns-university-a.html?mcubz=1

Kotakis, P. N. (2016). Army ROTC at one hundred. *Military Review*, *96*(3), 104–110.

Murray, M., Mann, B., & Mead, J. (2010). Leadership effectiveness and decision making in coaches. In J. M. Williams (Ed.), *Applied sport psychology: Personal growth to peak performance* (6th ed., pp. 106–131). New York, NY: McGraw-Hill.

Neiberg, M. S. 2000. *Making citizen-soldiers: ROTC and the ideology of American military service*. Cambridge, MA: Harvard University Press.

Pershing, J. L. (2006). Men and women's experiences with hazing in a male-dominated elite military institution. *Men and Masculinities*, *8*(4), 470–492.

Sosis, R., Kress, H. C., & Boster, J. S. (2007). Scars for war: Evaluating alternative signaling explanations for cross-cultural variance in ritual costs. *Evolution and Human Behavior*, *28*(4), 234–247.

Sutters, P. (2007, October 10). UNH hazing incident probed. *Seacoast Online*. Retrieved from www.seacoastonline.com/article/20071010/NEWS/710100369

United Press International. (1984, September 1). *ROTC training halted at Texas A&M following hazing death*. Retrieved from www.upi.com/Archives/1984/09/01/ROTC-training-halted-at-Texas-AM-following-hazing-death/9623462859200/

Part 3
Hazing Policies

Chapter 7

Lessons Learned About Hazing From an Executive Director of National Organizations

Mary Peterson

Fraternity and sorority life is a defining experience in the lives of many students in higher education. It is a place where lifelong relationships are built, leadership is developed, and growth is fostered. Fraternities and sororities are places where students build on-campus families and nationwide networks. Fraternity and sorority chapters are places where successes are celebrated and struggles are navigated. They are also places of joy and sometimes of sadness. Through it all, I have faith in the potential of these organizations to help students figure out who they are and to actively pursue their best selves.

Fraternity and sorority life have provided me with opportunities for my own growth and learning. I have learned how to advise and navigate administrative tasks. I have learned the importance of relational and emotional leadership in serving as a liaison between fraternity and sorority chapters, between chapters and institutions, between different types of student organizations, and beyond.

I have also learned the value of conflict—because conflict only happens when people care about something. When people do not care, they are more likely to not engage, debate, or demonstrate their emotions. Conflict can be a catalyst for transformation. Throughout my career within higher education and as an executive director of two national organizations, I have helped facilitate that transformation; sometimes we have not achieved that transformational point. Still, I have learned that in order to make a positive and effective transformational change within national organizations, one must have a clear vision and outcomes. The vision and outcome will direct the goals and initiatives for the organization. Furthermore, dialogue among all stakeholders is a key principle of success and necessary to make and achieve a transformational change within national organizations.

I have also learned about the importance of getting to know students. I understand their desperate need to connect, to find a sense of belonging and be validated. I understand their desire to find success as students and leaders. Students want to succeed and to achieve their own goals, and sometimes they need some support through that process. Students are the spirit of student organizations, campus, and student life.

During my experience working with two national organizations, I have been challenged to disrupt the hazing culture and habits. As a former executive director, I have had to make the decision to suspend and close fraternity and sorority chapters due hazing allegations. In this chapter, I reflect on my lived experiences and provide key notes from the lessons learned about hazing as a former executive director for two national organizations. I know that fraternity and sorority life is not about hazing. Fraternity and sorority life is about belonging and community. Fraternity and sorority life is about brotherhood, sisterhood, service, academics, and leadership.

In this reflection, it is clear to me that what I know and what students believe does not always align with the larger narrative. When we are bombarded with stories about hazing incidents across the country, then that is what many outside of the fraternity and sorority chapters believe to be true about our organizations. When students die trying to join our ranks, then that is the bigger picture the nation knows of who we are.

MARY'S BACKGROUND

I have worked in fraternity and sorority life for more than 30 years. I began my journey at the University of Iowa, where I became a member of Alpha Phi National fraternity in 1976 as an undergraduate student. I earned a bachelor of arts in elementary education in 1979 and a master's degree in planning, policy, and leadership in 1988, both from the University of Iowa. After completing graduate school, I worked at the University of Iowa in the Office of Student Life, where I oversaw many campus life programs, including the Greek community, for 24 years.

During my tenure at the University of Iowa, I helped found Sigma Lambda Beta International Fraternity (a Latino-based fraternity with a multicultural membership) in 1986. In 1990, I helped start Sigma Lambda Gamma National Sorority (a Latina-based sorority with a multicultural membership). Due to my involvement in and support of both organizations, I became a member and served as the first president of each of these organizations and then continued to serve as their executive director. Additionally, for the last 12 years, I have advised the National Asian Pacific Islander American Panhellenic Association. Its mission is as follows:

> A collective group of leaders within the Asian Pacific Islander Desi American community who work together to advocate, collaborate, and educate our members and constituency for the greater good. We represent our member organizations within the fraternal and university communities.
>
> (National Asian Pacific Islander American Panhellenic Association, 2017, para. 1)

Throughout my work with this association, and with Sigma Lambda Beta and Sigma Lambda Gamma, among many other fraternal organizations, I have gained a better understanding of organizational change, leadership, and hazing training and prevention.

For me, fraternity and sorority life is about community, diversity, and a sense of belonging. These experiences not only have shaped my own development but also have inspired my work and my ways of contributing to higher education. Fraternity and sorority life is a place of safety and trust, not a place of fear and pain.

I also had the pleasure of working with many national and international fraternal organizations in developing education materials, strategic planning, and speaking to their membership. Many times I was the first woman to speak at fraternity national events. I knew I was entering into new territory. I knew I had to navigate carefully and cultivate relationships. I was the *pledge*, if you will, and I had to connect with the established members to help them see me as a member with value to add to their organizations.

I have been very passionate in my work with undergraduate students. The fraternal experience is value based and can be one of the best experiences young people can have to help them grow and develop into responsible and engaged citizens. It can also be challenging. The satisfaction of helping undergraduates maneuver through these challenges is what has driven me.

HAZING

Hazing has been one of the biggest hurdles for students, organizations, and colleges and universities to overcome. It is a set of practices and habits that have historically violated the true meaning of fraternal life. I have seen it in many forms and in all fraternal organizations. The bonds of brotherhood and sisterhood can be forged in a variety of ways. Unfortunately, some organizations feel that pain and suffering—physical, emotional, or psychological—are the best ways to assess a potential member's dedication to the organization.

In truth, the dedication emerges through the service members provide to their chapters, campuses, and communities. Dedication is not something you can do a pretest for. Dedication is shown over time and effort. The dedicated leader, follower, or member is not a bystander. The dedicated member is not a bully who beats members into submission. The dedicated member seeks out the best in all individuals and elevates them as a part of the group rather than denigrating and humiliating them.

There have been many attempts to stop hazing habits and to break those cycles over the years. Those attempts have varied from firm anti-hazing policies to shorter new member/pledge programs. There has been constant education from national and international fraternity and sorority chapters as well as institutions of higher education. The efforts made, the education that has happened, and the policies that have been drafted have been effective and have worked to curb some of that behavior over the years. I know from my own experiences that we have minimized a great deal of bad hazing behavior.

For example, in my time working with organizations and organizational leadership, I have seen marked changes in the intake process. Most organizations today focus on belonging rather than on marginalizing others. Whereas in the past when organizations used hazing practices to call out certain potential members, today chapters use a variety of outreach and information to help new members find the right chapter for them based on their individual goals, needs, and values.

That said, there are outliers among us who cling to the old ways. There are groups that engage in underground hazing practices. There are organizations that use pain and humiliation as the test for who is worthy of joining a given fraternity or sorority chapter. In order to disrupt this national narrative around hazing, we have to be accountable to ourselves broadly and not in isolation. It is not about what happens only in our individual chapters but also what we see, hear, or suspect is happening in other spaces in the fraternal community and beyond. Everyone must be accountable to one another. We may not be our brother's or sister's keepers, but we should be dedicated to being their protectors when hazing habits victimize individuals.

ORGANIZATIONAL CHANGE

It is imperative that we look at the disruption of hazing culture from both the ground up and the top down. Although much has been written about work at the campus level or even the chapter level when it comes to hazing, what I propose is that we start with organizational change. National organizations send messages in the face of hazing tragedies, and these are important. We must move beyond dollars and liability and lawsuits. Instead, a focus on accountability throughout the intake process and membership experiences is essential. We have to move away from a check-this-box mentality around training, leadership development, and hazing education. Instead, aligning organizational values with organizational actions—in regard to hazing and other activities—is essential.

Although ritual and tradition matter, these practices do not and should not oblige organizations to internal or external secrecy. Activities or requirements that are hidden have to be eliminated. An organizational culture change is necessary for those organizations that continue to haze. As stated in Chapter 1, hazing is not a tradition of any fraternity or sorority; hazing is a habit that continues to hinder, hurt, and even take the lives of individuals every year.

Just as the past informs the present in terms of hazing or culture or tradition, so do past members have the power to inform current organizational behavior. The presence of older alumni not only protects the integrity of the organization but also the safety of potential and new members. These alumni have the opportunity to be a source of positive transformation in our chapters.

In order to make organizational change at the national level, executive or headquarter offices must have a clear vision and mission that states that hazing is not tolerated at any level of the organization. Although all fraternities and sororities have statements prohibiting hazing, it is clear that many student organizations still practice hazing habits. Leaders—chapter, campus, and national—must confront hazing experiences and apply sanctions to both individuals and organizations that haze other individuals.

If student organizations engage in hazing, then they should be closed and not allowed to return to campus, and individuals should be disaffiliated from the organization. Additionally, individuals who engage in hazing should be held accountable through college and university policies as well as state and federal laws. From leadership to sanctions, a transformation of cultural is imperative at the organizational level in order to disrupt histories of abuse through hazing habits in our chapters.

LEADERSHIP

Organizations are a reflection of their leaders. Hazing habits that are encouraged by leaders will be perpetuated by chapters. Leaders who align organizational activities with the values of the chapters will cultivate organizations that seek to build on those values for stronger chapters and stronger individual members.

Let's think about the executive boards of our undergraduate fraternity and sorority chapters—especially the president. Institutions of higher education not only hold the organizations accountable but also the individuals and the leaders are held accountable for organizational behaviors and activities. These young leaders—maybe 20 years old on average—are expected to manage and hold their members accountable. All fraternal organizations have strong values and expectations on which they are founded. This means all your members must have strong academics, community and campus involvement, senses of brotherhood/sisterhood within the organization, and aspire to develop leadership skills in the chapter and beyond. Members are respectful of one another and those outside the organization and are always willing to help a brother or sister with personal issues.

In addition to these positive attributes and organizational values, there is an expectation of the university as well as of the national organization that members avoid negative behaviors. In other words, no one engages in drugs, underage drinking, bad behavior of any kind, violation of campus policies, and so forth. Additionally, these young leaders are not only responsible for managing undergraduate members but also often called on to deal with alumni who are not sending good messages—especially regarding hazing. I know that most chapter leaders do not want the hazing culture to continue. It is usually a group of members or alumni who help keep the cycle going.

That is a lot of expectation on young leaders, especially if they do not receive the education and training needed. I encourage everyone to have more dialogue about hazing at the core of the conversation. These conversations need to be created where a fraternity or sorority chapter can have these discussions without shame or fear. They do not need another webinar, speaker, or manual training. These students need a true and honest conversation where the leadership and organizational culture will change for the positive well-being for all members.

EDUCATIONAL TRAINING AND PREVENTION

There is not one all-encompassing magical program or intervention. Organizations exist on different campuses with incredibly diverse students and student experiences. Too often one bombards students with prepackaged webinars or trainings just so that they can check something off on the list of things they have to do. As new educational training and hazing prevention workshops are offered, one must be intentional and continue these conversations with students. It is my hope that this book and all the resources listed within it are used to engage student affairs professionals and all students in critical conversations about how to disrupt the hazing culture.

Additionally, could it be that the professionals who work with these organizations are hazing in a sense? What sorts of practices and policies are in place that require organizations to "prove themselves" before becoming members? How do we arrange a hierarchy based on power that diminishes individual chapters? Are our policies and practices equitable? Is there access for everyone in fraternity and sorority life?

We have created many trainings and workshops for our young leaders, but are we missing something? Before any programs, trainings, outreach, or even accountability can be put in place, it is important to ask some key questions:

1. What is the campus hazing culture around a particular organization at a particular college?
2. How have people and organizations been held accountable in the past? How do we assess the effectiveness of those measures of accountability?
3. Who are our students/members? What are members' past experiences?
4. What conversations are happening in chapters related to bullying? How do members connect hazing and bullying in an effort to prevent both?
5. Do we talk about dealing with anger or anger management in any of our programming?
6. How do members define groupthink? How do they see it playing a role in the perpetuation of hazing culture in their organizations, across fraternity and sorority life, and in other organizations across campus and the nation?

I knew that as a fraternity and sorority adviser and executive director of two national organizations that hazing was happening in most colleges and universities. As the adviser, I had to build trust with each chapter president. I did this over time by focusing on relationships and instilling trust. Just as dedication in membership takes time, so does fostering a sense of connection between administrators and organizations. I could have threatened, used my status with the institution, or engaged in other problematic practices (hazing practices, perhaps), but that is not who I am or what I wanted in terms of a relationship with the chapters.

Instead, I needed to be transparent and vulnerable with them, rather than forcing them to be vulnerable while I remained distant and powerful. I was compelled to model leadership in the hope that they would replicate that example in their organizations. If there were alternatives to hazing when it came to building relationships and developing connections and community, I had to show them what those alternatives might look like.

When hazing situations emerged, I talked honestly with the chapter presidents about their hazing cultures and how I could help them to start creating change to transform those cultures into healthy communities. You need to own the resistance and to start with students where they are at. Let me repeat: You need to *own that resistance*. That is their job as students, as young adults, and as citizens emerging with their own senses of self and who they are as leaders. We do not want students blindly following other students and making poor decisions. We stress that we want students to be critical thinkers. If that is true, then we want them to be critical of and resistant to our solutions as well—critical and resistant but trusting and able to listen.

Do not misunderstand me and think that I am saying that they have to make their decisions and that I have no control over or input on that process. That is not at all the case. No doubt I shared the rules, laws, and consequences of their actions if they continued to haze and were caught. They had to decide, and they had to choose. If they were up for consequences, I could not back them.

That is how I saw my job then and that is how I see the job today. As an adviser, I am ultimately a communicator. My job is to inform students of the potential implications of their actions. My job is to keep people informed and educated and to provide resources and support. Today there is another step in that process, as higher education professionals have the responsibility to report incidents of hazing or harm to students. On the national and international levels, staff and volunteers also have that responsibility. Ultimately much of this comes down to legal liability and risk management. In our litigious society, this is our reality.

How do we help student leaders who want to change their cultures if they fear sharing the truth with us?

I recently spoke at a leadership institute for a fraternal organization. The seminar was on leadership skills. During seminars, I do not speak at attendees but rather create conversations with them. One young woman had the courage to stand up and admit her chapter hazed, and she struggled with how to stop that cycle. The regional volunteer in the room was in a quandary as to whether she should she report this or not, even though the young woman was desperately asking for help. We agreed to keep it in the room. It did not follow all the rules, but it was necessary.

While respecting the needs of the women in that room and protecting the vulnerability they showed, I also knew there was more to do. Education is essential. In order for real learning and growth to happen, there must be risk taking and authenticity. The young woman took the risk of sharing, and the regional volunteer took the risk of prioritizing what was right over what was in the rules. As a result, we were able to address this in a more holistic way with a focus on the entire organization rather than on a single chapter. We did a lot of work in that space with the people present, but I knew it could not simply end there.

I took this experience a bit farther and made suggestions to the national leadership. Could we create a team of alumni who were not official leaders or volunteers who could help chapters that wanted assistance and guidance? There would be lots of questions related to what the liability would be, along with many others. How would we navigate issues of liability for organizations, alumni who were involved, institutions, and others? It is daunting to know that students want this help but are afraid to ask due to liability. I truly believe this was not unique to this organization.

But beyond that, how liable are we as individuals for *not* helping? What burdens do we put on members, leaders, advisers, and others when we shy away from the conversation? Whom do we put at risk when we shut down dialogue? If we know things are happening, we are obliged to take action. Turning away from incidents, failing to investigate suspicions, and backing down from the largest responsibility of all—the safety of students—does not work. We see it in headlines every day from Louisiana State to Penn State to Texas State. Pretending hazing does not happen is not an effective strategy.

We have opportunities every day to disrupt hazing habits. We can change the future of hazing as we continue to eliminate practices and transform cultures. There is great work being done by the national and international fraternal community and higher education professionals. More important are the student leaders and new members/pledges who are speaking out. Sisterhood or brotherhood is not remaining silent in the face of tragedy but is instead speaking out.

REFLECTION QUESTIONS

1. Who are the faculty, staff, and alumni whose perspectives you most value when it comes to work in your organization? What conversations could you have with those individuals to understand the larger picture of your group and your organizational history?

2. Who are leaders outside of your organization whom you trust to partner with you in reflecting on the work of members, leaders, advisers, and alumni? How might those individuals serve as a sort of advisory board to your organization to provide insight that those affiliated with your group may not have enough distance to see?
3. How is the history of your organization on your campus shared? What successes and areas of excellence do you celebrate? What past mistakes and errors can you learn from, and what reforms could (or have) taken place as a result?
4. How do people within your organization define leadership and integrity? How do the practices, events, and service your organization offers align with those definitions?

CONCLUSION

Proactive action to prevent hazing is leadership—not hazing as others were hazed. Speaking up in the face of allegations is leadership—not falling into silence to protect perpetrators. Sharing new ideas related to service, academics, and leadership as strategies for inducting members rather than relying on a person's willingness and ability to be hurt and humiliated is what membership is about. Creating bonding and team-building initiatives related to lifting up rather than putting down, related to serving others rather than hurting others, and related to pride rather than humiliation is leadership.

We cannot stop our work on eliminating hazing. We need to take a serious look at the way we approach it. Rather than examining our hazing practices from the history of "this is the way it's always been done" and the "why not?" perspective, we have to look at hazing from the true human perspective and ask ourselves why. Only then can we treat one another as brothers and sisters rather than as dominant and subordinate groups. Only then can we aspire to our best selves as members, leaders, and human beings.

REFERENCE

National Asian Pacific Islander American Panhellenic Association. (2017). *Welcome to NAPA*. Retrieved from www.napahq.org/

Chapter 8
Policy and Hazing at the Federal and State Levels

Cristóbal Salinas Jr., Michelle L. Boettcher, and Jennifer Plagman-Galvin

Hazing is prevalent in today's society in part because anti-hazing policies and laws are unclear (Hosansky, 2013). Allan and Madden (2008) found in a national study that 1.5 million high school students are hazed each year, more than one in five students reported they have personally witnessed hazing, and 40% of athletes who reported being involved in hazing said a coach or adviser was aware of the activity. Hazing may cause physical, emotional, or mental harm and in some cases results in death. With that in mind, what policies and legislation exist around hazing in education?

PUBLIC POLICY ON HAZING

The numbers on hazing deaths are inconsistent, as there are no centralized records of hazing incidents or hazing-related deaths. According to Alvarez (2015), in a period of 10 years, between 2005 and 2015, more than 60 students died in hazing incidents. Contrary to these statistics, Chamberlain (2013) reported that there were only 35 deaths related to hazing between 2000 and 2013. Regardless, both authors asserted that students die from hazing incidents each year, and it is this reality that serves as a catalyst for the work in this chapter and throughout this text.

STATE DEFINITIONS

Forty-four states have anti-hazing laws, the exceptions being Alaska, Hawaii, Montana, New Mexico, South Dakota, and Wyoming (Allan & Madden, 2008; Bailey & Hughey, 2013; Hazing Statutes, 2007; StopHazing.org, 2000). Hazing Statutes (2007) showed evidence that 22 states with anti-hazing laws use the same language to define hazing. Alabama, Colorado, Connecticut, Delaware, Florida, Iowa, Kentucky, Maine, Massachusetts, Michigan, Mississippi, Missouri, Nebraska, Nevada, New York, Oklahoma, Pennsylvania, Rhode Island, South Carolina, Utah, West Virginia, and Wisconsin's state laws define hazing as "any activity in which a person intentionally or recklessly endangers the physical health [or safety of an individual] for the purpose of initiation into or admissions into, affiliation with, or continued membership with any organization" (e.g., Nebraska § 28-311.06).

The other 22 states that have anti-hazing laws use different terminology, and definitions of hazing can vary from state to state (Dixon, 2001). For example, Indiana law defines hazing as "forcing or requiring another person: with or without the consent of the other person; and as a condition of association with a group or organization; to perform an act that creates a substantial risk of bodily injury" (Hazing Statutes, 2007, p. 24). Indiana's state law definition of hazing recognizes that regardless of a person's willingness to participate in any events to be part of a group, hazing is only physical. In Arkansas, hazing "is limited to those actions taken and situations created in connection with initiation into or affiliation with any organization" (Hazing Statutes, 2007, p. 11). Although Indiana limits hazing to physical acts, Arkansas limits its definition to the initiation process. Both state definitions use broad terminology to identify where can hazing can occur, such as in groups or organizations, while other anti-hazing state policies specify that hazing includes customary athletic events, contests, and competitions.

Indiana, New Jersey, New York, and Texas proposed supplemental notes to legislation concerning hazing. In 2007, Indiana Senate Bill 343 proposed more severe punishments for hazing occurring in a highway work zone. New Jersey Assembly Bill 1173 proposed in 2006 to revise the law concerning hazing to upgrade criminal penalties, provide certain immunities, and create civil offense and require written policies. In 2007, New York proposed Assembly Bill 2795, which called for increases in the severity of hazing in several areas, including making it a felony charge when hazing results in injury or death. In 2007, hazing was added to an additional section of the education code of the Texas Senate Bill (Hazing Statutes, 2007). Furthermore, hazing may constitute additional criminal violations, such as sexual assault, physical assault, and domestic abuse (Hennessy & Huson, 1998).

LACK OF FEDERAL GUIDANCE

There is currently no federal legislation regarding hazing practices. However, it is important to keep in mind that there are federal protections granted to persons that overlap into hazing behaviors. Issues of protected class come into play when those engaging in hazing practices use language, target individuals, or engage in other behaviors targeting members of a protected class. As the Office of Civil Rights stated in its Dear Colleague Letter (2010) on bullying in academic settings,

> The label used to describe an incident (*e.g.*, bullying, hazing, teasing) does not determine how a school is obligated to respond. Rather, the nature of the conduct itself must be assessed for civil rights implications. For example, if the abusive behavior is on the basis of race, color, national origin, sex, or disability,

and creates a hostile environment, a school is obligated to respond in accordance with the applicable federal civil rights statutes and regulations enforced by OCR [Office of Civil Rights].

(p. 3)

Again, currently the impetus is on institutions and states to manage hazing issues. Federal guidance is lacking in regard to hazing policy and law, which may inform why national statistics are absent from the dialogue. Without federal requirements, there is little reason for organizations, institutions, or states to track hazing incidents in and beyond higher education.

ORGANIZATIONAL HAZING PRACTICES

Although federal oversight is missing and state law provides broad oversight for hazing, the bulk of the responsibility for hazing oversight rests with organizations themselves. Clubs, groups, and organizations implement their own policies, practices, and rituals related to the induction and acclimation of new members. These processes vary not only by organizational type but also among similar organizations. For example, not all athletic teams foster community through hazing. Similarly, as discussed earlier, not all fraternity and sorority life organizations utilize hazing, and those that do haze do not all haze in the same ways. Here we explore different organizational types and the role of hazing in their development.

Hazing in Athletics

Although some organizations—fraternity and sorority life organizations and the military—may use hazing practices to foster connections, the scenario can be very different in athletics. Athletes compete for positions on a team. Hazing can potentially be used to introduce athletes to the team culture or to set the stage for athletes to compete in making teams or earning starting positions (Hosansky, 2013).

Hazing in athletics has a long history and begins when athletes try out for a team and continues through practice, competition, and beyond their first season. These behaviors can surface as hazing habits, humiliation, and victimizing new team members (Peluso, 2006). Athletic teams haze in a variety of ways, including requiring new members to carry equipment or run errands for coaches or more senior players, being forced to pay for senior player or team meals, being forced to dress in drag, or being given unflattering haircuts. Sports hazing can be more violent and unpleasant than other student organization hazing activities (Hosansky, 2013).

Hazing Statutes (2007) showed that 26 of the 44 states with anti-hazing laws either do not reference athletics in the context of hazing or single athletics out as uniquely different from hazing. For example, anti-hazing laws in Alabama, Arizona, Arkansas, California, Colorado, Florida, Michigan, South Carolina,

Tennessee, and Washington state that "hazing does not include customary athletic events or other similar contest or competition" (e.g., Florida § 1006.63). Still other states used different terminology and definitions to indicate that hazing does not apply to athletic teams of or within the college or university. Connecticut law states that "hazing shall not include an action sponsored by an institution of higher education, which requires any athletic practice, conditioning, competition or curricular activities" (Hazing Statutes, 2007, p. 15).

Military Hazing

The military setting is unique among potential hazing environments, as members eat, sleep, live, and work with one another. As Pershing (2006) said of the experience at military service academies (much of which translates to other military organizations and settings),

> A fundamental component of military training at DOD [Department of Defense] service academies is the indoctrination system for fourth classmen (freshmen), which includes traditions and rituals passed down through several generations. Because these systems are primarily student-run by upperclassmen (juniors and seniors), and since the distinction between hazing and legitimate military training has sometimes been ambiguous in the past, the fourth class indoctrination systems are subject to potential abuse.
>
> (p. 471)

With that in mind, hazing is relevant in military organizations at all levels. The settings range from military schools to basic training and carry over into other official and unofficial military activities. As in other settings, the stress related to being hazed not only directly harms individuals but also can be so severe that individuals engage in self-harm behaviors as a means of escape.

On August 4, 2010, Army Pvt. Keiffer Wilhem of Willard, Ohio, killed himself 10 days after he arrived in Iraq with a platoon based out of Fort Bliss, Texas. Whilhem's family said he was being bullied and hazed, including being forced to run for miles with rocks in his pockets (Whitley, 2009; Seewer, 2009). Similarly, Army Pvt. Daniel Chen of New York City was found dead from a self-inflicted gunshot wound on October 3, 2011. Chen had endured racially motivated taunts and physical attacks from his superiors and comrades before he died. According to Chen's diary, he was dragged by soldiers across the floor, pelted with stones, and forced to hold liquid in his mouth while hanging upside down (Hawley, 2011).

Eight U.S. Army soldiers were charged with Chen's death; five soldiers received demotions and brief prison sentences, and two others received demotions but avoided prison. The final soldier, Chen's platoon leader, was accused of failing to create a climate in which everyone is treated with dignity and respect, regardless of race" and failure to prevent his subordinates from maltreating and engaging in racially abusive language (Brooks, 2012; Cheng, 2011; Semple, 2012). The Chen case was reported as a hazing incident, and it forced the military to review its hazing policies (Hosansky, 2013).

Additional responses to these types of cases have gained traction at the national level. U.S. Congresswoman Judy Chu and other house members introduced the Harry Lew Military Hazing Accountability and Prevention Act of 2012 to prevent hazing in the military and to ensure that the Department of Defense has effective hazing and harassment prevention and accountability policies. This law provided the Pentagon with the necessary tools to effectively address the problem of hazing and harassment in the armed services and to guarantee that our brave service members can safely and honorably defend the citizens and the Constitution of the United States (Chu et al, 2012).

Fraternity and Sorority Life Hazing

Of all hazing settings and scenarios, perhaps the most common and most stereotypical setting is in the context of fraternity and sorority life. As has been mentioned, hazing in an educational context—particularly in settings involving secret societies or fraternity and sorority life organizations—has a long history (Lipkins, 2006).

Although the rationale for many of these activities is the need to work through difficulty as a means of bonding and cultivating brotherhood or sisterhood, there are significant risks when college students engage in these behaviors. Hazing activities can be exhausting, humiliating, degrading, demeaning, and intimidating and include significant physical and emotional discomfort (Lipkins, 2006). Hazing activities can cause harm or create risk of harm to the physical or mental health of individuals (Keim, 2000; Office of Fraternity and Sorority Life, 2017).

The specific demographics and history of a chapter can influence the type of hazing in an organization as well. Nuwer (2001) noted that in "the late '80s and '90s, pledging deaths in historically black fraternities occurred as a result of beatings and physical tests of endurance, while pledging deaths in historically white fraternities were associated with alcohol-related incidents and so-called road trips" (pp. 176–177). Pledging is an ongoing underground recruitment process and subculture of hazing to initiate members into a fraternity or sorority or any other organization (Ruffins, 1997).

Hazing Statutes (2007) indicate that Michigan, Texas, and Vermont are the only three states with anti-hazing laws that constitute pledging as a form of hazing. These states define pledging as "any action or activity related to becoming a member of an organization" (Hazing Statutes, 2007, p. 35). This leaves much of the oversight for these groups with the national offices for organizations or with university policies where the student organization chapters are located.

A SPECIAL CASE: THE OBLIGATION OF EDUCATIONAL INSTITUTIONS IN REGARD TO HAZING

Historically most hazing events are affiliated with educational institutions, including but not limited to student, academic, honorary, athletic, and fraternal organizations (Allan & Madden, 2008). Due to the location of many reported hazing events, most states' anti-hazing laws refer to hazing by persons at educational institutions. For example, Michigan law states that an educational institution "shall not engage in or participate in the hazing of an individual" (Hazing Statutes, 2007, p. 35) and defines an educational institution as a "public or private school that is a middle school, junior high school, high school, vocational school, college, or university located in this state" (Hazing Statutes, 2007, p. 35).

Educational institutions have played a major role in creating anti-hazing policies and laws. In another example from 1986, the board of trustees of the University of Kentucky and the University of Louisville adopted policies that prohibit hazing that intentionally endangers an individual's mental or physical health. On August 1, 1995, the board of trustees of the University of West Virginia and the board of directors of the state college system created guidelines for anti-hazing policies. In 1996, the board of trustees of the Vermont state colleges adopted policies and procedures to ensure the enforcement of policies prohibiting harassment and hazing. The state of Maine allows the board of trustees of an educational institution to maintain public order and to prohibit hazing by any members affiliated with the institution, either on or off campus. Minnesota State Colleges and Universities were directed by the state to adopt a clearly written policy on hazing (Hazing Statutes, 2007).

Despite this, hazing continues to be an ongoing problem for colleges and universities. Kaplin and Lee (2009) introduced legal guidance for college and university professionals:

> Given the existence of state laws against hazing, and the lack of any rational relationship between hazing that exposes a student to danger and the educational mission of the institution, it is likely that courts will expect institutions to prevent hazing to make hazing a violation of the students' code of conduct, and to hold students who engage in hazing activities strictly accountable for their actions, whether or not they result in physical or mental injury to students.
>
> (pp. 600–601)

State laws hold colleges and universities responsible for regulating student conduct and monitoring the behavior of every student on campus (Kaplin & Lee, 2009).

For example, the Arizona hazing prevention law outlines that "every public educational institution in this state shall adapt, post and enforce a hazing prevention policy. The hazing prevention policy shall be printed in every student handbook for distribution to parents and students" (Hazing Statutes, 2007, p. 10).

Similar to Arizona's anti-hazing law, Florida, Kentucky, Maine, Massachusetts, Oklahoma, Texas, and Vermont have state laws that hold the educational institution responsible for adapting, posting, and enforcing a hazing prevention policy printed in the institutions' student codes of conduct. These codes set forth the specific authority and responsibilities of the institution in maintaining discipline, establishing guidelines that facilitate a civil campus community, and outlining the educational process for determining students' responsibilities for alleged violations of institutions' regulations (Iowa State University, 2012).

DISRUPTING HAZING PRACTICES

Challenging hazing practices and harmful habits continues within many student, campus, fraternal, academic, honorary, athletic, and military organizations nationwide. Although many assume that severe hazing practices, pranks, and acts are stereotypes from the past or are exaggerated by the media, hazing activities are still prevalent within our communities.

These ideas are contradicted by a study at Alfred University (1999). The study illustrated a regional context and the cultural activities related to hazing that occur in each area of the United States. Rural, residential campuses with Greek systems in eastern or southern states with no anti-hazing laws were the most likely to experience hazing. Eastern and western campuses had the most alcohol-related hazing, and southern and Midwestern campuses had the greatest incidence of the dangerous and illegal practice of hazing (Alfred University, 1999). Although each region may vary in severity or type of hazing, it is still present in each area of the country.

Barriers to Reporting Hazing

Although many colleges and universities promote reporting hazing events to police, there are barriers to reporting hazing through the criminal process. Due the diverse definitions contained in specific federal and state anti-hazing laws, reporting hazing becomes a challenge for individuals, as there is no clear process to know and understand the implications of hazing. Allan and Madden (2008) found that "25% of coaches or organization advisors were aware of the group's hazing behaviors; 25% of the behaviors occurred on-campus in a public space; in 25% of hazing experiences, alumni were present; and students talk with peers

(48%, 41%) or family (26%) about their hazing experiences" (p. 2). This is important to note because many individuals are award of hazing events but do not report them.

Failing to report hazing activity can be a result of more than unfamiliarity with local, state, or federal legislation or ignorance of the policies and positions of academic institutions or member organizations. Failure to report can also be due to the lack of awareness of the process of reporting hazing. Individuals may be afraid of the consequences of reporting hazing, including consequences for themselves or their organizations. Reporters of hazing incidents may be fearful of getting their teams or groups in trouble, the negative consequences that occur to individual students, the larger team or group finding out who reported the incident(s), or being physically hurt or otherwise retaliated against by a member of their teams or groups (Allan & Madden, 2008).

Hazing Penalties

When individuals *do* choose to report hazing, the outcomes can vary significantly by state, academic institution, or role with an organization. Just as there are many different definitions of and contexts for hazing, there are also different charges, penalties, and punishments for individuals and organizations that commit hazing. Rhode Island policies provide insight in regard to penalties for individuals versus school officials. If an individual is convicted of hazing in Rhode Island, that person can be fined a maximum of $500 dollars, imprisoned for 30 days to 1 year, or both. The penalty for a school official is a fine of not less than $10 dollars and not more than $100 dollars. Penalties also vary by state. Utah penalties are different from Rhode Island's, where hazing can be a class C (fine not exceeding $750), class B (fine not exceeding 1,000), or class A (fine not exceeding $2,500) misdemeanor. Additional penalties can include imprisonment of up to 15 years for felony charges in some states (Hazing Statutes, 2007).

Additional Consequences of Hazing

Beyond the criminal or organizational sanctions imposed on individuals and groups, there are other significant consequences of hazing that affect large numbers of students in the country each year. Allen (2012) stated that 47% of high school students experience hazing, and 55% of college students experience hazing (Allan & Madden, 2008). Alfred University (1999) found that more than a quarter of a million college students have experienced some form of hazing to join a college athletic team. Some were forced to destroy property, make prank phone calls, or harass others; others participated in drinking competitions or alcohol-related events, including consumption of alcohol on recruitment visits; and others were humiliated and deprived of sleep for extended periods of time.

IMPLICATIONS FOR PRACTICE AND FUTURE RESEARCH

Given the persistence of hazing in higher education and the lack of centralized information and legislation on the topic, there is a tremendous opportunity for work on this problem. Practitioners working with teams, organizations, advisers, coaches, and other faculty, staff, and students around student on-campus activities have the opportunity to fill the gap in best practices related to hazing prevention, education, campus policy, and policy enforcement. Similarly, without a centralized source of hazing incidents, the door is wide open for research on this topic. As this text has attempted to do, the opportunity exists for scholars to examine hazing in a variety of organizations, in diverse geographical regions at different types of institutions, and in delving more deeply into the role of gender, race, sexual orientation, and other identities.

Implications for Practice

As highlighted throughout this text, hazing practices are present in many aspects of American culture, from the military to athletic teams to marching bands to honor societies. Hollmann (2002) offered eight specific strategies that institutions should explore: (1) communicate, (2) offer educational programs, (3) monitor behavior and attack high-risk alcohol consumption, (4) monitor student organization activities, (5) investigate and enforce hazing policies, (6) form local and national relationships, (7) develop positive student organization team building, and (8) focus on leadership transition. These strategies combined with other guidance falls into four primary categories: culture and climate assessment, prevention and education, oversight, and enforcement and accountability. Institutions can begin to transform their campus cultures and organizations by following these steps.

Culture and Climate Assessment

Institutions and individual organizations must be familiar with the history of hazing on their campuses. First, staff and student leaders must engage in an examination of hazing policies and regulations currently in place. Second, institutions and leaders need to review past incidents of hazing to understand the culture on their campuses. This should not simply involve reviewing documented cases but talking with organizational members, leaders, and advisers in ways that make it safe for individuals to share their experiences.

Prevention and Education

Individuals and organizations must be made aware of institutional expectations. Consistent language leaves little room for misinterpretation of the definition of hazing. Additionally, staff and leaders must communicate clearly and offer educational programs. Institutions must provide a clear message of consequences and the seriousness of hazing activities on campus. Institutions should offer training for student leaders, staff, and faculty on confronting hazing behaviors.

Hollmann (2002) stressed the importance of leadership education and alternative ways of team building to disrupt hazing habits in organizations. Institutions, administrators, and advisers should not simply impose new initiation and membership processes and rituals. Rather, to be effective, students—members and leaders—must be involved in this transformation of culture.

Oversight

Monitoring behavior is a key element in the next item on the list. The third aspect highlighted is that institutions need to focus on attacking high-risk alcohol consumption both in hazing activities and across campus. Monitoring the activities of student organizations will lead to a better understanding of what is being seen and said within these organizations.

Additionally, campus staff and student leaders must build relationships with local and national organizations, such as athletic conferences and the National Collegiate Athletic Association, national fraternity and sorority chapters, or national band organizations. Specifically, institutions should work closely with organizations and their leadership to utilize language consistent with organizational and institutional goals and to have a shared definition of hazing. Other organizations might consist of conference and athletic organizations to apply pressure where the institution cannot.

Enforcement and Accountability

Once communication and strategies for oversight are in place, investigation and enforcement of all hazing reports is essential. Institutions must treat hazing reports in a timely manner both in investigation and in disciplinary response. All individuals and organizations must understand that hazing carries risks and that they will be held accountable. Potential risks for both organizations and individuals include a civil lawsuit, criminal prosecution for an illegal act, discipline or sanctions from the national organization, discipline or sanctions from the college or university, and possible loss of insurance coverage (Office of Fraternity and Sorority Life, 2017).

Additionally, processes should be transparent, and outcomes for organizations should be shared when appropriate and when doing so does not violate FERPA. At the institutional level, a centralized location for tracking hazing incidents of all types should be identified. This may make the most sense in the student conduct office, but there may be other appropriate options as well.

Although these strategies are broad, they provide an understanding of the ways in which institutions can begin to approach issues related to hazing. These strategies are applicable to any organizational type and provide a coordinated system for education, monitoring, and accountability around hazing. These are some of the foundational steps institutions must take to create cultural change around habits of hazing.

Implications for Further Research

It is imperative for the safety of students and the success of the cocurricular educational experience that research continue around hazing law and policy, hazing practices, and the impact of hazing on individuals and groups. To change the culture and habits of hazing in schools and organizations and to protect individuals from being hazed, states must develop clear anti-hazing laws and policies. Dixon (2001) asserted that if laws are passed and policies enacted, students will be more likely to report and to tell others about hazing incidents. Empowering students to report is an essential step in the transformation and elimination of hazing on college campuses.

Most hazing scholarship focuses on fraternity and sorority life contexts. It is important to study hazing in other settings to better understand the role it plays in other organizations, across our campuses, and in our society. Specifically, research in the areas of military organizations, marching and other bands, athletics, and student organizations beyond fraternity and sorority life is important. Similarly, studies on the development of community, brotherhood, sisterhood, and group bonding without the use of hazing practices can help foster successful and healthy organizations in the future.

Additionally, case studies are needed to help members, advisers, leaders, administrators, and legislators explore the concepts of hazing. Case studies based on both actual events and fictionalized situations can inspire more dialogue around this critical issue. These can be used proactively to educate members, as education is essential given that the leadership of organizations changes each year as new students come onto campuses.

CONCLUSION

Hazing is a dangerous and serious crime with significant consequences. All states need to develop and propose policies and laws against hazing (Hosansky, 2013). College and university administrators need to be aware of the danger, seriousness, and prevalence of hazing on campus and in organizations. Furthermore, administrators need to be aware of the many different aspects of hazing and how they relate to legal issues, student development, and student awareness. It is important to be knowledgeable of hazing laws and policies and for active members in the community to combat the negative hazing habits that permeate our campuses and society.

Campus and university administrators must be aware of the danger of hazing practices in student organizations, athletic teams, and other groups. By understanding what implications hazing practices have for student success on campus, administrators and practitioners can be better equipped to provide support or referrals for victims of hazing activities while challenging harmful habits and practices.

College and university administrators need to confront the hazing epidemic with tenacity, courage, and a deep sense of responsibility for the success of their institutions and students. The dignity of those seeking admission into student organizations must be protected and respected at all times in order to achieve organizational missions and adhere to foundational beliefs and core values. College and university administrators must remember that hazing is a crime.

Additionally, administrators need resources to educate staff and students. From educating student leaders during the process of recognition and funding of student organizations to providing appropriate sanctions when policies are violated, administrators must work with groups to ensure student safety. The same holds true for working with organizational advisers, coaches, and other staff leaders who engage in students' cocurricular experiences.

Training must be based on clear and accessible policies provided by the institution to students, staff, and administrators.

Ultimately, policy is useless without enforcement and accountability. Students and others working around student organizations and teams must be aware of how policies will be enforced and what the potential outcomes are—on campus and beyond. Enforcement must include consistent outcomes and high levels of accountability for individuals and organizations when policies are violated.

Only when policies are clear and consistent, when leaders are educated, and when students are aware of expectations, policies, laws, and outcomes can we provide safe, hazing-free experiences for college students. Joining an organization should be a highlight of any student's experience in college. Although new members have a responsibility for the benefits of organizational membership, those benefits should not be earned by enduring hazing. The price of membership should never include physical, mental, or emotional harm. Until there is clear legislation and policy, students continue to be at risk.

HAZING T-CHART ACTIVITY

Building on the resources provided in Chapter 1 (see Figures 1.1 and 1.2), here we introduce the hazing T-chart (see Figure 8.1). This chart assists individuals and organizations in engaging in reflection about their perceptions of hazing and the law. This activity is provided to start a conversation on hazing. We suggest that each participant be provided with two copies of the hazing T-chart. The first

Perceived understanding of hazing	Perceived understanding of hazing laws

FIGURE 8.1 Hazing T-Chart

T-chart is for program participants to complete before hazing presentations to capture members' understanding of hazing. A second copy is for note-taking during the training or educational program.

Once individuals have independently completed the first T-chart (before the educational programming), they engage with learning partners or in small groups to discuss their reflections. At the end of each educational program, we encourage that participants reflect on and compare their first hazing T-charts to their second hazing T-charts based on notes taken during the presentation.

REFERENCES

Alfred University. (1999). *Initiation rites and athletics: A national survey of NCAA sports teams.* Alfred, NY: Author.

Allan, E. J. (2012, September, 21). FAMU's town hall call for hazing to be reported. *National Public Radio.* Retrieved from www.npr.org/2012/09/21/161523342/famus-town-hall-calls-for-hazing-to-be-reported

Allan, E. J., & Madden, M. (2008). *Hazing in view: College students at risk.* Retrieved from www.stophazing.org/wp-content/uploads/2014/06/hazing_in_view_web1.pdf

Alvarez, D. M. (2015). Death by hazing: Should there be a federal law against fraternity and sorority hazing? *Journal of Multidisciplinary Research, 7*(2), 43–75.

Bailey, H. E., & Hughey, A. H. (2013, January 16). A realistic, pro-active approach to eradicating hazing for Greek organizations. *Diverse Issues in Higher Education.* Retrieved from http://diverseeducation.com/article/50714/#

Brooks, D. (2012, August 24). Soldier demoted in Chen hazing case. *Military News.* Retrieved from www.military.com/daily-news/2012/08/24/soldier-demoted-in-chen-hazing-case.html?comp=7000023317843&rank=4

Chamberlain, B. W. (2013). Am I my brother's keeper: Reforming criminal hazing laws based on an assumption of care. *Emory Law Journal, 63*(4), 925–977.

Cheng, P. (2011, December 22). 8 U.S. army men charged in NYC soldier's death. *NBC NewYork.* Retrieved from www.nbcnewyork.com/news/local/Danny-Chen-Soldier-Death-Hazing-Asian-American-Charged-Criminal-Probe-Military-135988423.html

Chu, Cumming, Honda, & Other House Members. (2012, May 7). Reps. Chu, Cumming, Honda, and other House Members to introduce legislation to prevent hazing in the military. *U.S. Congresswoman Judy Chu, Veterans.* Retrieved from http://chu.house.gov/press-release/reps-chu-cummings-honda-and-others-introduce-legislation-prevent-hazing-military

Dixon, M. (2001). Hazing in high schools: Finding the hidden tradition. *Journal of Law And Education, 30*(2), 357–363.

Hawley, C. (2011, December 21). Danny Chen death: Eight U.S. soldiers charged after alleged taunted led to apparent suicide. *Huffington Post Politics.* Retrieved from www.huffingtonpost.com/2011/12/21/danny-chen-army-suicide-bullying-chinese-american_n_1163629.html?view=print&comm_ref=false

Hazing Statutes. (2007, June 30). *Hazing statutes.* Retrieved from http://b.3cdn.net/raproject/969346b764b11860f9_70m6ivefo.pdf

Hennessy, N. J., & Huson, L. M. (1998). Legal issues and Greek letter organizations. *New Directions for Student Services, 81,* 61–77.

Hollmann, B. B. (2002). Hazing: Hidden campus crime. *New Directions for Student Services, 99,* 11–23.

Hosansky, D. (2013). Preventing hazing: Can tougher laws stop violent rituals? *CQ Researcher, 23*(6), 133–156.

Iowa State University. (2012). *Student disciplinary regulation (code of conduct).* Retrieved from http://policy.iastate.edu/policy/SDR

Kaplin, W. A., & Lee, B. A. (2009). *A legal guide for student affairs professionals* (2nd ed.). San Francisco, CA: Jossey-Bass.

Keim, W. (2000). *The power of caring.* Retrieved from www.stophazing.org/definition

Lipkins, S. (2006). *Preventing hazing: How parents, teachers and coaches can stop the violence, harassment and humiliation.* San Francisco, CA: Jossey-Bass.

Nuwer, H. (2001). *Wrongs of passage: Fraternities, sororities, hazing, and binge drinking.* Bloomington: Indiana University Press.

Office of Civil Rights. (2010). *Dear colleague letter: Harassment and civil rights.* Retrieved from www2.ed.gov/about/offices/list/ocr/letters/colleague-201010.pdf

Office of Fraternity and Sorority Life, University of Nebraska–Lincoln. (2017). *Resources.* Retrieved from www.unl.edu/greek/resources

Peluso, A. R. (2006). Hazing in sports: The effects and legal ramifications. *The Sport Journal, 19.* Retrieved from http://thesportjournal.org/article/hazing-in-sports-the-effects-and-legal-ramifications/

Pershing, J. L. (2006). Men and women's experiences with hazing in a male-dominated elite military institution. *Men and Masculinities, 8*(4), 470–492.

Ruffins, P. (1997). Are African American fraternities beating themselves to death? *Black Issues in Higher Education, 14*(8), 18–25.

Seewer, J. (2009, August 28). GI in Iraq made 2 calls telling of abuse before his suicide. *Military Times*. Retrieved from www.federaljack.com/gi-in-iraq-made-2-calls-home-telling-of-abuse-before-his-suicide/

Semple, K. (2012, February 15). Court-martial urged for two in the death of a private. *The New York Times*. Retrieved from www.nytimes.com/2012/02/16/nyregion/courts-martial-urged-for-2-in-death-of-pvt-danny-chen.html?_r=1&

StopHazing.org. (2000). *States with anti-hazing laws*. Retrieved from www.stophazing.org/states-with-anti-hazing-laws/

Whitley, M. A. (2009, August 28). Private Keiffer Wilhem of Ohio took his life in Iraq; now family learns his superiors are charged with bullying him and other. *Cleveland.com*. Retrieved from http://blog.cleveland.com/metro/2009/08/private_keiffer_wilhelm_of_ohi.html

Chapter 9

Preventive or Reactionary?
Emerging Policies on Hazing in Postsecondary Education

Cameron C. Beatty

As defined in Chapter 1 of this book, hazing is forcing individuals to engage in activities that are potentially harmful, demeaning, degrading, or embarrassing in the process of joining a group or organization. Although hazing habits have been consistent elements in higher education, increasing numbers of high-profile incidents and hazing-related litigation have given rise to major efforts to prevent hazing by stakeholders and administrators (Allan & Madden, 2012; Nuwer, 2004, 2018). Although effective policy on hazing is important in any organization to try to curb the sting of hazing, implementing policy alone is not enough (Lipkins, 2006).

However, campus officials must be cautious with education opportunities and policy changes. Students may respond to efforts to curb their behavior with psychological reactance (Brehm, 1966), a process in which individuals respond by doing the opposite of what is advocated in order to protect their own attitudes and actions. This can lead to increased hazing and/or decreased reporting of hazing behaviors (Allan & Madden, 2012; Bensley & Wu, 1991). This chapter highlights the recent emergence of postsecondary institutions' hazing policies in response to highly publicized campus incidents. Although reactionary university anti-hazing policies have become the standard, many universities are moving to full disbanding or suspension. This chapter concludes with considerations advocating for a preventive approach to policy creation, implementation, and practice.

Reactive policy is developed in response to a concern, problem, or emergency. It is designed to remedy problems that already exist. Reactive policy development often happens more quickly than proactive policy, as the problems can be pressing or even urgent. Reactive policy debate centers mostly on whether a certain policy mechanism is the best way to handle a situation, not whether the situation will ever become a problem. Proactive policy is deliberately chosen and often designed to prevent a concern, problem, or emergency from occurring. Proactive policies can be more challenging in that it is often difficult politically to get lawmakers to commit money and resources to a problem that has not yet occurred. Even so, there are many examples of proactive measures in energy policy.

Preventive and proactive approaches aim to prevent hazing from happening. In the past 5 years, there has been reemerging encouragement and lobbying to federalize hazing laws and connect them to students' eligibility to receive federal financial aid (Wilson, 2012). As stated in Chapter 8, six states still have no hazing laws at all (Alaska, Hawaii, Montana, New Mexico, South Dakota, and Wyoming). Richardson (2014) noted that higher education institutional hazing policies must align with state laws. Policies and statutes must be clearly and consistently reinforced through continued development of educational practices that actively engage students and student organizations (Richardson, 2014). There must be more collaboration among educators, law enforcement officials, and alumni associations about the development and implementation of preemptive anti-hazing initiatives.

Recently, the move in reactive policy development to address high-risk behavior has shifted toward suspending or expelling all organizations and activity. In the fall of 2017, for example, Florida State University, Louisiana State University, Texas State University, the University of Michigan, and Ohio State University each suspended all or part of their fraternity and sorority life activities. Lee (2017) pointed out the rise in hazing-related deaths nationwide on postsecondary campuses and stressed that for decades institutions have struggled with how to address hazing while states have implemented laws. However, the fact remains that high-risk behavior continues, resulting in student deaths each year.

REACTIONARY CAMPUS POLICIES

In the past 15 years, several colleges and universities have developed stronger hazing policies to address the ongoing and evolving issue of hazing. Many of the new and emerging edits to university hazing policies have been reactionary to address highly publicized hazing allegations. The following highlights a few cases in order to address the process of how postsecondary institutions continue to develop and implement hazing policies.

The University of Massachusetts Amherst (UMass) has a very comprehensive and informative section of its campus policies website that provides extensive information about Massachusetts hazing law, university hazing policy, directions on how to report hazing, the impact of hazing, hazing myths, and other resources. In 2006, North Pleasant Street, also known as Frat Row, was demolished, which marked a drastic change in the partying and hazing culture of undergraduates at UMass. In 2012, the *Daily Collegian*, the university's campus newspaper, published an article about the rising standards of UMass admissions and the recent financial investment the state has put into improving the flagship university's facilities, which has led to an overhaul of the "Zoomass" public image. Both administrators

PREVENTIVE OR REACTIONARY?

and students have driven this change, with members of fraternities now rejecting the frat label, citing negative connotations with the abbreviation (Hoff, 2012).

The Massachusetts Institute of Technology (MIT) has an entire website dedicated to hazing, with a similar breadth of information as is available on the UMass website and more. There is extensive detail on apathy or acquiescence in the face of hazing as constituting hazing as well as definitions for subtle hazing, harassment hazing, and violent hazing. Its university policy goes into great detail as to what constitutes hazing and what does not, and the sanctions for engaging in hazing are stated as disciplinary suspension or expulsion. MIT also has a Hazing Prevention and Education Committee that was formed in 2013 under the Division of Student Life that includes bystander intervention-based trainings, prevention social marketing campaigns, reporting forms and systems, and more.

MIT's current hazing policy is likely (in part) a result of the 2013–2014 investigation and ultimate 2-year suspension of the Delta Upsilon fraternity (reinstated in spring 2016) that was found to be engaging in hazing activities. The investigation and ultimate decision to suspend the fraternity raised many questions about Greek life oversight, university involvement, and student safety (Brent, 2014). By making changes within MIT's fraternities, sororities, and independent living groups to create a comprehensive, prevention-based effort, MIT has demonstrated the severity of hazing and identified precautionary methods.

Rutgers University has embedded its hazing policy within the fraternity and sorority affairs section of its student life website, and the university requires all fraternity and sorority organizations to file hazing compliance forms each year with a deadline for submission. The policy also lists very specific activities and behaviors that are explicitly prohibited, and it outlines New Jersey hazing law and the Pledge's Bill of Rights. Unlike UMass and MIT, the website does not offer extensive outside resources for additional information on hazing or its impact. In 2015, Sigma Phi Epsilon was shut down as the result of an incident where a 20-year-old fraternity member was hospitalized due to alcohol intoxication, which happened only 6 weeks after the alcohol-poisoning death of a 19-year-old Rutgers University student after a party at the Delta Kappa Epsilon house. Hazing policies have been updated and strictly enforced after high-profile investigations.

Like Rutgers University, Montclair State University includes hazing prevention and policy information in the Greek life section of its Division of Student Development and Campus Life. In 2011, two Tau Kappa Epsilon fraternity members were charged with aggravated hazing. The information provided now includes a detailed list of prohibited activities as well as an overview of New Jersey hazing law and the Pledge's Bill of Rights. Although there is little information about additional resources on the impact of hazing, there is a link to HazingPrevention. org and a section for hazing prevention workshops.

The hazing policy at Young Harris College is embedded in the Greek life portion of the campus activities and student life section of the college's web page, but it is limited compared to some of the other websites referenced earlier. There is a list of examples of hazing behaviors and activities as well as a five questions to ask to determine if something could be construed as hazing. There is also a brief overview of Georgia State law on hazing. There are no additional resources, and no other information is provided. The lack of an extensive hazing policy or other information at Young Harris College is curious, as its hazing culture has been a topic of conversation in recent years after *Jezebel* published a damning article about extreme hazing happening at the school and the lack of administrative intervention to protect students (Baker, 2013). Two instructors were allegedly terminated for attempting to uncover the pervasive hazing culture at Young Harris College (Straumsheim, 2013).

Like MIT, Florida Agricultural and Mechanical University (FAMU) has an entire website dedicated to education and information about hazing. FAMU has a zero-tolerance policy on hazing in its student code of conduct, a procedure for reporting hazing, and an online anti-hazing agreement. The website details how different university stakeholders are committed to ending hazing, including student organizations, parents, athletes, administrators, and campus leaders. There is a plethora of educational information and resources available as well as links to Florida State law on hazing and explicit details on FAMU's policies and procedures for handling hazing allegations.

The comprehensive nature of this visible push to end hazing at FAMU is likely (at least in part) a result of the 2011 death of FAMU student and drum major Robert Champion. In 2015, three FAMU students were convicted of manslaughter in Champion's death, who was a victim of a band hazing initiation that included a severe beating that left him with blunt force trauma to the head, killing him within an hour of the ritual.

These recent cases of hazing in higher education highlight the obvious high-risk behaviors and sometimes fatal consequences of hazing. But are there preventive policy and practice approaches available to minimize hazing in postsecondary education? Are higher education educators and professionals doing everything they can to protect students from this hazing culture? What does a postsecondary learning environment look like without hazing?

KEY CONSIDERATIONS FOR DEVELOPING HAZING PREVENTION POLICIES

What should institutions be doing? Although this chapter has focused on how different colleges and universities responded after incidents in terms of hazing prevention and hazing policy development, for institutions without major incidents, there are important considerations as well. This section highlights how other administrators, staff, advisers, and organizational leaders can learn from what the institutions highlighted here have and are experiencing.

Two recent cases highlight the continued emergence of new policies developed in response to highly publicized hazing incidents on their campuses. After the death of Tim Piazza on the Penn State University campus in February 2017, Penn State President Eric J. Barron submitted an op-ed the following August calling for more university oversight and less self-governance of student organizations, fraternities, and sororities that engage in hazing activities. He proposed ongoing safety initiatives that included unannounced drop-in monitoring at fraternity houses by university-hired and trained staff; eligibility requirements for new members that do not allow first-semester freshmen to join; a reformed and shortened new member (pledging) process; an informational scorecard making public critical information about each chapter; strong social restrictions that limit alcohol availability and use; strict limits to the size and number of social gatherings; increased parent and new member education; and a no-tolerance policy regarding hazing. He proposed that for chapters that violated these guidelines and as a result put students in jeopardy that the university would immediately and permanently revoke Penn State recognition for the organization.

Similarly, the death of 18-year-old Maxwell Raymond Gruver at Louisiana State University in September 2017 has implications for reactionary and preventive policies. Authorities believed the death to be a result of fraternity hazing, leading to all fraternity and sorority activities and recruitment at the university to be suspended indefinitely and the closure of Phi Delta Theta. Additionally, as a result of this incident, 10 students from Phi Delta Theta were arrested in the death of Maxwell Gruver.

Individual and organizational accountability is important, but after a student has died, it is too late to help him or her. Although there has been a trend of suspension and expulsion of student organizations, fraternity and sorority chapters, and athletic team members and coaches, there needs to be continued efforts to develop prevention policies in order to stop high-risk behaviors and keep students safe. Some considerations for postsecondary institutions moving forward in anti-hazing work and policy development include the following:

1. *Information sharing.* The higher education community must streamline information sharing about best practices, effective prevention and intervention initiatives, and successful anti-hazing programs among institutions. Think tanks are needed to develop strategies to enhance anti-hazing best practices already being engaged. Educators must become involved at a personal level, facilitate the flow of information, and engage in honest dialogue with students and student organizations.
2. *Individual accountability.* Yale's Hazing Prevention Task Force (2011) recommended that hazing policies include student accountability for initiation practices, hazing, and the effects of hazing on witnesses and third parties. The task force encouraged the university to hold witnesses

of hazing just as accountable as offenders. No longer can institutions afford to tolerate bystanders as innocent in hazing processes, but rather they must be held accountable as enablers of these hazing habits.
3. *Organizational accountability*. Institutions must require a structure of shared accountability among administration, campus leadership, and student leadership. A structure of accountability involves creating collective ownership among administrators, campus leadership, and student leadership in eliminating acts of hazing and high-risk behaviors (drinking and drug use). Accountability extends beyond having campus policies, programs and practices, and interventions in place to creating structures that lead to a sustained cultural change with regard to hazing and high-risk behaviors.
4. *Hazing audit*. Colleges and universities should establish campus-wide anti-hazing coalitions or task forces under the Division of Student Affairs to oversee a review of the campus hazing policy and practices and to provide continuous emphasis on and improvement in hazing prevention measures. Review committees such as these should not only be implemented in times of crisis but also be charged with developing proactive initiatives to help prevent these crises from happening.
5. *Cultural transformation*. The University of Texas System implemented preventive educational programming as part of an overall campus culture shift from simple awareness programs to more active and engaging prevention programs. Environmental management is the new framework used by the institution. In seeking to change the environment around hazing, the task force encouraged the use of environment-focused strategies to "examine policies, campus culture, and norms around hazing and binge drinking, available campus programs, services and intervention efforts, and national research" (University of Texas System, 2014, p. 5). In short, working toward cultural transformation is a cumulative result of all the previous items on this list.

Traditionally, some campus prevention activities focused only on awareness of individual choices and behaviors, assuming that students would make healthier behavioral choices when faced with facts about alcohol and the impact of hazing behaviors. Strategies for cultural transformation include efforts related to individual decision making but also focus on interpersonal and group processes designed not only to change student behaviors but also social norms, thus creating an environment where positive behaviors are encouraged. Moving beyond the people involved, this approach also seeks to address policy issues on campus and within the community. A blended policy approach that allows for a combination of accountability, amnesty policies, awareness, and other mechanisms can best encourage students to seek help for severely intoxicated students in life-threatening or dangerous situations and report hazing when they witness or are made aware of incidents (University of Texas System, 2014).

ORGANIZATIONAL REFLECTION QUESTIONS

1. What are the anti-hazing policies on your campus? In your organization (locally and nationally)?
2. Who is responsible for knowing hazing policy in your organization (members, advisers, etc.)?
3. What resources can you identify to provide more information about hazing policies, processes, and consequences on your campus and in the larger organization?
4. Do you believe that anti-hazing policies prevent hazing? Why or why not? What is most effective in addressing hazing habits?

CONCLUSION

Although effective anti-hazing policy is important in higher education to try to curb the harm and destruction that results from hazing, implementing policy alone, as indicated by the approach taken by most universities and colleges with seemingly effective hazing policies, may not be enough. This chapter highlighted recent campus reactionary policies to hazing and calls for preventive policy and practice approaches in order to have the most substantial impact on the problem. Anti-hazing education is important; students need to understand in their groups and organizations that hazing is not a beneficial activity. A policy simply stating "no hazing" will not be effective on its own. Anti-hazing education should be ingrained in the culture of the institution, and students should be engaging in educational programming on an ongoing basis in order to truly comprehend the issues.

REFERENCES

Allan, E., & Madden, M. (2012). The nature and extent of college student hazing. *International Journal of Adolescent and Medical Health*, 24(1), 83–90. doi:10.1515/IJAMH.2012.012

Baker, K. (2013). Naked sweethearts & mud crawls: A small college's big hazing problem. *Jezebel*. Retrieved from http://jezebel.com/naked-sweethearts-and-mud-crawls-small-college-has-big-485060397

Bensley, L. S., & Wu, R. (1991). The role of psychological reactance in drinking following alcohol prevention messages. *Journal of Applied Social Psychology*, 21(13), 1111–1124.

Brehm, J. W. (1966). *A theory of psychological reactance*. New York, NY: Academic Press.

Brent, D. (2014, December 2). Behind the suspension of MIT Delta Upsilon. *The Tech*. Retrieved from http://tech.mit.edu/V134/N58/du/du.htm

Hoff, P. (2012, December 5). UMass fraternities no longer characterized with "Zoomas" party image. *Daily Collegian*. Retrieved from http://dailycollegian.com/2012/12/05/umass-fraternities-no-longer-characterized-with-%E2%80%98zoomass%E2%80%99-party-image/

Lee, K. (2017, November 15). So what's behind the recent fraternity hazing incidents on college campuses nationwide? *Los Angeles Times*. Retrieved from www.latimes.com/nation/la-na-fraternity-hazing-20171115-htmlstory.html

Lipkins, S. (2006). *Preventing hazing: How parents, teachers, and coaches can stop the violence, harassment, and humiliation*. San Francisco, CA: Jossey-Bass.

Nuwer, H. (Ed.). (2004). *The hazing reader*. Indianapolis: Indiana University Press.

Nuwer, H. (2018). *Hazing deaths*. Retrieved from www.hanknuwer.com/hazing-deaths/

Richardson, D. C. (2014). *University official's perceptions about felony hazing laws* (Unpublished doctoral dissertation). Barry University, Miami Shores, FL.

Straumsheim, C. (2013, May 1). Terminated for defending students? *Inside Higher Ed*. Retrieved from www.insidehighered.com/news/2013/05/01/instructors-say-anti-hazing-push-led-termination

University of Texas System. (2014, April). *Recommendations from the task force on hazing and alcohol*. Retrieved from www.utsystem.edu/sites/default/files/documents/Recommendations%20from%20the%20Task%20Force%20on%20Hazing%20and%20Alcohol/hazing-and-alcohol-task-force-report.pdf

Wilson, F. (2012). *Congresswoman Wilson announces framework for anti-hazing legislation*. Retrieved from http://wilsonhouse.gov

Part 4

Hazing Prevention, Awareness, and Education

Chapter 10

The Psychological Shadow of Hazing

Mental Health Issues and Counseling

Raquel Botello and Natalie Carlos Cruz

Media, research, and policy concerns related to hazing often highlight the physical damage and life-threatening situations that hazing can produce while the psychological aftermath of hazing is overlooked. Although hazing has been classified as either physical or nonphysical, the purpose of hazing is often to elicit psychological duress (Finkel, 2002). Due to lethality concerns, much more attention has been given to the physical impact of hazing practices (Finkel, 2002; Nuwer, 2001). It can be argued that whether intentional or not, hazing practices often primarily seek to elicit a psychological response from the victim. In a sense, the practice of perceived threat, humiliation, assault, and other hazing practices often aim at establishing power, instilling fear, or even generating a sense of survivorship that can promote loyalty or belonging to a specific group (Cimino, 2011).

It is difficult to understand why individuals who have never been aggressive or mistreated others would engage in often cruel and traumatic hazing practices. Simultaneously, the question of why individuals continue to volunteer for and conform to such difficult experiences remains a mystery. Thus, the threefold focus of this chapter includes, first, to unravel the psychological underpinnings that drive and promote hazing; second, to discuss how hazing can be addressed from a mental health perspective in terms of risk for psychological concerns and treatment; and third, to provide directions for future research and suggestions for university administration in addressing psychosocial approaches to decreasing hazing and the psychological aftermath of hazing.

DIFFERENTIATING HAZING FROM BULLYING

Hazing practices differ from other forms of aggressions, such as bullying. Bullying has been more recently defined as a repetitive verbal or physical behavior that focuses on the imbalance of power and impotence of victims in fending for themselves (Espelage & Swearer, 2003). In contrast, hazing is less likely to be repetitive or long lasting. As defined in Chapter 1, hazing can be perceived to have an end goal of formalized group membership, where as bullying does not include a perceived positive end goal. However, hazing and bullying do have same similarities in that they are both classified as a type of proactive aggression. Proactive aggression is a form of aggression whose focus is to elicit such a response as intimidation and power (Espelage & Swearer, 2004).

Unlike hazing, bullying is a type of interpersonal aggression that has been more easily reported and researched and one that became an issue addressed within schools and society. Given the similarities between hazing and bullying, an overview is necessary in order to distinguish the negative psychological consequences between bullying and hazing. For example, bullying literature has identified various roles involved in this phenomenon (Holt & Espelage, 2007; Levy et al., 2012), including the bully, victim, bully-victim, and bystander. Although different, these roles are often intercorrelated (Levy et al., 2012). There are negative outcomes for bullies, including deteriorations in academic performance (Schneider, O'Donnell, Stueve, & Coulter, 2012), sexual harassment perpetration (Espelage, Basile, & Hamburger, 2012), poor school adjustment (Nansel et al., 2001), and substance use (Haynie et al., 2001). For victims of bullying, studies have found clinically significant high levels of depression (Espelage, Low, & DeLaRue, 2012), suicide ideation and attempts (Klomek, Marrocco, Kleinman, Schonfeld, & Gould, 2007), and anxiety (Holt et al., 2014). Further, those who are dually involved as bully-victim demonstrate an even greater complexity of severe psychological impairment (Holt & Espelage, 2007).

In contrast, hazing is unspoken, highly underreported, and often denied by both perpetrators and victims. For example, some reports have noted that fewer than 10% of hazing victims identify their experience as hazing (Allan & Madden, 2012). Additionally, victims often view their own hazing as a necessary component of their membership in a group or organization (Allan & Madden, 2008; Diamond, Callahan, Chain, & Solomon, 2016). One reason for this is that hazing is a passage to a supposedly purposeful ending. The illusion of purpose and meaning can hide the true nature of the often traumatic or abusive hazing experience. Hazing victims may accept their experience as purposeful and necessary and do not view themselves as being victimized per se.

From a psychological perspective, when individuals find purpose to any sort of difficult experience, they are less likely to be experience it as negative, abusive, or traumatic (Tedeschi & Calhoun, 2004; Triplett et al., 2012). Making sense of an experience is a way of coping with and decreasing the cognitive dissonance (i.e., morals and values incongruent with actions) that may develop (Cooper, 2011). Thus, it is likely that victims of hazing may not perceive their experience as harmful, as their pursuit for purpose and congruency undermines that actual impact. Instead, victims may need to later confront the lingering effects of these experiences. Literature on assault victims has noted that delayed negative appraisal of memories of traumatic event predicts the severity of posttraumatic mental health concerns (Halligan, Michael, Clark, & Ehlers, 2003).

Why nonaggressive and socially responsible individuals would harm someone during the practice of hazing habits may be explained by the phenomenon of moral disengagement. Bandura, Barbaranelli, Caprara, and Pastorelli (1996) identified moral disengagement as the reason why individuals engage in acts that often go against their values and morals. McCreary, Bray, and Thoma (2017) have linked fraternity membership to higher likelihood of moral disengagement and less likelihood to intervene in hazing situations. That is, perpetrators of hazing may be more inclined to justify their actions if their beliefs align with value in the process and they themselves experienced being hazed (Hamilton, Scott, LaChapelle, & O'Sullivan, 2016). It is likely that many perpetrators and victims would not engage in these harmful activities outside of the current context. However, findings have indicated a difference between non-fraternity members and fraternity members to reported moral disengagement (McCreary et al., 2017).

HAZING OBEDIENCE AND CONFORMITY

How did the value of community and belonging devolve to suffering being a requirement of belonging? Some researchers have traced hazing back centuries and even to evolutionary rationale (Cimino, 2011). Administrators have tried to understand why hazing continues and more specifically why individuals will participate in the act of hazing toward themselves and others. The famous and classic psychological study conducted by Milgram (1963) sought to determine how good people can do terrible things as a way to understand why historic atrocities like the holocaust could occur. Milgram (1963) found that under pressure and with the presence of clearly perceived authority, the majority of individuals follow orders and act in ways that are harmful and even potentially lethal to others.

Given these findings, it is likely that hazing continues because authoritative forces (older members, advisers, or leaders of organizations) encourage or initiate hazing or simply allow it to happen. For example, a quarter of college students who reported hazing believed that coaches and advisers were aware of hazing activities (Allan & Madden, 2012). Additionally, social conformity theory demonstrates that individuals will conform to group pressure even when they are certain that it is faulty judgment or the wrong choice (Keating et al., 2005). Hazing often happens within a group context; thus, social conformity is likely a factor that promotes hazing activities and hazing culture. As an example, fraternity and sorority organizations often "cross" or admit individuals in cohorts; thus, it is likely that the conformity of the newcomers is generated and reinforced by existing and previous cohort members.

BELONGING AND GROUP MEMBERSHIP

Belonging is often regarded as the finish line for the hazing victim, whether it is voluntary or not (Diamond et al., 2016). Achieving a sense of belonging is one of the most basic and natural human needs. Developmentally, group memberships are particularly important for college students who are often in the midst of identity formation (Montgomery & Côté, 2003). Researchers have suggested that past negative school experiences (i.e., bullying) do not impact college students' perceived engagement, as they may see college as a blank slate or place to reinvent themselves and form group connections (Holt et al., 2014). Students may view the joining of an organization or sport as a way to socialize, make new friends, and continue to expand their school adjustment and identity. College students with a greater sense of social integration and adjustment have been linked to higher retention (Gerdes & Mallinckrodt, 1994)

Hazing can occur in a variety of groups or settings, but it is most frequent during the college years when students have unique individual and contextual factors that make them more susceptible to the potentially traumatic effects of hazing (Arnett, 2004). Arnett (2004) argued that many 18- to 25-year-olds in Western countries are within a distinct life phase in between adolescence and adulthood that he referred to as emerging adulthood. Advances in technology and the U.S. shift from a manufacturing economy to a knowledge- and information-based economy has contributed to this change. Therefore, emerging adults find themselves in an unstructured, open exploration of a variety of possible life directions. This is true not only in education but also in personal relationships (including romantic relationships), work, and worldviews. Deprived of financial self-dependency and the security of marriage and parenthood, emerging adults are more susceptible to doing whatever it takes to create a strong social support network (Arnett, 2004).

In this same light, schools may often promote connection and involvement as a way to enhance the college experience and smooth the adjustment process. Thus, condemning a practice that is linked to social status and inclusion (hazing as a part of group intake processes) creates complexity, eliminating these practices as a whole. For administrators and institutions, it is important for the need for connection and belonging to be validated as a positive value outside of hazing practices. Thus, interventions should be clear in promoting practices of belonging and groups while distinguishing hazing as an unnecessary and detrimental activity.

Thus, because individuals naturally seek connection and belonging, hold a high value in group membership, respond to authority, and conform to groups, practices like hazing continue to be rationalized and promoted (Diamond et al., 2016; Keating et al., 2005; Milgram, 1963). Along with perceived authority and power gained, the hazee may often become the hazer once he or she is in the organization. In other words, individuals who are hazed as newcomers often take on the perpetrator role in future scenarios (Hamilton et al., 2016). This combination creates a vicious cycle that fuels hazing into a sustained practice.

PSYCHOLOGICAL CONSEQUENCES

The psychological consequences of hazing are underresearched and not clearly understood in part as a result of it being unrecognized and underreported. Hoover (1999) found that 60% of hazed university athletes would not report hazing. Major reasons given by participants include believing that it's not a problem, simply not wanting to tell on their friends, and thinking that the administration would not handle the issue correctly and possibly make things worse. Moreover, some participants did not believe they were victims of hazing. The cognitive dissonance that evolves between seeing oneself as a strong and moral individual and being a victim of hazing may be a deterring factor in reporting hazing among student-athletes. Hoover and Pollard (2000) explored the effects of hazing among high school students in data from 1,541 respondents. Results from their study indicated that of those who experienced hazing, 71% reported negative consequences, including relationship difficulties in addition to physical and psychological symptoms (Hoover & Pollard, 2000). Common impacts on both the victim/person being hazed and the perpetrator/those who haze are listed in Table 10.1.

Bystanders may also walk away with intense feelings of powerlessness, remorse, and acute stress related to what they witnessed. Bystanders often fear being victimized themselves and will experience a heightened level of anxiety (Rivers, Poteat, Noret, & Ashurst, 2009). Research on bystanders also highlights the cognitive dissonance experienced between their desire to have intervened without having acted on that intent (Bannon, Brosi, & Foubert, 2013; Rivers et al., 2009). Further research on the different roles of hazers, hazees, hazer-hazee, and bystanders is warranted to better understand the negative psychological consequences specific to this phenomenon.

TABLE 10.1 Psychological Impacts on Hazee/Victim and Hazer/Perpetrator

Victim/Impact on Person Being Hazed	Perpetrator/Impact on Those Who Haze
• Physical, emotional, and/or mental instability • Sleep deprivation • Loss of sense of control and empowerment • Decline in grades and coursework • Difficulty concentrating • Relationships with significant others suffer • Posttraumatic stress syndrome • Loss of respect or interest in organization • Erosion of trust among group members • Illness or hospitalization	• Decline in grades and coursework • Relationships with significant others suffer • Loss of connection • Media scrutiny • Damage to one's personal reputation • Warped sense of leadership • Feelings of shame and guilt

Adapted from HazingPrevention.org (2015).

TRAUMATIC HAZING

Hazing itself can be defined and recognized as abuse and may be experienced as a traumatic event (Cimino, 2011). The Substance Abuse and Mental Health Services Administration (SAMHSA; 2014) defines trauma as

> an event, series of events, or set of circumstances that is experienced by an individual as physically or emotionally harmful or life threatening and that has lasting adverse effects on the individual's functioning and mental, physical, social, emotional, or spiritual well-being.
>
> (para. 2)

Therefore, it is important to carefully consider the significant mental health disorder often associated with trauma. The American Psychiatric Association's (APA; 2013) *Diagnostic and Statistical Manual of Mental Disorders* recognizes posttraumatic stress disorder (PTSD) as a condition that occurs following the experience or witnessing of a traumatic event in which a person is exposed to actual or threatened death, serious injury, or sexual violence. A severe hazing incident in which a student's physical integrity was directly or indirectly threatened qualifies as a traumatic event according to both definitions.

In order to meet a diagnosis for PTSD, symptoms from four criteria need to be present for more than 1 month. These include symptoms of intrusion (i.e., involuntary memories, nightmares); avoidance of trauma-related thoughts, feelings, and reminders; negative alterations in cognitions and mood (i.e., persistent shame, feeling alienated); and alterations in arousal and reactivity (i.e., irritability, hypervigilance). The severity, frequency, and duration of hazing can intensify and prolong the negative psychological consequences of hazing (APA, 2013). The dismal psychological shadow of hazing may follow young adults' lives unless assessed and treated appropriately.

FACTORS INCREASING VULNERABILITY TO HAZING

Young men and women with specific characteristics or who belong to specific groups are particularly vulnerable to perpetrating or falling victim to different hazing practices. Campo, Poulos, and Sipple (2005) completed a web-based survey to examine university students' attitudes, behaviors, and beliefs related to hazing. Results indicated that fraternity or sorority affiliations, males, varsity athletes, leaders, and upperclassmen were more likely to engage in hazing. Studies indicate that men are more likely than women to be subjected to unacceptable activities (Allan, 2003; Pershing, 2006). Examples include destroying or stealing property, beating up others, being tied or otherwise restrained, being confined in a small space, and being paddled, beaten, kidnapped, or abandoned (Hoover & Pollard, 2000).

In addition to organizational affiliation and gender, college students' vulnerability for the negative outcomes of hazing is significantly increased via their own prior mental health issues. In fact, it is estimated that one in four students suffers from a diagnosable mental health issue, including anxiety disorders, depression, eating disorders, attention deficit and hyperactivity, and schizophrenia (National Institute of Mental Health [NIMH], 2017). According to NIMH (2017), 18- to 25-year-olds have one of the highest rates of severe psychological illness and, unfortunately, the lowest rate of seeking help. Additionally, researchers have found that various factors impact whether a person who experiences traumatic events responds with positive growth and meaning making versus psychological distress (Tedeschi & Calhoun, 2004; Triplett et al., 2012). The combination of these factors, along with stress, lack of sleep, and multiple issues relating to transitions to college life, contribute to suicide being the second leading cause of death on college campuses (Haas et al., 2002).

Furthermore, a student's prior childhood trauma, including emotional, physical, and sexual abuse, neglect, and prior bullying, can increase the cyclical nature of victimization and risk of experiencing psychological distress from being involved in hazing (Finkelhor, Turner, & Hamby, 2012). A history of substance use is also important to consider given that alcohol contributes to a reduction in social inhibitions and is a common factor in hazing incidents (Owen, Burke, & Vichesky, 2008). Even one hazing incident alone may trigger a relapse of a prior mental health issue or cause a breakdown that can take years from which to recover.

ASSESSMENT, CRISIS INTERVENTION, AND TREATMENT

Prevention is the best intervention when addressing hazing. Conversely, when many studies indicate that more than half of college students involved in clubs, teams, and organizations experience hazing, additional measures must be in place to address and screen the needs of those affected (Allan & Madden, 2008). Proper assessment, crisis intervention, and mental health treatment are critical in supporting those students who have been severely hazed. Victims may be experiencing clinically significant distress and disrupted functioning in their homes, schools, relationships, and day-to-day activities. Mental health professionals can help address the emotional distress caused by hazing and alleviate the symptoms endured by those who are affected. Roberts's (2002) Integrative Assessment, Crisis Intervention, and Trauma Treatment (ACT) model may provide helpful guidelines to consider.

Assessment

The ACT model stresses the importance of a thorough assessment of needs prior to any mental health intervention. Such a potentially traumatic event as hazing may influence trauma, crisis response, or overall stress. It is not the event that is causal of a trauma but rather the individual's unique perception and experience of an event. Determining whether an event is experienced as traumatic for a student will be influenced by personal characteristics and event dimensions. Personal characteristics include a client's gender, culture, personality, resilience, perceived social support, and coping. Event dimensions involve hazing frequency, duration, and severity. A thorough biopsychosocial assessment can help to adequately determine risk issues and needed referrals.

Thorough assessment of an individual's past or ongoing hazing experiences should be conducted in a delicate manner. If a college student is asked in a straightforward manner, "Have you ever been hazed?," it is very likely that he or she will say no. Instead, mental health professionals and counselors should adopt an approach similar to that taken when inquiring about other sensitive topics, such as substance use or domestic violence. Questions and prompts should be phrased in a very open and nonjudgmental manner and become more specific dependent on the responses received. For example, a mental health professional may first explore openly about any groups a student is connected with at the college. Then he or she can begin to narrow down the questions to ask how a student's experience in the group has matched or differed from what he or she expected and so on. I strongly recommend that a brief assessment measure be constructed and evaluated for use at college campuses to better screen for those individuals at high risk and in need of mental health services to address the effects of hazing.

Crisis Intervention

The ACT model stresses the importance of intervening in a crisis situation to best help offer students support as needed. Roberts's (2002) seven-stage crisis intervention model provides a helpful framework to consider for students actively involved in hazing and in crisis.

1. Assess lethality and risk of harm to self or others as an important initial step.
2. Establish rapport to create a collaborative relationship where a student can feel he or she can trust the mental health professional and open up about his or her experiences.
3. Identify problems, including the last-straw situation or precipitating event, to understand the student's present needs.
4. Address the student's feelings through active listening and validation.
5. Explore alternatives, untapped resources, and coping skills.
6. Develop an action plan to resolve the crisis.
7. Follow up with the plan and problem solve any barriers that may have occurred.

Trauma Treatment

The ACT model indicates that when individuals are experiencing significant trauma-related symptoms, a longer and more intensive treatment approach is required. SAMHSA (2014) has established six key principles to utilizing a trauma-informed approach that can be applied across multiple types of settings and may be helpful in guiding the interventions aimed at addressing the needs of students recovering from hazing experiences. First, the physical and psychological *safety* in terms of an individual's physical setting and interpersonal interactions must be a priority. Second, *trustworthiness and transparency* should be communicated to the students being served in order to best form a therapeutic alliance that will promote healing. Third, *peer support* and promoting mutual self-help can further reduce the secrecy and shame surrounding survivors of hazing via utilizing others' stories and lived experiences to promote recovery. Fourth, *collaboration and mutuality* through partnering and leveling power differences between a mental health professional and the client can further foster the healing that takes place through relationships. Fifth, *empowerment, voice, and choice* guides interventions that recognize and build on individuals' strengths, and clients are supported in regaining their voice to make choices and set goals to determine the plan of action they need to move forward. Sixth, *cultural, historical, and gender issues* are identified, and services consider the racial, ethnic, and cultural needs of individuals served while recognizing and addressing historical trauma (Roberts, 2002). The APA (2005) advises clinical psychologists and other mental health professionals to utilize evidence-based practices that integrate "the best available research with clinical expertise in the context of patient characteristics, culture, and preferences" (p. 3). Although there are no well-established evidence-based interventions developed specifically to address the needs of individuals having experienced hazing incidents, the APA recommends using specialized knowledge, skills, and training in treatments with the strongest research support.

IMPLICATIONS FOR RESEARCH

The phenomenon of hazing is not as widely researched or clearly understood as other forms of interpersonal aggression. The definitions of hazing vary, and at times hazing policies themselves are not clearly defined. The lack of definition and identification of hazing make it very difficult for researchers to fully investigate and understand the mental health consequences related to hazing (for more on hazing definitions, see Chapter 1). Yet there is a need for research that clearly identifies the potential impact of hazing on mental health. Although many students experience significant and long-lasting negative effects, some students are able to recover and move forward from their experiences. Additionally, the lack of research, the lack of reporting, and the lack of ability to identify hazing is a huge barrier in understanding this social issue. Campo et al. (2005) found that a major resilience factor that reduces the risk of participating in hazing is having friends outside the organization in which they may be hazed. Using a client's present strengths and helping him or her learn to identify the differences between healthy and unhealthy relationships can lighten the psychological shadow of hazing.

There is a gap in the literature between the scholarship about students who discontinued the initiation process and those who experienced hazing before dropping out of the initiation. Because these numbers are likely not reported, it is unclear whether hazing is a factor in why students drop out of initiation and whether they have prolonged negative consequences. It is also unclear what type of university-sanctioned organization accountability different student groups have for sharing information about students who begin but do not complete the intake process. Observing the individuals who dropped out of student organization intake processes may shed light on understanding why hazing is underreported and how it can lead to psychological distress. Another potential avenue to explore is to address other non-hazing initiation practices and how these can lead to positive experiences and promote student adjustment. One way to address hazing is to find healthy alternatives that help groups build cohesion and belonging and then disseminate these alternatives to groups and institutions.

IMPLICATIONS FOR PRACTITIONERS

The amount of students with psychological distress has increased in number and severity of distress, and concerns for "harm to self" (i.e., suicidal ideation, nonlethal harming) are also on a continuous rise (Center for Collegiate Mental Health, 2015). With this increase, it is crucial for administrators to continue to address the impact of hazing. Potentially, new and future generations of students may exhibit greater psychological precursors that could lead to negative psychological distress in the event of hazing experiences. As indicated briefly, individuals with higher reported distress may carry more risk factors for mental health concerns if they experience hazing (Finkelhor et al., 2012). Students deserve to have positive college experiences that will foster their growth and identity instead of facing the risk of developing a new potential trauma, such as a negative hazing experience.

University and college administrators may already have existing resources that can be used in new ways to attend to the impact of hazing. For example, university counseling centers may not be screening for hazing experiences. This can be a missed opportunity to address the hazing issues and its impact on students. Many counseling centers already assess for history of traumatic experiences; however, it is unclear if conversations about experiences related to hazing are part of that intake process. Opening more venues that directly address hazing may help individuals report hazing and give light to this unspoken harmful college tradition. Similarly, anonymous hotlines or phone applications for reporting assaults and bullying concerns are already available to students.

Additionally, faculty, staff, coaches, and family members can become more sensitive to students' engagement in social groups and ask about their experiences from a neutral stance. This neutral stance can allow students to share both positive and negative experiences that can include hazing. Asking open-ended questions can help individuals elaborate on and share experiences more openly. Holistically academic institutions can provide direct training to employees to continue to normalize the screening and reporting of hazing events in the same manner that trainings are conducted for students in distress and sexual misconduct.

Finally, preventive measures must focus on an institutional or a group-level attitude change toward hazing. Such an approach may often be focused on reprimanding those who violate and on a group-by-group basis. However, a psychosocial perspective may provide a more systemic way of preventing hazing from its continued practice and development.

REFLECTION QUESTIONS

Given the multifaceted nature of this topic in the context of student organizations, we provide some reflection questions here. It can be easy to speak in generalizations about mental health issues that become much more challenging when an actual incident involving real students surfaces.

1. What are the resources on your campus for training and response related to mental health issues?
2. What workshops or trainings have your organization had in the past related to wellness—particularly in regard to mental health?
3. When do you think high-stress times are for students involved with your organization? How do you prepare for and provide support during those times?

CONCLUSION

Organizational culture is built on individual understanding. This is as true for mental health in a hazing context as for the other elements of hazing. One potential barrier for system change is that institutions or groups will have a cohort effect, whereas old members will be less likely to change their attitudes than newer ones who can be socialized differently. Thus, this creates issues, as hazing occurs in the context of others and there are often no gaps or blank slates for organizations to work from—older members have one frame of reference and newer members may have another. The only way to bridge this gap is to make the issues related to mental health transparent and part of ongoing organizations as they transition from one year (or term) to the next.

The understanding of hazing continues to be very theoretical and assumptive, as many view it only as a harmful tradition. It may be helpful to understand the symbolism and meaning that it creates in an effort to decrease abusive hazing and replace it with a new era of nonaggressive, growth-oriented alternatives that can generate similar purpose and meaning. Engaging members, leaders, advisers, faculty, and others in dialogue about how building team or group cohesion intersects not only with the physical but also the mental health of individuals is essential to creating healthy organizations.

REFERENCES

Allan, E. J. (2003). Gender and hazing: Analyzing the obvious. In H. Nuwer (Ed.), *The hazing reader: Examining the rites gone wrong in fraternities, professional and amateur athletics, high schools, and the military*. Bloomington: Indiana University Press.

Allan, E. J., & Madden, M. (2008). *Hazing in view: College students at risk*. Retrieved from www.stophazing.org/wp-content/uploads/2014/06/hazing_in_view_web1.pdf Allan, E. J., & Madden, M. (2012). The nature and extent of college student hazing. *International Journal of Adolescent Medicine and Health*, *24*(1), 83–90.

American Psychiatric Association. (2005). *Report of the 2005 Presidential Task Force on Evidence-Based Practice*. Retrieved from www.apa.org/practice/resources/evidence/evidence-based-report.pdf

American Psychiatric Association. (2013). *Diagnostic and statistical manual of mental disorders* (Vol. 5). Arlington, VA: Author.

Arnett, J. J. (2004). *Emerging adulthood: The winding road from the late teens through the twenties*. New York, NY: Oxford University Press.

Bandura, A., Barbaranelli, C., Caprara, G. V., & Pastorelli, C. (1996). Mechanisms of moral disengagement in the exercise of moral agency. *Journal of Personality and Social Psychology*, *71*(2), 364.

Bannon, R. S., Brosi, M. W., & Foubert, J. D. (2013). Sorority women's and fraternity men's rape myth acceptance and bystander intervention attitudes. *Journal of Student Affairs Research and Practice*, *50*, 72–87. doi:10.1515/jsarp-2013–0005

Campo, S., Poulos, G., & Sipple, J. W. (2005). Prevalence and profiling: Hazing among college students and points of intervention. *American Journal of Health and Behavior*, *29*, 137–149. doi:10.5993/AJHB.29.2.5

Center for Collegiate Mental Health. (2015). *2014 annual report* (Publication No. STA 15–30). University Park, PA: Author.

Cimino, A. (2011). The evolution of hazing: Motivational mechanisms and the abuse of newcomers. *Journal of Cognition and Culture*, *11*(3–4), 241–267.

Cooper, J. (2011). Cognitive dissonance theory. *Handbook of Theories of Social Psychology*, *1*, 377–398.

Diamond, A. B., Callahan, S. T., Chain, K. F., & Solomon, G. S. (2016). Qualitative review of hazing in collegiate and school sports: Consequences from a lack of culture, knowledge and responsiveness. *British Journal of Sports Medicine*, *50*(3), 149–153.

Espelage, D. L., Basile, K. C., & Hamburger, M. E. (2012). Bullying perpetration and subsequent sexual violence perpetration among middle school students. *Journal of Adolescent Health*, *50*, 60–65. doi:10.1016/j.jadohealth.2011.07.01

Espelage, D. L., Low, S., & DeLaRue, L. (2012). Relations between peer victimization subtypes, family violence, and psychological outcomes during early adolescence. *Psychology of Violence*, *2*, 313–324. doi:10.1037/a0027386

Espelage, D. L., & Swearer, S. M. (2003). Research on school bullying and victimization: What have we learned and where do we go from here? *School Psychology Review*, *23*, 365–385.

Espelage, D. L., & Swearer, S. M. (2004). *Bullying in American schools: A social-ecological perspective on prevention and intervention*. Mahwah, NJ: Erlbaum.

Finkel, M. A. (2002). Traumatic injuries caused by hazing practices. *American Journal of Emergency Medicine*, *20*(3), 228–233.

Finkelhor, D., Turner, H. A., & Hamby, S. (2012). Let's prevent peer victimization, not just bullying. *Child Abuse & Neglect*, *36*, 271–274. doi:10.1016/j.chiabu.2011.12.001

Gerdes, H., & Mallinckrodt, B. (1994). Emotional, social, and academic adjustment of college students: A longitudinal study of retention. *Journal of Counseling & Development*, *72*(3), 281–288.

Haas, A., Koestner, B., Rosenberg, J., Moore, D., Garlow, S. J., Sedway, J., . . . Nemeroff, C. B. (2002). An interactive web-based method of outreach to college students at risk for suicide. *Journal of American College Health*, *57*(1), 15–22.

Halligan, S. L., Michael, T., Clark, D. M., & Ehlers, A. (2003). Posttraumatic stress disorder following assault: The role of cognitive processing, trauma memory, and appraisals. *Journal of Consulting and Clinical Psychology*, *71*(3), 419.

Hamilton, R., Scott, D., LaChapelle, D., & O'Sullivan, L. (2016). Applying social cognitive theory to predict hazing perpetration in university athletics. *Journal of Sport Behavior*, *39*(3), 255.

Haynie, D. L., Nansel, T., Eitel, P., Crump, A. D., Saylor, K., Yu, K., & Simons-Morton, B. (2001). Bullies, victims, and bully-victims: Distinct groups of at-risk youth. *Journal of Early Adolescence*, *21*, 29–49. doi:10.1177/0272431601021001002

HazingPrevention.org. (2015). *Hazing and its consequences*. Retrieved from http://hazingprevention.org/home/hazing/hazing-and-its-consequences/

Holt, M. K., & Espelage, D. L. (2007). Perceived social support among bullies, victims, and bully-victims. *Journal of Youth and Adolescence*, *36*, 984–994.

Holt, M. K., Greif Green, J., Reid, G., DiMeo, A., Espelage, D. L., Felix, E. D., & Sharkey, J. D. (2014). Associations between past bullying experiences and psychosocial and academic functioning among college students. *Journal of American College Health*, 62(8), 552–560.

Hoover, N. C. (1999). *National survey: Initiation rites and athletics for NCAA sports teams*. Retrieved from www.alfred.edu/sports_hazing/docs/hazing.pdf

Hoover, N. C., & Pollard, N. J. (2000). *Initiation rites in American high schools: A national survey*. Retrieved from www.alfred.edu/hs_hazing/docs/hazing__study.pdf

Huitt, W. (2007). Maslow's hierarchy of needs. In *Educational psychology interactive*. Valdosta, GA: Valdosta State University. Retrieved from www.edpsycinteractive.org/topics/conation/maslow.html

Keating, C. F., Pomerantz, J., Pommer, S. D., Ritt, S. J., Miller, L. M., & McCormick, J. (2005). Going to college and unpacking hazing: A functional approach to decrypting initiation practices among undergraduates. *Group Dynamics: Theory, Research, and Practice*, 9(2), 104.

Klomek, A. B., Marrocco, F., Kleinman, M., Schonfeld, I. S., & Gould, M. S. (2007). Bullying, depression, and suicidality in adolescents. *Journal of the American Academy of Child & Adolescent Psychiatry*, 46(1), 40–49.

Levy, N., Cortesi, S., Gasser, U., Crowley, E., Beaton, M., Casey, J., & Nolan, C. (2012). *Bullying in a networked era: A literature review*. Cambridge, MA: The Berkman Center for Internet and Society at Harvard University.

McCreary, G., Bray, N., & Thoma, S. (2017). Bad apples or bad barrels? Moral disengagement, social influence, and the perpetuation of hazing in the college fraternity. *Oracle: The Research Journal of the Association of Fraternity/Sorority Advisors*, 11(1), 1–15.

Milgram, S. (1963). Behavioral study of obedience. *Journal of Abnormal and Social Psychology*, 67(4), 371.

Montgomery, M. J., & Côté, J. E. (2003). College as a transition to adulthood. In G. R. Adams & M. D. Berzonsky (Eds.), *Blackwell handbook of adolescence* (pp. 149–172). Malden, MA: Blackwell.

Nansel, T., Overpeck, M., Pilla, R. S., Ruan, W. J., Simons-Morton, B. G., & Scheidt, P. (2001). Bullying behaviors among U.S. youth: Prevalence and association with psychological adjustment. *Journal of the American Medical Association*, 285, 2094–2100.

National Institute of Mental Health. (2017). *NIMH: Statistics*. Retrieved from www.nimh.nih.gov/health/statistics/index.shtml

Nuwer, H. (2001). *Wrongs of passage: Fraternities, sororities, hazing, and binge drinking*. Bloomington: Indiana University Press.

Owen, S. S., Burke, T. W., & Vichesky, D. (2008). Hazing in student organizations: Prevalence, attitudes, and solutions. *Oracle: The Research Journal of the Association of Fraternity Advisors*, 3, 40–58.

Pershing, J. L. (2006). Men's and women's experiences with hazing in a male dominated elite military institution. *Men and Masculinities*, 8, 470–492. doi:10.1177/1097184X05277411

Rivers, I., Poteat, V. P., Noret, N., & Ashurst, N. (2009). Observing bullying at school: The mental health implications of witness status. *School Psychology Quarterly*, *24*, 211–223.

Roberts, A. (2002). Assessment, crisis intervention, and trauma treatment: The integrative ACT intervention model. *Brief Treatment & Crisis Intervention*, *2*(1), 1.

Schneider, S. K., O'Donnell, L., Stueve, A., & Coulter, R. W. (2012). Cyberbullying, school bullying, and psychological distress: A regional census of high school students. *American Journal of Public Health*, *102*, 171–177. doi:10.2105/AJPH.2011.30030

Substance Abuse and Mental Health Services Administration. (2014). *SAMHSA's concept of trauma and guidance for a trauma-informed approach*. Retrieved from http://store.samhsa.gov/shin/content/SMA14-4884/SMA14-4884.pdf

Tedeschi, R. G., & Calhoun, L. G. (2004). Posttraumatic growth: Conceptual foundations and empirical evidence. *Psychological Inquiry*, *15*(1), 1–18.

Triplett, K. N., Tedeschi, R. G., Cann, A., Calhoun, L. G., & Reeve, C. L. (2012). Posttraumatic growth, meaning in life, and life satisfaction in response to trauma. *Psychological Trauma: Theory, Research, Practice, and Policy*, *4*(4), 400.

Chapter 11

An Appreciative Approach to Hazing Prevention

Jennifer L. Bloom and Amanda E. Propst Cuevas

Hazing has been a practice used to initiate group members for time immemorial. However, the practice of hazing has recently gained greater public attention because of the negative press that has emerged following hazing incidents on college campuses involving athletic teams, marching bands, and fraternities and sororities. The ritual of hazing over the past century has developed a more negative connotation given such adverse consequences of hazing as bullying, harassment, and even death.

The call for hazing prevention efforts has sounded loudly and clearly (Allan & Madden, 2008; Holmes, 2013; National Collegiate Athletic Association [NCAA], 2007; StopHazing.org, 2018). The purpose of this chapter is to provide an additional definition of hazing, explore the reasons groups haze new members and the alleged benefits of the practice, and offer an approach to successfully transition new members into their groups.

WHAT IS HAZING?

Cimino (2011), a leading scholar on hazing and initiations, defined hazing as "a phenomenon that occurs around the time that new members are integrated into an extant coalition . . . staggered group entry over time. This process produces overlapping membership generations" (p. 246). In other words, hazing involves bringing new members into an organization and teaching them its traditions and values. However, what is the difference between hazing and positively building a team? The National Collegiate Athletics Association (2007) made distinctions between hazing and team building, as shown in Table 11.1.

Why Do Groups Haze New Members?

Although there are a variety of reasons why groups may haze new members, Cimino (2011) identified three themes or macro theories: "(a) hazing generates group solidarity; (b) hazing is an expression of dominance; and (c) hazing allows

TABLE 11.1 Hazing Versus Team Building

Hazing	Team Building
Humiliates and degrades	Promotes respect and dignity
Tears down individuals	Supports and empowers
Creates divisions	Creates real teamwork
Lifelong nightmares	Lifelong memories
Shame and secrecy	Pride and integrity
A power trip	A shared positive experience

for the selection of group members" (pp. 243–244). The activities that comprise hazing rituals, whether benign or severe, are often passed down through organizations from one generation or cohort to another. A pervasive mode of thinking exists that "because I had to go through this experience and survived, so should you." The uncertainty, challenge, and adventure surrounding hazing activities often create a common bond among members.

Furthermore, hazing rituals enable senior members to dominate and establish power over new initiates and establish a hierarchy among those members who hold established leadership rank within the organization and those seeking membership to the organization (Cimino, 2011; Keating et al., 2005). This perceived power differential may add psychological value to initiates' desire to comply and conform with hazing rituals to ultimately belong (Cimino, 2011). In other words, incoming members are willing to do whatever it takes to become full-fledged members of the organization. Those who pay the price of admission through the successful completion of hazing rituals, often through demonstration of some form of physical and psychological endurance, prove to be among the survival of the fittest and gain the prized reward of then becoming an equal member within the group. As Cimino (2011) assessed,

> In summary, certain characteristics of hazing appear to allow for the selection of members with high levels of intrinsic valuation. Specifically, in a market of prospective members, a high-cost induction will presumably discourage those who desire only short-term association (and, thus, short-term benefits). That said there are other characteristics of hazing (e.g., coercion), as well as hazing's presence in nonvoluntary associations, that suggest that generating accurate inferences of intrinsic valuation is not the only function of hazing and may not be its primary function. (p. 250)

The price of hazing is often set high to create a selective environment in which those truly interested in and committed to joining the organization are identified

(Cimino, 2011). As best as they can understand entering into the hazing process, newcomers ultimately weigh the costs and benefits of association regardless of how benign or extreme they may be.

The Downside of Hazing

The adverse consequences of hazing are steep and warrant attention. Collins (2017) reported, "Since 2017, there has been at least one hazing-related death on a college campus each year, not including all the incidents that go unreported due to the secret nature of these organizations" (para. 16). Similar to inroads being made with bullying, college and university faculty, staff, and students must continue to educate and inform others about hazing in order to finally change the culture and behavior that has permeated college life for so long.

Bruce and Deering (2016) stated that the myths of hazing behavior include notions that "bonding activities will bring the team closer together; new teammates need to earn their spot and prove themselves worthy of the jersey; activities are all in good fun and people can always choose not to participate" (para. 1). However, Van Raalte and Cornelius (2007) found that hazing in athletic teams correlated with lower levels of team cohesion. Furthermore, whether for a sports team, fraternity or sorority, or other campus student organization, the consequences to the organization of participating in hazing rituals are severe, including liability risks, academic discipline, and group sanctions or banning (Cornell University, 2017). The consequences to individuals participating in hazing rituals are also serious and can include academic sanctions or criminal or civil charges (Cornell University, 2017). Finally, those hazed can also pay a high cost, including psychological or physical harm, and in some cases, even death (Cornell University, 2017). Advocates of hazing prevention encourage group leaders to dispel hazing myths and embrace methods and means by which to build a positive team and create lasting bonds.

However, how newcomers rationalize participation in adverse activities confounds practitioners and scholars. As Holmes (2013) summarized,

> Finally, it is still unclear why our children and young adults allow themselves to be hazed. In order to more fully understand the realities surrounding hazing, we must accept the fact that we have generations of students who are "Dying to belong." That is, they are so eager to associate themselves with a particular organization that they are willing to be beaten, kicked, slapped, drowned in alcohol and sexually assaulted all for the purposes of "belonging." We must teach our children and young adults that brotherhood and sisterhood is not connected to abuse. Bullying does not signify love. We do not tell the domestic violence victim that they are being loved when they are being smacked around

or verbally assaulted. Instead, we encourage them to get far away from their abuser as quickly as they can. So, we must instill the same value in our children. We must also discourage the culture of silence that is associated with the need to belong. Students must have a safe haven to report such abuse without fear of backlash from their peers and other organization affiliates.

(p. 19)

What Are the Benefits of Hazing Rituals?

Although hazing rituals often carry a negative connotation given the possible physical and/or psychological harm to newcomers, these rituals do provide positive benefits to the group as well as to incoming (persons hazed) and existing (hazers) members (see hazing.cornell.edu). Specifically, hazing rituals serve to develop stronger group identity, forge greater team building and bonding, and establish a sense of belonging.

Stronger Group Identity

One of the positive outcomes of hazing is the development of a stronger group identity. Through participation in hazing activities, group members share a lived experience unique to the membership and culture of the organization. In 1959, researchers Aronson and Mills conducted a study in which they applied Festinger's theory of cognitive dissonance to test the effect of the severity of initiation on members' liking of the group. Aronson and Mills (1959) concluded that those who experienced a more severe initiation developed a stronger liking for the group. That is, because of the greater effort exerted, the initiates navigated the cognitive dissonance by developing a stronger affinity for the group and deemed the sacrifice worth the cost. Metaphorically speaking, the pain was worth the gain. The price of membership was more valuable to those who had to exert more effort and consequently developed a stronger group identity (Kamau, 2013). This pattern has been confirmed through subsequent studies (Keating et al., 2005; Lodewijkx, van Zomeren, & Syroit, 2005).

Team Building and Bonding

Another benefit to hazing rituals is that they serve as team-building and bonding tools (Cimino, 2011; Cornell University, 2017; Keating et al., 2005). Ultimately, newcomers seek entry to a specific group because they perceive that the group members share similar interests and values. By engaging with others in hazing rituals, team members can build bonds quickly.

Sense of Belonging

Newcomers opt to participate in hazing rituals because they have a fierce need to belong. One may recall that belongingness and love comprise the midway point in Maslow's hierarchy of needs (1954). A sense of belonging is a deeply rooted psychological need that manifests in times of transition, such as starting college and establishing new friendships and connections with others. In the book *Big Questions, Worthy Dreams: Mentoring Emerging Adults in Their Search for Meaning, Purpose, and Faith*, author Sharon Daloz Parks (2011) encouraged the establishment of "places of dependable connection, where we have a keen sense of the familiar: ways of knowing and being that anchor us in a secure sense of belonging and social cohesion" (p. 116).

Research on college student thriving, defined as academic, psychological, and social well-being (Schreiner, 2010a) demonstrates that a psychological sense of community is the number one driver to thriving (Schreiner, 2013). Schreiner (2010b) outlined the following four elements of a sense of community that we believe can be positively applied to developing an appreciative approach to hazing prevention: (1) *membership* or a feeling of being at home, (2) *ownership* or a sense that both one as a person as well as one's voice are valued by a community or group, (3) *relationship* or building strong and positive emotional connections with others who share similar interests and passions, and (4) *partnership* or "mutual goals that require collaboration with others in order to succeed" (p. 49). An appreciative approach to hazing prevention is one way for organizations to meet members' psychological sense of community needs.

AN APPRECIATIVE APPROACH

How can college and university faculty, staff, and students educate group members on other ways to attain the benefits they are seeking? Part of the answer to the question "How do we prevent hazing?" is to reframe it by changing the question itself to "How can we encourage members to create alternatives that provide the same 'benefits' as hazing?" This reframing of the question mirrors the groundbreaking work of Dr. Martin Seligman, past president of the American Psychological Association (APA), who challenged the association's members to shift the focus of their work from a problem-based approach to mental health to figuring out what makes people mentally well (Fowler, Seligman, & Koocher, 1999). This shift led to the positive psychology movement, and we agree with other practitioners and scholars that education must be part of the solution to addressing hazing.

Drawing on the organizational development theory of appreciative inquiry (Cooperrider & Whitney, 2005) and the appreciative inquiry summit process (Ludema, Whitney, Mohr, & Griffin, 2003), appreciative advising has six phases: disarm, discover, dream, design, deliver, and don't settle (Bloom, Hutson, & He, 2008). These six phases are a powerful framework for facilitating positive discussions about how best to welcome/initiate new members into the organization. This appreciative approach has proven to be a powerful theory-to-practice framework for talking about other such potentially delicate issues as diversity (Bloom, Weiser, & Buonocore, 2012). Therefore, we propose taking an appreciative approach to helping organizational members create safe alternatives to successfully initiate members into the organization.

Disarm

Many student organization leaders and members have endured hours of anti-hazing workshops. Students often are reluctant to attend and/or participate in anti-hazing workshops because they do not appreciate the presumption of guilt that their organization is engaging in hazing practices. Also, the tone of many hazing prevention workshops is such that participants may feel they are being lectured at and/or talked down to by the facilitators. Lastly, more time is often spent telling participants what not to do instead of what they can do. In sum, it is no surprise that students are reluctant to engage in educational workshops designed to eradicate hazing. It is important to share the why and how of the training without ignoring the realities of hazing, which the facilitator can accomplish by acknowledging participants' reticence through an introductory statement such as the following:

> I understand that you are likely not thrilled to be attending today's workshop. However, I want to assure you that today's workshop is going to be very different from past hazing workshops you have attended. Instead of lecturing you about the dangers of hazing, we are going to explore why organizations initiate members and have you brainstorm positive ways to initiate people into your organization to create a strong brotherhood/sisterhood. For the rest of your lives, you will be welcoming people into workplaces, nonprofit organizations, and the like, so the ideas we cocreate today are going to be strategies you can use throughout your careers. We're going to walk you through a six-phase process that will help you create the sense of community we are all seeking.

Discover

The discover phase is focused on building trust among participants by sharing stories. The facilitator will divide the group into pairs and assign one person to serve as the question asker and the other to answer one of the following questions:

- Tell me about a time when you felt like you really had a strong sense of belonging in an organization? How was that sense of belonging created?

- Describe a time when you were new to an organization. What emotions did you feel? How did people make you feel welcome?
- What motivates you in terms of wanting to contribute to the success of this organization?

After 2 minutes, the facilitator will stop the conversations and have participants switch roles.

The facilitator then asks participants, "Who was inspired by their partners' stories? Please raise your hands." Then the facilitator should ask for volunteers who are willing to share their partners' stories and why they were inspiring. After three or four people have shared their stories, the facilitator should highlight some of the themes that arose from them. Additionally, the facilitator should point out the power of stories: "Stories have a depth and breadth that allows meaning to be conveyed much more effectively than would a list of key points or other more analytical reports. Stories engage the imagination in ways that analytic discussions cannot" (Watkins & Mohr, 2001, p. 77). The facilitator should also highlight examples from the stories that involve non-hazing alternatives.

Dream

Once a positive stage has been set during the discover phase by sharing stories, the facilitator will shift the conversation to the dream phase. The purpose of the dream phase is to have the group come together to create a joint dream of an idealized future for the organization (Cooperrider & Whitney, 2005). The facilitator breaks the audience into groups of three to five and gives each group a large Post-it pad with markers. The facilitator then leads them through the activity, asking as many of the following questions as appropriate and encouraging them to draw or write down their answers on the large Post-it pad:

- If you could make this into the perfect organization where every member is engaged in helping the organization and all its members be successful, what would that look like?
- If we wanted to plan the ideal way to bring new members into our organization and integrate them successfully into the organization, what would that look like?
- As people, we all want to feel like we matter, belong, and are valued. How can we make our organization one that fulfills those goals?
- If we were to dream about ways new members thrive and do not merely survive during our initiation process, what would that look like?

After giving the small groups an appropriate amount of time to create their visions of what the initiation process can become, each group should be invited to the front of the room to share what their groups created and discussed. After the groups share their respective dreams, a break should be given to the participants while the facilitators get together and come up with the shared major themes that emerged from the dream phase activity. The top three to five themes should be shared with participants after they return from the break. Participants should then have the opportunity to edit or add other themes that emerged or important considerations that did not emerge during the initial group conversations.

Design

Once a shared dream has been established, the design phase is where the group cocreates a plan for making the results of the dream conversations a reality. The facilitator should ask the participants to come up with specific steps that will need to be taken to make the dream happen. The facilitator can provide prompts or ask questions such as the following:

- Now we are switching modes from dreaming to doing. I want each group to come up with a list of specific steps that can be taken to positively welcome and initiate new members into our organization.
- What components of our initiation process can we use as building blocks for making the initiation process both safe and memorable?
- If you were totally in charge of transforming the initiation process, what role(s) would you assign to yourself? What roles would you assign to others?

Once each group has compiled a detailed plan, they should share their ideas with the larger group. After the groups have presented, the larger group can be assigned to come up with a new design plan based on the ideas that have emerged. After those groups have shared their plans, participants should agree on an organizational plan to achieve what has been outlined and identify priorities in working toward the fulfillment of the organizational plan. The top three to five priorities that emerge should then be identified.

Deliver

Coming up with a plan and executing it are two different things. Now that the top priorities have been identified in the design phase, participants should be asked to identify which priority is most exciting to them personally. The key to the deliver phase is to assign people to groups to work on the priority about which they are most genuinely excited. Each priority group should then be asked to come up with steps and deadlines for following through on their priority as a part of the plan that was created in the design phase.

An important aspect of the deliver phase involves reminding participants that in executing the plan there will be obstacles and barriers that emerge. One way to prepare participants for these barriers is to ask them deliver questions such as the following:

- When we run into setbacks as we deliver on the plan we designed, how are we going to regroup quickly and learn from our mistakes?
- What strategies can we use to deal with unexpected challenges that may arise in carrying out our plan?
- Who are people we can go to for assistance if we run into unexpected barriers?
- Are there other organizations that have done this work whose experiences might inform what we are about to take on?

The goal is not to avoid mistakes—it is to learn from them. The event concludes by highlighting the new ideas that have emerged for safely initiating members into the organization and to finalize the plan as each priority group shares its work in order to build a cohesive plan for the future.

Don't Settle

The don't settle phase is an important reminder that we must always strive to continuously improve. The facilitator should schedule a follow-up meeting 3 to 4 months after the initial plan has been devised. The purpose of the follow-up meeting is to celebrate the successes that the group has enjoyed as well as to encourage participants to seek to continuously improve and update the plan. The following questions may be posed and explored:

- What is your biggest success to date in terms of executing the plan? What specific actions led to the success?
- If we could improve the effectiveness of our plan by 50%, how would we achieve this goal?
- What would it look like if we wanted to improve the effectiveness of our plan by 100%?

CONCLUSION

Although hazing provides benefits to organizations and their members, including building a stronger group identity, team building, and increasing members' sense of belonging, there are dangers to individuals and risks to organizations as a result of these behaviors. Additionally, the benefits related to hazing habits can be accrued in ways other than engaging in such unhealthy behaviors as excessive drinking and dangerous physical acts. This chapter has provided an alternative way for organization members to engage in an appreciative process for creating healthier ways of welcoming new members into the organization. By leading students through the six phases of appreciative advising, members will not only create healthier ways to increase new members' sense of belonging but also enhance their own sense of belonging in the organization.

REFERENCES

Allan, E. J., & Madden, M. (2008). *Hazing in view: College students at risk*. Retrieved from www.stophazing.org/wp-content/uploads/2014/06/hazing_in_view_web1.pdf

Aronson, E., & Mills, J. (1959). The effect of severity of initiation on liking for a group. *Journal of Abnormal and Social Psychology*, 59, 177–181.

Bloom, J. L., Hutson, B. L., & He, Y. (2008). *The appreciative advising revolution*. Champaign, IL: Stipes.

Bloom, J. L., Weiser, G., & Buonocore, V. (2012). An appreciative approach to diversity training. *Journal of Appreciative Education*, 1(1), 25–34.

Bruce, S., & Deering, H. (2016). *Addressing student-athlete hazing*. Retrieved from www.ncaa.org/sport-science-institute/addressing-student-athlete-hazing

Cimino, A. (2011). The evolution of hazing: Motivational mechanisms and the abuse of newcomers. *Journal of Cognition and Culture*, 11, 241–267. doi:https://doi.org/10.1163/156853711X591242

Collins, I. (2017, May 30). *Hazing: The dark side of belonging*. Retrieved from https://belongingworks.com/2017/05/30/hazing-the-dark-side-of-belonging/

Cooperrider, D., & Whitney, D. D. (2005). *Appreciative inquiry: A positive revolution in change*. San Francisco, CA: Berrett-Koehler.

Fowler, R. D., Seligman, M. E. P., & Koocher, G. P. (1999). The APA 1998 annual report. *American Psychologist*, 54, 537–568.

Cornell University. (2017). *Hazing at Cornell*. Retrieved from www.hazing.cornell.edu/

Holmes, R. W. (2013). *How to eradicate hazing*. Bloomington, IN: AuthorHouse.

Kamau, C. (2013). What does being initiated severely into a group do?: The role of rewards. *International Journal of Psychology*, 48(3), 399–406.

Keating, C. F., Pomerantz, J., Pommer, S. D., Ritt, S. J. H., Miller, L. M., & McCormick, J. (2005). Going to college and unpacking hazing: A functional approach to decrypting initiation practices among undergraduates. *Group Dynamics: Theory Research & Practice*, 9(2), 104–126.

Lodewijkx, H. F. M., van Zomeren, M., & Syroit, J. E. M. (2005). The anticipation of severe initiation: Gender differences in effects of affiliation tendency and group attraction. *Small Group Research*, 36(2), 237–262.

Ludema, J. D., Whitney, D., Mohr, B. J., & Griffin, T. J. (2003). *The appreciative inquiry summit: A practitioner's guide for leading large-group change*. San Francisco, CA: Berrett-Koehler.

Maslow, A. (1954). *Motivation and personality*. New York, NY: Harper.

National Collegiate Athletic Association. (2007). *Building new traditions: Hazing prevention in college athletics*. Retrieved from www.ncaa.org/sites/default/files/hazing%20prevention%20handbook%2057315.pdf

Parks, S. D. (2011). *Big questions, worthy dreams: Mentoring young adults in their search for meaning, purpose, and faith* (2nd ed.). San Francisco, CA: Jossey-Bass.

Schreiner, L. A. (2010a). The "thriving quotient": A new vision for student success. *About Campus*, *15*, 2–10.

Schreiner, L. A. (2010b). Thriving in community. *About Campus*, *15*, 2–10.

Schreiner, L. A. (2013). Thriving in college. *New Directions for Student Services*, *143*, 41–52.

StopHazing.org. (2018). *Alternatives to hazing*. Retrieved from www.stophazing.org/alternatives-to-hazing/

Van Raalte, J. L., & Cornelius, A. E. (2007). The relationship between hazing and team cohesion. *Journal of Sport Behavior*, *30*(4), 491–507.

Watkins, J. M., & Mohr, B. J. (2001). *Appreciative inquiry: Change at the speed of imagination*. San Francisco, CA: Jossey-Bass.

Chapter 12

Preventing Hazing
Promising Practices for College and University Administrators and Professionals

Michelle L. Boettcher, Cristina J. Perez, and Cristóbal Salinas Jr.

This book has focused on an examination of hazing in a variety of organizational contexts and its impact on college students' experiences. Although it is important to understand historical and current hazing events, ultimately the goal of this book is to provide information to transform the hazing culture in higher education. In an effort to do this, we close the book with this chapter focused on what has been done effectively in the past, lessons learned by higher education and organization administrators, and how to anticipate and proactively address hazing-related behaviors in the future. Rather than closing with case studies as in other chapters, this chapter and the book conclude with a list of reflective questions to guide professionals and organizations as they seek to foster student involvement in safe and community-focused ways. The reflective questions provided in this chapter can be used in conjunction with the case studies throughout the book, but they can also be used as stand-alone tools as organizations and campuses examine their own hazing cultures and practices.

CONSIDERATIONS

This chapter is built on key considerations facing not only organizations but also issues with which higher education grapples daily. Biddix (2016) engaged in an extensive review of research related to issues facing fraternities, including and beyond hazing issues. His recommendations, although specific to fraternal organizations, translate across organizational types when looking to reform hazing culture on campus. These recommendations include linking organizational values to campus priorities. Biddix (2016) states, "An essential first step for the fraternity community is to demonstrate that core fraternity values directly parallel and support institutional priorities" (p. 802). The same statement could be said for marching bands, military organizations, athletics, and other student groups and organizations.

In addition to higher education and institutional considerations, there are issues related to student populations that require specific attention when proactively educating students, organizations, and advisers about hazing behaviors. Other recommendations Biddix (2016) made to educated individuals about hazing include mobilizing stakeholders, focusing on peer education, connecting efforts among organizations, and publishing results of effective initiatives for reducing hazing behaviors. Again, each of these recommendations can be applied to organizations dealing with hazing issues. The next section focuses on how addressing these future considerations is informed by existing scholarship and practice related to hazing prevention.

Hazing-Related Issues in Higher Education

There are several key issues related to hazing in higher education, including Title IX legislation in the context of sexual misconduct, mental health issues on campus, toxic masculinity, and the use of alcohol and other drugs by college students. In the future, as new issues emerge, it is essential that students, administrators, leaders, organizations, alumni, and other stakeholders invested in the sustainability of these organizations exercise vigilance in terms of education, outreach, and support to students.

Title IX

In Sanday's (2007) exploration of rape culture in a fraternity context, the author specifically identified hazing habits and rituals as contributing to sexual aggression and the perpetuation of rape myths in that culture. Additionally, Allan and Madden (2008) include sex acts as common elements of hazing involving young men in educational settings. Dunn (2013) wrote, "Colleges and universities should consider broadening the definition of fondling to ensure that sexual touching for the purpose of humiliation is included in the definition to adequately address sexual violence that occurs during hazing" (p. 570). As Title IX issues related to sexual misconduct continue to emerge across higher education, it is imperative that organizations be aware that in addition to hazing violations, some hazing habits involving sexual aggression, sexual contact, or sexual humiliation and embarrassment may violate additional policies and laws.

Mental Health

As has been explored in Chapter 10 of this book, the impact of hazing experiences on students' mental health is an essential element in any discussion of hazing culture on college campuses. A 2015 report from the Center for Collegiate Mental

Health found that the number of students seeking counseling services and the number of counseling appointments was increasing more than five times faster than enrollment. The Center for Collegiate Mental Health (2015) also reported steady growth in depression, anxiety, and social anxiety compared to previous years and an increase in nonsuicidal self-injury and suicidal ideation. Allan and Madden (2012) described the mental health impact of hazing as creating situations "where embarrassment, humiliation and degradation can take an emotional toll and lead to what has been referred to as the hidden harm of hazing—the emotional scars resulting from the humiliating and degrading aspects of hazing" (p. 7). Part of the work of this book has been to address hazing issues in order to help students have safe experiences in their involvement in higher education.

Toxic Masculinity

These hazing-related considerations disproportionately affect men in higher education (Campo, Poulos, & Sipple, 2005; Hoover, 2000; Knutson, Akers, Ellis, & Bradley, 2011). Dowd (2010) explained toxic masculinity as one of multiple masculinities that is dominant and hegemonic in contemporary American society. According to Evans, Frank, Oliffe, and Gregory (2011), Western culture has socialized individuals to associate masculinity with being "heterosexual, middle class, and possessing stereotypical masculine traits of assertiveness, dominance, control, physical strength, and emotional restraint" (p. 8). Men tend to be more constrained to gender expectations than their female counterparts and are thus more prone to subordination or marginalization when not exemplifying masculine ideals. Additionally, "Men are only as masculine as their last demonstration of masculinity," further increasing their engagement in behaviors that can cause harm and pain (Evans et al., 2011, p. 8). The type of masculinity described here is highlighted and tested throughout the hazing process—whether the hazing involves competitive drinking or stoicism in the face of pain and humiliation.

Young men and boys are often socialized to take it like a man or to man up, equating emotional expression and vulnerability with weakness. Anger is one of the few acceptable male emotions, and it has connections to violence and oppression of others. This is problematic because it creates an environment where emotions are suppressed and decreases individuals' likelihood of seeking help in times of emotional or physical distress (Evans et al., 2011). Understanding the impact gender expectations and toxic masculinity has on hazing behaviors is key when working with and responding to situations among men's organizations.

Cantalupo (2013) expanded on these ideas and examined hegemonic masculinity specifically in the context of hazing. She noted that this traditional form of masculinity includes behaviors related to "bullying, sexual harassment, hazing, and sexual and dating violence" (Cantalupo, 2013, p. 904). As referenced in the earlier section on Title IX's relationship to hazing, the role of toxic masculinity directly connects sexual misconduct and hazing.

Alcohol and Other Drugs

Researchers have noted that alcohol and other drugs play a key role in hazing, with participation in drinking games as the leading hazing behavior across organization types (Allan & Madden, 2008; Finkel, 2002; Parks, Jones, Ray, Hughey, & Cox, 2015). In the 2015 National Institute on Alcohol Abuse and Alcoholism survey, just under 60% of college students between the ages of 18 and 22 drank alcohol in the month prior to taking the survey, and two out of three engaged in binge-drinking behaviors in that time frame. Additionally, the Higher Education Center for Alcohol and Drug Misuse and Prevention (2017) stated that more than one third of college students have used an illicit drug (i.e., marijuana, amphetamines, and narcotics other than heroin) in the past year. The combination of drug and alcohol use in higher education and drug and alcohol activities related to hazing is a dangerous combination.

Furthermore, substances are often used as "social lubricants," but rapid consumption can lead to memory loss, injury, and death. Several recent studies continue to highlight the role of alcohol in hazing and the need to address the use of alcohol and other drugs for the safety of students (McGinley, Rospenda, Liu, & Richman, 2016; Parks et al., 2015; Rosenberg & Mosca, 2016; Scott-Sheldon, Carey, Kaiser, Knight, & Carey, 2016). This clearly is not a problem of the past but persists into hazing cultures today and as such it is a major concern to be addressed in higher education.

Student Demographic Considerations

The role of inclusivity in terms of race, gender, sexual orientation, and other intersecting identities is a key consideration in advising, educating, and training organizations. Although not exclusive to men's groups, hazing among men tends to lean toward physical and degrading behaviors, often with the intent to emasculate the individual. These behaviors can include but are not limited to forced calisthenics, paddling, viewing pornography, sleep deprivation, homoerotic rituals, and alcohol consumption (Parks et al., 2015). The use of homoerotic rituals to emasculate members and the impact of this behavior on LGBT+ individuals should be considered because it can affect their sense of safety and belonging within their organizations and on campus. Parks et al. (2015) also found evidence of physical abuse to discourage LGBT+ identifying new members from continuing with the membership process.

As we consider the various ways hazing can impact students and their intersecting identities, Parks et al. (2015) stressed that the first step to reaching a solution regarding hazing is to recognize that all organizations, teams, and student groups do not have the same history, thus creating an environment where hazing does not look the same across the board. Although there is a gap in research on hazing in predominately white sororities, hazing often takes the form of psychological or emotional abuse with the intent to minimize the new member, pick at her self-confidence by attacking appearance, and push her into a subordinate role. Examining hazing practices across the intersectionality of identity is an important way to further dismantle hazing culture. Research shows that the experience of group members varies depending on race (Edwards, 2009; Harper & Harris, 2010; Patton, Bridges, & Flowers, 2011) and that sexual orientation and homophobia play an important role in the experiences of college fraternity men (DeSantis & Coleman, 2008; Hesp & Brooks, 2009; Trump & Wallace, 2006). The role of identity in hazing cultures and contexts increasingly emerges in issues on college campuses, and this chapter is designed to address those and the other issues highlighted as needs in the literature.

EFFORTS TO REDUCE AND ELIMINATE HAZING

Understanding the context of hazing culture in higher education is important to developing strategies for addressing hazing behaviors and culture. In order to transform organizational culture, leaders, staff, and students must work together to increase awareness, provide effective education and training, and develop strong organizational leadership and healthy team dynamics. This section focuses on strategies for achieving these goals in efforts to reduce and eventually eliminate hazing in higher education. Key questions are also presented with the purpose to transform the hazing culture in higher education. Furthermore, the next section emphasizes the role of awareness, education, leadership, and community in disrupting hazing habits.

Increased Awareness

Allan and Madden (2008) found that 55% of college students experience hazing, but 9 out of 10 do not consider themselves to have been hazing victims. This gap presents an opportunity for campuses and organizations to increase awareness of hazing behaviors and to recognize them as a problem. Hazing habits can take a variety of forms across different organizations, and hazing affects individuals differently. Understanding the perpetrators' methods and "rationale" for hazing will also help tailor education and training to varying audiences.

Recognizing Warning Signs

Although many hazing activities occur in the secrecy of members-only spaces, there are possible warning signs that hazing is taking place. By teaching administrators, students, parents, volunteers, and coaches to recognize these signs, steps can be taken to intervene. HazingPrevention.org (2015) identifies the following as possible warning signs:

- Physical changes—exhaustion, weight loss, unexplained illness or injury, changes in sleeping or eating habits
- Psychological changes—exhaustion, withdrawal, expressed feelings of sadness or worthlessness
- Changes in communication—decrease in communication with friends or family, increased secrecy, unwillingness to share details about life or events
- Changes related to organizational membership—sudden change in behavior or attitude after joining an organization, wanting to leave an organization with no explanation

(HazingPrevention.org, 2015, para. 2)

By recognizing these warning signs, administrators, educators, peers, and parents can take initial steps to address or intervene in potential hazing situations. Additionally, members who may be questioning whether they are experiencing or perpetrating hazing can ask themselves the following questions:

- Would I feel comfortable participating in this activity if my parents were watching?
- Would we get in trouble if a school or college administrator walked by?
- Am I being asked to keep these activities secret?
- Am I doing anything illegal or against college or university policy?
- Does participation in this activity violate my values or those of the organization?
- Is this causing emotional or physical distress or stress to myself or to others?
- Am I going to be able to get a job if I have to put a criminal arrest on my application?

(HazingPrevention.org, 2015, para. 2)

Encouraging reflective and critical thinking about the behaviors and possible consequences can help students think about the long-term impact while also developing the ability to recognize problematic situations.

Hidden Harm

Although some students may believe hazing is harmless team building, it is important to encourage students to think about the long-term impact and consequences of hazing. Hidden harm describes the effects of previous trauma, both physical and psychological, and the long-lasting effects on an individual (Allan & Madden,

2012; HazingPrevention.org, 2015). Hidden harm can occur from the acts of hazing themselves but can also exacerbate students' previous experiences, including mental health issues, military service, sexual assault, abuse, alcohol or other drug addictions, or prior experiences with hazing and bullying. Therefore, it is important to elevate awareness of hidden harm on college campuses by creating space for open dialogue around mental health, developing positive communities, and personalizing the issue (Apgar, 2013).

Awareness Campaigns and Programs

To help bring hazing to light, campuses and organizations can plan awareness campaigns and programs to foster conversation and increase awareness. One such campaign is National Hazing Prevention Week organized by HazingPrevention.org and usually facilitated on campuses in the last full week of September. In the 40 days leading up to the event, Sigma Nu fraternity began the #40answers campaign that engages individuals online with a daily tweet of a commonly heard justification for hazing. Twitter users can then respond to the tweet in a way that discourages hazing behaviors and promotes healthy relationship building and congruence with organizational values (HazingPrevention.org, 2015).

Other organizations provide hazing awareness information as well. For example, in 2007, the National Collegiate Athletic Association released a resource guide, *Building New Traditions: Hazing Prevention in College Athletics*, to help deter hazing among athletic teams. The document includes guidance for administrators, coaches, student-athletes, and team captains and their role in hazing prevention. Also, the music fraternity Phi Mu Alpha provides risk management and anti-hazing information through its website (www.sinfonia.org/operations/risk-management-policies/). Similarly, campus Reserve Officers' Training Corps provide guidance about hazing and responses to reports of hazing through *The Military Commander and the Law* issued by the Judge Advocate General's School (Bernstein, 2016).

Education and Training

To further build on awareness campaigns and programs, it is important to reach out to key constituent groups and to intentionally train on hazing recognition and response. These groups can include but are not limited to campus administrators, conduct officers, fraternity and sorority life staff, alumni volunteers, coaches, residence life staff, counselors, academic advisers, and student leaders.

Assessment

Prior to developing comprehensive training programs, completing institutional, organizational, and individual assessments can help identify areas of strength and opportunity around hazing cultures. Initial reflection questions, such as those listed at the end of this chapter, can be used to begin initial reflection. Institutions and organizations can also choose to form a task group or coalition of key constituents and/or external experts and consultants to help initiate hazing climate surveys and self-assessments. Data can be used to inform training, policy development, and education initiatives.

Institutional Policy

Before developing or refining policy, institutions should develop a hazing philosophy statement that drives policy, response, and education. Institutions and organizations should provide clear information on hazing policy, but the key to prevention success is effective enforcement. In a study conducted by Holman and Johnson (2015), athletes acknowledged signing paperwork agreeing to the no-hazing policy but disregarded it because of past hazing instances with no repercussions.

Adequately training administrators on reporting channels can also help support students with hazing concerns. Allan and Madden (2008) found that 95% of students who identified a hazing experience did not report it to campus officials. This has to be resolved in order to transform the hazing culture on campus. McCreary (2015) stressed the importance of adequately training administrators and conduct officers to facilitate hazing investigations. By equipping administrators to handle thorough investigations, organizations can be held accountable when hazing allegations arise.

Training Key Constituent Groups

Trainings can begin with pre-assessment of participants' abilities to recognize hazing, knowledge of reporting processes, and awareness of institutional policies and state and local laws. Results can be used to tailor the training to participants. Topics covered in these trainings should include warning signs, examples of hazing activities, state and local laws related to hazing, college and university policies, support resources, and response protocols. Facilitators of the training should incorporate learning strategies that engage participants and provide an opportunity to apply content to their roles and environments. A post-assessment can be used to measure learning and identify follow up or areas for improvement in future trainings.

Although there may be resistance to a post-assessment because of the additional work it creates for organizations and their members, in the current litigious climate, a post-assessment is essential. Parks and Spencer (2013) stated, "In recent years, courts have increasingly gone against the precedent of holding that universities are not liable for physical injury to students on their campuses" (p. 131) as the concept of in loco parentis has eroded. Student safety has emerged in recent college cases in both curricular and cocurricular activities (Lake, 1999) and specifically in connection with fraternity and sorority life organizations (Jones, 2000).

As universities and organizations plan communications to students' families, they can also provide information on warning signs, reporting, and resources to help constituents recognize and deter hazing. Parents or guardians may be hesitant to share student or organization information for fear of repercussions their students may face, so it is important to address protections from retaliation for reporting students. By providing information at the front end of the reporting process, a barrier to hazing prevention can be removed.

Changing Mind-Sets Around Hazing

One of the main obstacles to hazing prevention and intervention education is getting participants to understand hazing as a problem. McCreary (2015) stated that the lack of progress when using traditional prevention models is due to the fact that perpetrators rarely see hazing as a problem. Training can reframe prevention education with students by starting with naming the purpose of hazing (e.g., relationship building, respect, unity) and then providing alternate strategies to foster positive outcomes (McCreary, 2015).

Develop Strong and Responsible Leadership

Hazing prevention must be driven from strong leadership in organizations and on campuses in order to develop buy-in from student organizations and teams. By training administrators and student leaders (e.g., athletic team captains, drum majors, leadership boards of student organizations, fraternity and sorority student members), students can recognize hazing as a problem, follow effective response protocols, and educate members about potential consequences.

Eliminating the Need to Establish Hierarchy

Although perpetrators often cite building unity and fostering relationships as a reason for hazing, one of the root causes lies in the need to establish hierarchy. Hazing is used as a tool to solidify the internal hierarchy of a group and to establish new members on the lowest rung (Parks et al., 2015). By "surviving" the hazing process, new members prove to active or older teammates that they are worthy of membership. McCreary (2015) stated that this thought process on hierarchy and power dynamics will persist as long as traditional pledging and new member induction processes continue, meaning that the sole responsibility of member induction cannot fall on the 19- to 22-year-old who continues to perpetuate the problem. McCreary (2015) suggested that an authority figure, such as a coach, administrator, alumni volunteer, or international representative, intervene to prevent toxic behaviors from continuing.

Bystander Intervention

Once students acknowledge hazing as a problem, administrators and organizations can empower individuals to intervene and report occurrences of hazing. For a bystander to intervene, Deitch-Stackhouse, Kenneavy, Thayer, Berkowitz, and Mascari (2015) identified five stages individuals must move through.

Noticing the Event

The first step to intervening is noticing that hazing is taking place through direct experience, recognizing warning signs, and having the experience recounted by a peer.

Interpreting the Event as a Problem

The bystander must then recognize that a behavior is a problem even if it seems silly or harmless (e.g., embarrassing outfits, carrying items) because any instances that violate hazing policies could indicate deeper underlying issues.

Feeling Responsible for Finding a Solution

All students should feel a responsibility to intervene or report instances of harm even if they are not the ones experiencing or engaging in hazing behaviors.

Having Skills to Intervene

Individuals must understand the reporting process, know which resources are available to address hazing, and discuss the issue with their peers to challenge them to reconsider negative practices.

Intervening

The next step is to take action whether through reporting or directly addressing the issue with peers.

Fostering Healthy Community Dynamics

In order to eradicate hazing from campuses, administrators and organizations must strive to develop a strong sense of belonging. Sweet (1999) suggested that "hazing is the result of group interaction processes that are linked with students' need for belonging [and] their isolation from other social relations on campus" (p. 355). Many hazing behaviors isolate members from social groups outside of their organization, thus establishing the perpetrators as their main social connection on campus (Parks et al., 2015). Considering the role hazing takes in isolating new members and the need of students to find a sense of belonging and connection (Hoover, 2000), some individuals may feel they have no other choice than to participate in hazing activities.

Practices to Create a Welcoming and Inclusive Environment

In attempt to create a welcoming and inclusive environment, we pose the following questions: What is to be done about the situation? How do organizations foster a sense of belonging and build community while also keeping members safe? There are a variety of best practices to creating environments that foster a sense of belonging among students.

Peer Mentor

One of the first strategies is connecting new members of a group with a peer mentor. The peer mentor can be an upper-class or established member who provides guidance throughout a new member period. Peer mentors should be trained on resources that can help support a successful transition, policies and guidelines for membership, and communication skills needed to stay connected with mentee(s).

Shared Vision and Goals

Providing an opportunity for new members to understand or develop a shared vision and goals for their experience also fosters a sense of belonging. This provides space for new and active members to collaborate and can be done by utilizing individual and organizational missions and values.

Open, Effective Communication

Creating open channels of communication between organization leaders and new members mitigates power dynamics that can lead to hazing behaviors. Rather than viewing leaders as "untouchable," effective communication establishes relationships among members and opportunities for mentorship and helps support the continued success of an organization.

Creating Positive Traditions

Some organizational members view hazing has the only way to build respect and unity among members. Administrators and educators need to identify opportunities to develop relationships in congruence with organizational values and institutional policies. The following items are some examples of alternatives to prevent hazing: community service, positive rituals like a uniform presentation ceremony before the first game, rope courses or team-building activities, having alumni call and welcome new members, planning a group outing like a movie night or bowling, or conducting a food drive or fundraiser (National Collegiate Athletic

Association, 2007). Although not an exhaustive list, these are initial ways for organizations to connect with one another and their campuses and local communities. Things to consider when planning activities are accessibility for all members, avoiding overprogramming, and staying in compliance with organizational and institutional policies.

REFLECTION QUESTIONS

The final section of this chapter is designed to provide resources for institutions, organizations, leaders, and professionals working with student organizations or other cultures vulnerable to hazing activity. In working to change the culture of hazing, it is essential to understand the role of history and units within the institution that inform how organizations and individuals interact on campus. Lastly, one must engage in dialogue and reflection about how to handle different challenges related to hazing culture.

Institutional Reflection Questions

Reflective Questions for Student Organizations and Organizational Leaders

1. How do the values, mission, and philosophy of your organization align with the priorities, mission, and values of the larger institution?
2. How do your events and activities reflect your values and the values of the larger institution?
3. How does your organization foster relationship building? Is this in line with organizational and institutional policies?

Reflective Questions for Professionals

1. What is the history of the organization(s) in which you work? How can you build on past experiences to inform future training, education, events, and responses?
2. What is the status of your relationship with organizational leaders and members? In what ways have you fostered community, transparency, honesty, and collaboration?
3. What education and training has been provided in the past? How have those activities been assessed?
4. Where are opportunities for current leaders and members to facilitate training and education on hazing in organizations?
5. What is your protocol for responding to incidents of hazing? (If you do not have one, develop one.)

6. How have previous hazing incidents been handled? What can you learn from those situations?
7. What traditions, rituals, myths, and histories do you need to disrupt to develop a hazing-free community?

CONCLUSION

Hazing prevention begins with an understanding of hazing and the organizational cultures on each campus. Engaging in intentional and specific reflection is a first step in preventing hazing and, as a result, transforming organizational and institutional culture. Considering the aspects of the organizations highlighted here is essential to understanding culture on a deeper level. Using the reflection questions provided at the end of this chapter can afford individuals and organizations the chance to engage in dialogue to develop a deeper understanding of hazing habits.

REFERENCES

Allan, E., & Madden, M. (2008). *Hazing view: College students at risk*. Retrieved from www.stophazing.org/wp-content/uploads/2014/06/hazing_in_view_web1.pdf

Allan, E. J., & Madden, M. (2012). The nature and extent of college student hazing. *International Journal of Adolescent Medicine and Health*, 24(1), 83–90.

Apgar, T. T. (2013). *Hidden harm of hazing: Engaging peers in this important discussion*. Retrieved from http://hazingprevention.org/hidden-harm-of-hazing-engaging-peers-in-this-important-discussion/

Bernstein, G. H. (Ed.). (2016). *The military commander and the law*. Maxwell Air Force Base, AL: Judge Advocate General's School.

Biddix, J. P. (2016). Moving beyond alcohol: A review of other issues associated with fraternity membership with implications for practice and research. *Journal of College Student Development*, 57(7), 793–809.

Campo, S., Poulos, G., & Sipple, J. W. (2005). Prevalence and profiling: Hazing among college students and points of intervention. *American Journal of Health Behavior*, 29(2), 137–149.

Cantalupo, N. C. (2013). Masculinity & Title IX: Bullying and sexual harassment of boys in the American liberal state. *Maryland Law Review*, 73(3), 887–986.

Center for Collegiate Mental Health. (2015). *2015 annual report*. Retrieved from http://ccmh.psu.edu/wp-content/uploads/sites/3058/2016/01/2015_CCMH_Report_1-18-2015.pdf

Deitch-Stackhouse, J., Kenneavy, K., Thayer, R., Berkowitz, A., & Mascari, J. (2015). The influence of social norms on advancement through bystander stages for preventing interpersonal violence. *Violence Against Women*, 20(10), 1284–1307.

DeSantis, A. D., & Coleman, M. (2008). Not on my line: Attitudes about homosexuality in black fraternities. In G. S. Parks (Ed.), *Black Greek-letter organizations in the 21st century: Our fight has just begun* (pp. 291–312). Lexington: University Press of Kentucky.

Dowd, N. E. (2010). Asking the man question: Masculinities analysis and feminist theory. *Harvard Journal of Law & Gender, 33*(2), 415–430.

Dunn, L. L. (2013). Addressing sexual violence in higher education: Ensuring compliance with the Clery Act, Title IX and VAWA. *Georgetown Journal of Gender and the Law, 15*, 563–584.

Edwards, J. T. (2009). Sorority chapter members' perspectives of chapter racial integration. *Oracle: The Research Journal of the Association of Fraternity/Sorority Advisors, 4*, 42–54.

Evans, J., Frank, B., Oliffe, J. L., & Gregory, D. (2011). Health, illness, men and masculinities (HIMM): A theoretical framework for understanding men and their health. *Journal of Men's Health, 8*(1), 7–15. doi:10.1016/j.jomh.2010.09.227

Finkel, M. A. (2002). Traumatic injuries caused by hazing practices. *American Journal of Emergency Medicine, 20*(3), 228–233.

Harper, S. R., & Harris, F., III. (2010). *College men and masculinities: Theory, research, and implications for practice.* San Francisco, CA: Jossey-Bass.

HazingPrevention.org. (2015). *Hidden harm.* Retrieved from http://hazingprevention.org/home/hazing/hidden-harm/

Hesp, G. A., & Brooks, J. S. (2009). Heterosexism and homophobia on fraternity row: A case study of a college fraternity community. *Journal of LGBT Youth, 6*, 395–415.

Higher Education Center for Alcohol and Drug Misuse Prevention and Recovery. (2017). *Other drug use.* Retrieved from http://hecaod.osu.edu/campus-professionals/prevention/other-drugs/

Holman, M., & Johnson, J. (2015). Moving from awareness toward prevention. *Physical & Health Education Journal, 81*(2), 1–27.

Hoover, N. C. (2000). *Initiation rites in American high schools: A national survey.* Retrieved from www.alfred.edu/hs_hazing/

Jones, C. M. (2000). In loco parentis and higher education: Together again? *Charleston Law Review, 185*(1), 185–206.

Knutson, N. M., Akers, K. S., Ellis, C. K., & Bradley, K. D. (2011). *Applying the Rasch model to explore new college sorority and fraternity members' perceptions of hazing behavior.* Retrieved from www.uky.edu/~kdbrad2/MWERA_Nikki.pdf

Lake, P. F. (1999). The rise and fall of in loco parentis and other protective tort doctrines in higher education law. *Missouri Law Review, 64*(1), 1–28.

McCreary, G. (2015, July). Five reasons we are failing to move the needle when it comes to hazing prevention. *Essentials, D*(6). Retrieved from https://c.ymcdn.com/sites/afa1976.site-ym.com/resource/collection/85281FF1-F44B-40A8-A44A-696D3A7E9867/Five_Reasons_We_Are_Failing_to_Move_the_Needle_When_It_Comes__to_Hazing_-_Researcher.pdf

McGinley, M., Rospenda, K. M., Liu, L., & Richman, J. A. (2016). It isn't all just fun and games: Collegiate participation in extracurricular activities and risk for generalized and sexual harassment, psychological distress, and alcohol use. *Journal of Adolescence*, *53*, 152–163.

National Collegiate Athletic Association. (2007). *Building new traditions: Hazing prevention in college athletics*. Retrieved from www.ncaa.org/sites/default/files/hazing%20 prevention%20handbook%2057315.pdf

National Institute on Alcohol Abuse and Alcoholism. (2015). *College drinking*. Retrieved from https://pubs.niaaa.nih.gov/publications/collegefactsheet/Collegefactsheet.pdf

Parks, G. S., Jones, S. E., Ray, R., Hughey, M. W., & Cox, J. M. (2015). White boys drink, black girls yell . . . a racialized and gendered analysis of violent hazing and the law. *Journal of Gender, Race and Justice*, *18*(1), 93–123.

Parks, G. S., & Spencer, D. (2013). Student affairs professionals, black "Greek" hazing, and university civil liability. *College Student Affairs Journal*, *31*(2), 125–138.

Patton, L. D., Bridges, B. K., & Flowers, L. A. (2011). Effects of Greek affiliation on African American students' engagement: Differences by college racial composition. *College Student Affairs Journal*, *29*(2), 113–123; 177–179.

Rosenberg, S., & Mosca, J. (2016). Risk management in college fraternities: Guidance from two faculty advisors. *Contemporary Issues in Education Research (Online)*, *9*(1), 7–14.

Sanday, P. R. (2007). *Fraternity gang rape: Sex, brotherhood and privilege on campus* (2nd ed.). New York: New York University Press.

Scott-Sheldon, L. A., Carey, K. B., Kaiser, T. S., Knight, J. M., & Carey, M. P. (2016). Alcohol interventions for Greek letter organizations: A systematic review and meta-analysis, 1987 to 2014. *Health Psychology*, *35*(7), 670–684.

Sweet, S. (1999). Understanding fraternity hazing: Insights from symbolic interactionist theory. *Journal of College Student Development*, *40*(4), 355.

Trump, J., & Wallace, J. A. (2006). Gay males in fraternities. *Oracle: The Research Journal of the Association of Fraternity/Sorority Advisors*, *2*, 8–28.

Chapter 13

Closing Discussion
Disrupting Hazing Myths as a Strategy to Changing Culture

Leslie Schacht Drey, Natalie Rooney, Michelle L. Boettcher, and Cristóbal Salinas Jr.

The final chapter of this book is designed to build on the case studies included throughout the text. In addition to organization- and topic-specific case studies, in order to truly transform culture related to hazing on campus, we must look at hazing more broadly. This final chapter presents a series of hazing myths in the form of case studies. Paired with the other chapters in this text, this section is designed to help organizations, members, leaders, and advisers critically examine and begin to dismantle hazing culture that may exist in their groups and on their campuses.

We have identified common myths related to hazing practices and hazing culture, along with questions and connections to specific chapters. These can be used in reflective practice not only in individual organizations but also across larger organizations and with staff and administrators to examine hazing culture on campus more broadly.

Hazing habits are perpetuated in a variety of different settings despite efforts to prevent, educate, address, and enforce policy and change culture. These behaviors persist largely due to the myths and misconceptions around hazing that exist. These myths and misconceptions can be toxic in organizations and can undermine efforts to eliminate or change behavior.

Throughout this chapter, we address several of the myths related to hazing in group settings and organizations. This is not an all-encompassing list; rather, these are a handful of the most popular and pervasive myths that exist today related to hazing behavior. Seven hazing myths and misunderstandings are presented next.

MYTH 1: EVERYTHING CAN BE CONSIDERED HAZING (CHAPTER 1)

The saying "everything can be considered hazing" is often used as an excuse for those groups that continue to utilize hazing as way to indoctrinate new members into the organization. Rather than choosing to recognize that hazing relates specifically to harmful and damaging activities, some members choose to reason that any

CLOSING DISCUSSION

group activity could be considered hazing. This claim is illogical, as there are many options for safer activities that can be implemented in place of hazing activities that still meet the same or similar intent. The rationale that everything is hazing is a poor excuse and shows a lack of interest in actually understanding the topic.

Create a list of new member activities that are part of the joining or intake process for your organization. Identify those that clearly *do not* constitute hazing, those that *could* constitute hazing, and those that truly *do* constitute hazing according to the definitions in this book (see Chapter 1).

Allan and Madden (2008): Any activity expected of someone joining or participating in a group that humiliates, degrades, abuses, or endangers them regardless of a person's willingness to participate.

(p. 2)

Cholbi (2009): Any method of initiation into a student organization, or any pastime or amusement engaged in with regard to such an organization that causes, or is likely to cause bodily danger or physical or emotional harm to any member of the campus community.

(p. 144)

Finkel (2002): Committing acts against an individual or forcing an individual into committing an act that creates a risk for harm in order for the individual to be initiated into or affiliated with an organization.

(p. 228)

Lipkins (2006): A process, based on a tradition [habit] that is used by groups to discipline and to maintain a hierarchy (i.e., a pecking order). Regardless of consent, the rituals require individuals to engage in activities that are physically and psychologically stressful.

(p. 13)

Discussion

1. How is your new member process designed to strengthen your organization?
2. How is your new member process designed to empower your new members?
3. When you hear of or witness hazing in your organization or others, why do you think those practices have emerged?
4. What is the purpose of having a joining or membership intake process for your organization?
5. What steps can or should you take if you witness or hear about hazing in your organization? In another organization?

MYTH 2: HAZING EXISTS ONLY IN FRATERNITIES AND SORORITIES (CHAPTERS 4, 5, 6, 7, 12)

Although fraternities and sororities have dominated popular culture related to hazing stereotypes and depictions and are perhaps some of the most public organizations to have high-profile hazing incidents, hazing is prevalent in a wide variety of groups and organizations. All organizations must be vigilant when it comes to monitoring their membership processes to ensure that hazing habits are not part of their organizational experience. Hazing perpetuates in group activities as early as junior high or high school and appears in athletic and sport teams, cheerleading and dance teams, band and performing arts, the military, and student organizations (including fraternities and sororities).

Discussion

1. What events currently exist on your campus where different organizations come together to discuss hazing habits across campus?
2. What new initiatives can you think of for different types of organizations to collaborate around disrupting and transforming hazing culture at your institution?
3. What are similarities in new member processes for different types of organizations on campus?
4. What are some particularly effective elements of new member processes, that do not include hazing, in different types of organizations on campus? How can those be adapted to other organizations?

MYTH 3: WOMEN ARE NOT HAZED (CHAPTER 11)

For many people, when they think about hazing, they imagine movies or TV shows that depict males forcing other males to engage in harmful behavior. However, hazing is not exclusive to male-identified people. According to Allan and Madden (2008), hazing is not as predominant in women's only organizations, but it does still occur with frequency. Of the 55% of overall respondents for their study who indicated they had experienced hazing within their organizations, 61% of those were male and 52% were female (Allan & Madden, 2008).

Women tend to utilize less physical forms of hazing that include yelling, emotional and mental abuse, and verbal abuse. Women also do not frequently identify many of their behaviors as hazing; however, when the behaviors are described, they do identify with them, confirming that hazing behavior is present. Hazing occurs with all genders in different forms.

Discussion

1. What is the role of gender in hazing? Why do you think men engage in more physical hazing and women tend to yell or engage in mental and emotional hazing?
2. How does the idea that gender impacts hazing affect groups with members who are both men and women?
3. In what ways can men and women come together to talk about hazing? Are there conversations groups should have where they need to be separated by gender? Why or why not?
4. In what ways can or should women be a part of disrupting men's hazing practices, and can or should men be a part of disrupting women's hazing practices?

MYTH 4: ONLY PHYSICAL HAZING IS HARMFUL (CHAPTERS 11, 12, 13)

Psychological forms of hazing include verbal, mental, and emotional hazing, such as tests, manipulation, servitude, sleep deprivation, verbal abuse, and more. According to LaRose (2014), "Those who have a history of trauma may be even more at risk for negative psychological reactions to hazing. The hazing may trigger reactions to previous victimization, which can have devastating consequences for the victim" (para. 10).

These types of hazing can have the same effects as physical abuse, can last as long as injuries from physical abuse, and are complicated by the fact that they leave no visible marks or scars. Those who have been hazed may have trouble with self-esteem, depression, anxiety, or issues within relationships. As Finkel (2002) reported, "Victims may require long-term support and psychological help to cope with the hazing episode(s)" (p. 232).

Discussion

1. Does all hazing have emotional, mental, or psychological effects? Why or why not?
2. How can leaders and advisers assess the potential damage of new member events or group rites of passage when it comes to these types of invisible injuries?
3. Who is available on your campus to help with stress, trauma, and mental, emotional, and psychological support, whether related to hazing or not?
4. Where is the line between anxiety and nervousness about joining an organization and mental, emotional, and psychological hazing perpetrated by the organization?

MYTH 5: HAZING BUILDS UNITY AMONG NEW MEMBERS (PREFACE, CHAPTERS 3, 11, 12)

The belief that hazing builds unity among new members is troubling and perhaps one of the most pervasive of the myths included here. Although proponents for hazing argue that it builds mental toughness, hazing can also build significant animosity between hazing victims and hazing perpetrators. Allan and Madden (2008) found that less than a third of students surveyed agreed that hazing helps students feel more like a part of the organization they were seeking to join. Animosity and a lack of community as a result of hazing have also been discussed in other studies (Johnson & Chin, 2015; Johnson, 2011).

Discussion

1. Why do you think people believe hazing creates community and membership bonds?
2. How can those same outcomes be achieved without hazing?
3. What are the potential risks to brotherhood, sisterhood, membership, and the organization when hazing habits are used as a means of bringing new members into your organization?

MYTH 6: NEW MEMBERS *WANT* TO BE HAZED (CHAPTERS 3, 11, 12)

"Hazing is the result of power, influence, and social hierarchies" (Burns, 2015, p. 100). In the vast majority of organizational and institutional hazing policies, the desire or approval to participate is not a defense when charged with a hazing offense. Willing participation can be a further illustration of the way hazing deeply infiltrates organizational culture and is seen as a means to be accepted and affirmed by the rest of the group as a full member. As hazing is further sensationalized in pop culture, students come into certain group settings expecting to be hazed, and some even request for it to occur to experience an "accepted" rite of passage.

Discussion

1. Wanting to belong to a group or wanting to be part of a community can easily be confused with new members wanting to be hazed. Discuss how this might look different in different contexts (joining a group, alcohol use, language related to sexual encounters, etc.).
2. What options exist for new members in your organization to raise concerns about how they are being treated? What are the realistic responses or outcomes for potential members who raise those concerns?

3. Research shows that people rationalize traumatic hazing experiences. In other words, "What I went through was so bad, it has to be worth it to be a part of this group." How does this belief reflect the value of belonging to an organization?

MYTH 7: IF YOU DO NOT HAVE THE SAME EXPERIENCE AS THOSE BEFORE YOU, THEN YOUR MEMBERSHIP IS NOT VALID (CHAPTER 12)

The notion that you must experience hazing activities in order to be a valid member of an organization is one of the deepest penetrating reasons that hazing continues to exist. As Bloom and Cuevas wrote in Chapter 12 of this text, "A pervasive mode of thinking exists that 'because I had to go through this experience and survived, so should you.'" When older members of an organization assert that new members' worth is based on their participation in dangerous hazing activities, it sets a harmful precedent that likely does not align with their organization's mission and purpose.

Often this myth of membership validity linked to hazing causes new members to believe in the previous myth in this chapter that they "desire" to be hazed so that they will be accepted as a valid member of the organization. Cimino (2011) has written about these issues and asserted that being hazed as a cost of admission for an organization instills in both established and aspiring members a sense of connection. Group members, especially older leaders, must think critically about the purpose of membership in their organizations to understand that hazing does not and should not have a purpose in their value as members.

Discussion

1. Reflect on your joining experiences for the organizations to which you belong. What were the key moments in those experiences? When did you first feel like a member? Why did you feel like a member?
2. How do the membership processes for your organizations align with what your stated values are as an organization? For example, if respect is a key aspect of your organization, how is respect modeled during the intake process? How is leadership modeled during those processes?
3. What non-hazing experiences can be established and new or incoming members share to forge lasting and genuine connections and bonds?

CONCLUSION

This chapter was designed not only to highlight existing myths around hazing but also to provide interactive ways for individuals, organizations, and administrators to talk about and disrupt those myths on their own campuses. Providing a successful intervention to prevent and address hazing behavior must be multi-faceted, and the place to start is understanding the intent of hazing habits. When hazing habits occur in an organization, the rationale is to recruit and shape a certain type of member, to foster a certain type of environment, and to meet the expectations, goals, and mission of an organization. By analyzing how hazing habits actually work against these outcomes and focusing instead on how these same goals can be achieved by doing more values-aligned, legal, and safe activities, dangerous and damaging behavior can be prevented and organizations will have the potential to thrive in new and more meaningful ways. The attraction of creating new traditions and leaving a legacy on an organization can be a convincing reason to end harmful behaviors and replace them with productive activities aligned with organizational values.

Myths have the power to shape a person's understanding of hazing, and as long as these myths are allowed to perpetuate, we will struggle to permanently eradicate hazing from our organizations. Educators and advisers of these organizations must work to dispel these myths by teaching group members how to recognize signs of hazing as well as how and where to report it. In partnership with advisers, organizational members, leaders, and alumni can provide groups with alternative ideas that will lead them to better outcomes without engaging in harmful behavior. This chapter is designed to provide tools for identifying and dismantling hazing habits while developing healthy recruitment and intake processes to foster stronger and more productive groups and organizations.

REFERENCES

Allan, E. J., & Madden, M. (2008). *Hazing in view: College students at risk*. Retrieved from www.stophazing.org/wp-content/uploads/2014/06/hazing_in_view_web1.pdf

Burns, J. M. (2015). Covering up an infection with a bandage: A call to action to address flaws in Ohio's anti-hazing legislation. *Akron Law Review, 48*(1), 91–126.

Cholbi, M. (2009). On hazing. *Public Affairs Quarterly, 23*(2), 143–160.

Cimino, A. (2011). The evolution of hazing: Motivational mechanisms and the abuse of newcomers. *Journal of Cognition and Culture, 11*, 241–267.

Finkel, M. A. (2002). Traumatic injuries caused by hazing practices. *American Journal of Emergency Medicine, 20*(3), 228–233.

Johnson, J. (2011). Through the liminal: A comparative analysis of communities and rites of passage in sport hazing and initiations. *Canadian Journal of Sociology, 36*(3), 199–227.

Johnson, J., & Chin, J. W. (2015). Hazing rites/rights: Using outdoor- and adventure education-based orientation to effect positive change for first-year athletes. *Journal of Adventure Education and Outdoor Learning, 16*(1), 16–30.

LaRose, L. (2014, October). *Beyond bullying: The long-term effects of hazing on young adults.* Retrieved from www.theravive.com/today/post/beyond-bullying-the-long-term-effects-of-hazing-on-young-adults-0001766.aspx

Lipkins, S. (2006). *Preventing hazing: How parents, teachers and coaches can stop the violence, harassment and humiliation.* San Francisco, CA: Jossey-Bass.

Author Biographies

Cameron C. Beatty, PhD, is an assistant professor of higher education and student affairs at Salem State University. He earned his PhD in higher education and student affairs at Iowa State University in 2014 and taught in their leadership studies program from 2013 to 2016. His research foci include the intersections of gender and race in leadership education, retention of students of color on historically white college campuses, and global leadership education for undergraduate students.

Jennifer L. Bloom, EdD, is an associate professor and coordinator of the higher education leadership MEd program in the educational leadership and research methodology department at Florida Atlantic University. Her research interests include appreciative advising, appreciative education, appreciate administration, and careers in higher education administration.

Michelle L. Boettcher, PhD, is an assistant professor at Clemson University. Prior to this role, she worked as assistant dean of students and director of the Office of Judicial Affairs at Iowa State University. She has also held housing positions at a variety of institutions. Her research focuses on senses of belonging and community in the context of higher education—specifically around faculty and marginalized populations.

Raquel Botello, PhD, is an assistant professor of psychology at Texas A&M University–Corpus Christi. Her research focuses on understanding multicultural factors that influence psychological well-being and educational outcomes specifically in ethnic and racial minority college students. Her work also emphasizes the clinical training of the developing therapist in working with diverse clients of various marginalized identities.

Natalie Carlos Cruz, PsyD, is a licensed psychologist who works in the Project Heal program at the University of Southern California's Center for Excellence in Developmental Disabilities at Children's Hospital of Los Angeles. She provides clinical intake assessments, trauma-informed psychological evaluations, and individual, collateral, and family

AUTHOR BIOGRAPHIES

therapy to children and families who are grieving and/or have experienced traumatic experiences by utilizing various evidence-based treatment models in English and Spanish. Her research interests include issues of diversity and mental health, especially grief, trauma, and resilience processes.

Amanda E. Propst Cuevas, PhD, is director of the Office of Appreciative Education at Florida Atlantic University, where she advances initiatives that apply the appreciative advising theory-to-practice framework to promote positive education. Her research interests are centered in the areas of appreciative education that intersect student success/thriving and organizational excellence.

Leslie Schacht Drey, MEd, is assistant dean of student life and director of the Center for Fraternity and Sorority Life at Oregon State University. She is a volunteer for her sorority, Alpha Chi Omega, and for Delta Sigma Phi Fraternity. She is a passionate advocate for the fraternity/sorority experience, and her research interests are in student governance, prevention, advocacy, and accountability work on college campuses.

S. Brian Joyce, PhD, is director of Greek life at Dartmouth College. He has served in various student affairs roles for more than 14 years. His research interests include exploring how privileged identities reify dominant structures in higher education and examining the production of hegemonic masculinity among college men.

Shawn Knight, MEd, is a judicial officer at the University of California, Davis. His background in student affairs involves working in student conduct administration, LGBTQ+ student services, and fraternity advising and facilitation. HIs areas of research interest include the intersectionality of gender expression, sexual orientation, and masculinities within single-gender organizations.

Jenny Nirh, PhD, is assistant director for academic success and achievement at the University of Arizona. Her research interests include student success, hazing, and fraternity and sorority life.

Cristina J. Perez, MEd, is the curriculum design coordinator at Alpha Delta Pi Sorority's executive office. In this role, she leads education, training, inclusion, and leadership initiatives for the sorority, reaching collegiate, alumni, and volunteer members.

Mary Peterson, MA, was the first executive director of Sigma Lambda Beta International Fraternity and Sigma Lambda Gamma Sorority National Sorority, and she served as the associate director of the Office of Student Life at the University of Iowa for 24 years. Her 35 years working in the fraternal community in a variety of roles has given her great insight into student success, leadership, hazing, and fraternity and sorority life.

AUTHOR BIOGRAPHIES

Jennifer Plagman-Galvin, MPA, is director of operations for the College of Human Sciences and a doctoral candidate at Iowa State University. Her professional experience includes student affairs, academic affairs, and nonprofit work serving as an assistant dean of students for Greek affairs, the National Panhellenic Conference Delegation for Pi Beta Phi, and a member of the Pi Beta Phi Grand Council. Her research includes multicultural competence development and multicultural work of student affairs educators.

Natalie Rooney, MEd, works in new student programs and family outreach at Oregon State University. She serves as a chapter adviser for Kappa Delta Sorority and cochaired a university task force on the health and sustainability of the fraternity and sorority community. Her research interests focus on the racial identity development of fraternity and sorority students of color in predominantly white institutions and on access to higher education.

Cristóbal Salinas Jr., PhD, is an assistant professor in the educational leadership and research methodology department at Florida Atlantic University. His research promotes access to and quality in higher education and explores the social, political, and economic context of educational opportunities for historically marginalized communities of people.

Jason M. Silveira, PhD, teaches a variety of music education classes at the University of Oregon and is also the conductor of the University of Oregon Symphonic Band. His research interests include music perception and cognition, psychology of music, teacher effectiveness, and psychophysiological responses to music.

Ethan Swingle is a doctoral student in the educational leadership and research methodology department at Florida Atlantic University's College of Education. His research interests include the faculty athletic representative's role in intercollegiate athletics, the impact student-athlete support systems have on student-athletes, and the academic progress rate for student-athletes.

Index

Note: Page numbers in bold indicate tables and those in italics indicate figures.

administrators, hazing prevention role of 33–34
Alabama 86, 88
Alaska 86, 102
alcohol-related hazing events 31–32, 140
Alfred University 31, 92, 93
Allan, E. J. 5, 29, 44, 54, 86, 92–93, 138, 139, 141, 144, 153, 154, 156
Alpha Delta Pi 53
Alpha Phi National 78
Alvarez, D. M. 86
American Literary, Scientific, and Military Academy 66
American Psychiatric Association (APA) 116, 119
American Psychological Association (APA) 130
Ammon, R. 34
appreciative advising, phases of 130–131; see also hazing prevention, appreciative approach to
Arizona 88, 92
Arkansas 87, 88
Arnett, J. J. 114
Aronson, E. 129
Ashton, Jeff 41
Asian American fraternities 54
Assembly Bill 1173 (New Jersey) 87
Assembly Bill 2795 (New York) 87
athletics hazing 17–19; organizational practices in 88–89
awareness campaigns/programs 143

band hazing 15–16
Bandura, A. 56–57, 113
Barbaranelli, C. 113
Barron, Eric J. 105
Baruch College 58
Bates College 34
Bauer, B. Y. R. 42
Be a Champion Foundation 47
belonging, group memberships and 114, 130
Berkeley, Edward Fairchild 52
Berkowitz, A. 146
Beta Theta Pi 58
Biddix, J. P. 137–138
Big Questions, Worthy Dreams: Mentoring Emerging Adults in Their Search for Meaning, Purpose, and Faith (Parks) 130
Black fraternities 53
Black Haze (Jones) 14–15
Bloom, L. R. 14
Bogenberger, David 8
Boster, J. S. 68
Bowdoin College 58

INDEX

Bray, N. 113
Bruce, S. 128
Brueckner, William C. Jr. 69
Building New Traditions: Hazing Prevention in College Athletics (NCAA) 143
bullying: defined 111; *vs.* hazing 111–113; as interpersonal aggression 112
Burning Sands (film) 58
bystander intervention 145

California 86, 88
California State University, Long Beach 35
Colorado 89
Campo, S. 54, 116, 120
Cantalupo, N. C. 139
Caprara, G. V. 113
Carter, B. A. 43–44
case studies: college marching bands, hazing and 47–49; fraternities and sororities 59–61; intercollegiate athletics, hazing and 36–37; military hazing 71–73
Center for Collegiate Mental Health 138–139
Chamberlain, B. W. 86
Champion, Robert 8, 40–41, 42, 45, 104
Chen, Daniel 89–90
Cholbi, M. 5, 153
Chu, Judy 90
Cimino, A. 126–128, 157
The Citadel hazing case 70
Clery Center 46–47
Clinton, George 66
coaches, hazing prevention role of 34
Cokley, K. 56
Colby College 58
College and University Athletic Band Guidelines 47
College Band Directors National Association (CBDNA) 47
college marching bands, hazing and 40–49; case studies 47–49; Champion, Robert example 40–41; future research for 45–47; history of 41–43;

literature review of 43–45; practice recommendations for 45–47
College of William and Mary 52
Collins, I. 128
conflict, value of 77
Connecticut 86, 89
consideration, group effectiveness and 65
Cornelius, A. E. 128
Cornell University 30, 52
Covey, S. 4
crisis intervention model 118
Crotty, M. 14
Crow, B. 34
cultural transformation 106–107
culture/climate assessment 94
Cumberledge, J. P. 41–42

Daily Collegian 102
Dartmouth College 30, 58
Dear Colleague Letter (Office of Civil Rights) 87–88
death toll, due to hazing 7–8, 54, 86
dedication 79
Deering, H. 128
Deitch-Stackhouse, J. 146
Delaware 86
deliver phase of appreciative advising 133–134
Delta Kappa Epsilon 103
Delta Upsilon fraternity 103
demographics 140–141
Deng, Chun Hsieng 58
design phase of appreciative advising 133
Diagnostic and Statistical Manual of Mental Disorders 116
disarm phase of appreciative advising 131
discover phase of appreciative advising 131–132
Divine Nine 53
Dixon, M. 96
don't settle phase of appreciative advising 134
Dowd, N. E. 139

dream phase of appreciative advising 132–133
drug-related hazing events 140
Drury University 31
Dunn, L. L. 138

educational institutions: defined 91; hazing obligation of 91–92
educational training, hazing and 82–84, 143–145
Ellsworth, C. W. 43
enforcement and accountability 95–96
ERADICATE model 46
euphemistic labeling, hazing as form of 57
Evans, J. 139

fagging 7
federal/state level hazing policies and legislation 86–98; in athletics 88–89; culture and climate assessment 94; disrupting hazing practices 92–93; educational institutions and 91–92; enforcement and accountability 95–96; federal guidance, lack of 87–88; in fraternity/sorority life 90; future research for 96; hazing T-chart activity 97–98, *98*; implications for practice 94–96; in military 89–90; organizational types and role of 88–90; oversight 95; prevention and education 94–95; public policy 86; state definitions 86–87
Finkel, M. A. 5, 153, 155
Firestone, J. M. 68
Fitzgerald, Thomas 69
Florida 86, 88, 89, 92, 104
Florida Agricultural and Mechanical University (FAMU) 8, 104; Champion, Robert hazing incident 40–41
Florida State University 102; Hazing Education Initiative 32
Fordham University 34
Frank, B. 139

fraternal organization hazing 16–17, 22–23
fraternities 52–61; Asian American 54; Black 53; case studies 59–61; challenges in 58–59; diversification of 53–54; exclusivity in 55; group member transition phases 55; hazing as ongoing issue in 54–55; hazing/tradition connections 56; history of 52; moral disengagement, hazing and 56–57; multicultural 53–54; opportunities in 59; organizational practices in 90; overview of 52; Peterson on 77–78; tradition in 55–56; trends in 57–58; women's 53
fraternity hazing 19–20

Ganellen, B. D. 42
Georgia 104
Gettysburg College 58
GI Bill 54
Goat (film) 58
Godfrey, R. 67
Goodrich, Bruce 69
Gregory, D. 139
group identity, hazing and 129
Gruver, Maxwell Raymond 105

habits: defined 4; hazing as 3–4, 80
Harris, R. J. 68
Harry Lew Military Hazing Accountability and Prevention Act of 2012 90
Harvard Phi Beta Kappa fraternity 7
#40answers campaign 143
Hawaii 86, 102
hazee/victim, psychological impacts on **115**
hazer/perpetrator, psychological impacts on **115**
hazing: alcohol-related **31**–32; barriers to reporting 92–93; benefits of 129–130; as bonding tool 129; *vs.* bullying 111–113; categories of 5–6; consequences of 93; death toll due to 7–8, 54, 86; definitions of 5–6, 9, 42, 45, 126; downside of

INDEX

128–129; educational institutions and, obligation of 91–92; educational training and 82–84; examples 8–9; federal legislation regarding 87–88; firsthand accounts of (*see* hazing testimonies); first reported case of 28; as form of euphemistic labeling 57; group identity and 129; as habit 3–4; history of 7–8; lessons learned about (*see* Peterson, Mary); marching bands and 41–43; moral disengagement and 56–57; moral justification of 57; myths, disrupting 152–158; organizational change and 80–81, 88–90; overview of 3; penalties 93; Peterson on 79–80; preventing 137–149; psychological shadow of 111–122; public policy on 86; reasons for 126–128; role of, in organizations (*see* organizations, role of hazing in); sense of belonging and 130; state definitions of 86–87; *vs.* team building **127**, 129; traumatic 116; vulnerability to, factors increasing 116–117

hazing audits 106

hazing box activity 10, *10–11*

hazing myths, disrupting 152–158; everything can be considered hazing 152–153; hazing builds unity among members 156; hazing exists only in fraternities/sororities 154; new members want to be hazed 156–157; only physical hazing is harmful 155; women are not hazed 154–155; you must experience hazing activities to be valid member 157

hazing policies: at federal/state levels 86–98; lessons learned 77–85; postsecondary education 101–107; *see also* Peterson, Mary

hazing practices, disrupting 92–93

hazing prevention, appreciative approach to 126–135; deliver phase 133–134; design phase 133; disarm phase 131; discover phase 131–132; don't settle phase 134;

dream phase 132–133; hazing, defined 126; hazing benefits 129–130; hazing downsides 128–129; overview of 130–131; reasons groups haze 126–128

Hazing Prevention Consortium 47

HazingPrevention.org 32, 33, 142, 143

Hazing Statutes 88–89, 90

hazing T-chart activity 97–98, *98*

hazing testimonies 14–23; athletics hazing 17–19; band hazing 15–16; Black Greek fraternities 14–15; fraternal organization hazing 16–17, 22–23; fraternity hazing 19–20; overview of 14–15; residential life hazing 21

hidden harm 142–143

hierarchy needs, eliminating 145

higher education: alcohol/drugs and 140; hazing related issues in 138–140; mental health and 138–139; military hazing and 65–66; Title IX legislation and 138; toxic masculinity and 139–140

Higher Education Center for Alcohol and Drug Misuse and Prevention 140

Hobart College 28

Hollmann, B. 7–8, 54, 94, 95

Holman, M. 144

Holmes, R. W. 46, 128–129

Hoover, N. C. 29, 115

Hudson, M. W. 20, 44–45, 47

Hughey, M. W. 55

Indiana 87

Indiana Senate Bill 343 87

information sharing 105

initiating structure, group effectiveness and 65

Initiation Rites and Athletics for NCAA Sports Teams (Hoover) 28

Integrative Assessment, Crisis Intervention, and Trauma Treatment (ACT) model 117–119

Intercollegiate Athletic Association 27

intercollegiate athletics, hazing and 27–37; administrators' role in preventing

33–34; case studies 36–37; coaches' role in preventing 34; current cases of 30–31; defined 27; history of 28–29; likelihood of 29; overview of 27; past cases of 29–30; prevention measures 32–33; student-athletes' role in preventing 34–35; trends in 31–32, **31–32**
interpersonal aggression 112
Inter-Sorority Council 53
Iowa 86

Jewett, R. 28–29
Jezebel 104
Johnson, J. 144
Jones, R. L. 14–15
Jones, S. E. 55

Kaplin, W. A. 91
Kappa Alpha Society 52
Kappa Kappa Psi 43
Keller, K. M. 67, 68
Kenneavy, K. 146
Kentucky 86, 92
Kerr, G. 28–29
Kihss, P. 69
Kleinknecht v. Gettysburg College 42
Kotakis, P. N. 65–66
Kowalski, C. L. 28
Kress, H. C. 68

LaRose, L. 155
leadership, hazing prevention through 81–82
Lee, B. A. 91
Lee, K. 102
Leggett, Mortimer 52
Lipkins, S. 5, 7, 153
Louisiana State University 102, 105
Luther, M. 7

MacPherson, E. 28–29
Madden, M. 5, 29, 44, 54, 86, 92–93, 138, 139, 141, 144, 153, 154, 156

Maine 86, 91, 92
Maine West High School 8
Mann, B. 65
Mascari, J. 146
Massachusetts 86, 92, 102
Massachusetts Institute of Technology (MIT) 103; Hazing Prevention and Education Committee 32, 103
Matthews, W. K. 46
McCreary, G. 113, 144, 145
McGlone, C. A. 5
Mead, J. 65
mental hazing 6
mental health 138–139
Michigan 86, 88, 90, 91
Middlebury College 58
Milgram, S. 113
Military Commander and the Law, The (Judge Advocate General's School) 143
military hazing 65–73; case studies 71–73; The Citadel case of 70; definition of 66–67; further research for 71; higher education and 65–66; Norwich University ROTC case of 69; organizational practices in 89–90; overview of 65; St. John's University ROTC case of 69; Texas A&M University ROTC case of 69; types of 67; University of New Hampshire ROTC case of 70; in university programs 67–68; Virginia Military Institute case of 70
Mills, J. 129
Mississippi 86
Missouri 86
Montana 86, 102
Montclair State University 103
moral disengagement, hazing and 56–57, 113
moral justification of hazing 57
Morehouse College 53
multicultural fraternities 53–54
Murray, M. 65
Mu Sigma Upsilon 53
myths *see* hazing myths, disrupting

INDEX

National Asian Pacific Islander American Panhellenic Association 78
National Association of Intercollegiate Athletics 27
National Association of Latino Fraternal Organizations 53
National Collegiate Athletic Association (NCAA) 27, 33, 95, 126, 143
National Defense Act of 1916 65
National Hazing Prevention Week 143
National Institute of Mental Health (NIMH) 117
National Institute on Alcohol Abuse and Alcoholism 140
National Junior College Athletic Association 27
National Multicultural Greek Council 53–54
National Panhellenic Conference 53
National Study of Student Hazing 54
Nebraska 86, 87
Neiberg, M. S. 66
Nesbitt, Henry 40–41
Nevada 86
New Jersey 87, 103
New Jersey Assembly Bill 1173 87
New Mexico 86, 102
New York 86, 87
North-American Interfraternity Conference 53
Northern Illinois University, Pi Kappa Alpha fraternity 8
Northwestern University 30, 35
Norwich University ROTC hazing case 69
Nuwer, H. 43, 45, 54, 90

Office of Civil Rights 87–88
Ohio State University 102
Oklahoma 86, 92
Oliffe, J. L. 139
open channels of communication 147
organizational accountability 106

organizational hazing practices 88–90; in athletics 88–89; in fraternity/sorority life 90; in military 89–90
organizations, role of hazing in: college marching band 40–49; educational training and 82–84; fraternities and sororities 52–61; intercollegiate athletics 27–37; military university programs 65–73; reflection questions 84–85
oversight 95

Parks, G. S. 55, 140–141, 144
Parks, Sharon Daloz 130
Pastorelli, C. 113
peer mentor 147
penalties, hazing 93
pennalism 7
Pennsylvania 86
Pennsylvania State University 58, 105; Phi Sigma Kappa fraternity 8
perpetrator, defined 4
Pershing, J. L. 68, 89
Pershing Rifles military society 69
Peterson, Mary 77–85; background of 78–79; educational training and 82–84; on fraternity and sorority life 77–78; on hazing 79–80; hazing prevention workshops and 82–84; leadership and 81–82; organizational change and 80–81
Phi Beta Kappa 52
Phi Delta Theta 105
Phillips, D. 34
Phi Mu Alpha 143
physical hazing 5
Piazza, Timothy 58, 105
Pi Beta Phi 53
Pledge's Bill of Rights 103
Pollard, N. J. 115
postsecondary education hazing policies 101–107; cultural transformation and 106; hazing audits and 106;

INDEX

information sharing and 105; organizational accountability and 106; overview of 101–102; prevention considerations 104–107; reactionary 102–104; student accountability and 105–106
posttraumatic stress disorder (PTSD) 116
Poulos, G. 54, 116
preventing hazing 137–149; alcohol/drugs and 140; assessments and 143–144; awareness campaigns/programs 143; bystander intervention and 145; changing mind-sets 145; community dynamics, building 145–148; considerations 137–138; education/training 143–145; hidden harm 142–143; hierarchy needs, eliminating 145; increased awareness and 141–143; institutional policy and 144; mental health and 138–139; overview of 137; reflection questions 148–149; student demographics and 140–141; Title IX legislation and 138; toxic masculinity and 139–140; training constituent groups 144–145; warning signs, recognizing 141–142
prevention/education 94–95
proactive aggression 112
proactive university anti-hazing policies 104–107; described 101–102
psychological shadow of hazing 111–122; ACT model and 117–119; assessment of needs 117–118; belonging, group memberships and 114; crisis intervention 118; hazing vs. bullying 111–113; implications for practitioners of 120–121; implications for research on 119–120; overview of 111; psychological consequences 115, **115**; reflection questions 121; social conformity, hazing obedience and 113; traumatic hazing 116; trauma treatment 119;

vulnerability to hazing, factors increasing 116–117
public policy on hazing 86

Ray, R. 55
reactionary university anti-hazing policies 102–104; described 101
reporting hazing, barriers to 92–93
Reserve Officers' Training Corps (ROTC) 65; founding institution of 66; indoctrination concept and 68
residential life hazing 21
Rhode Island 86, 93
Richardson, D. C. 102
Rider University 58
Roberts, A. 117–119
ROTC *see* Reserve Officers' Training Corps (ROTC)
Rutgers University 103

Sanday, P. R. 138
Schreiner, L. A. 130
Seligman, Martin 130
Senate Bill 343 (Indiana) 87
shared vision/goals 147
Shayne, E. 55
Sigma Alpha Epsilon, Iowa Beta Chapter 8
Sigma Lambda Beta International Fraternity 22, 78
Sigma Lambda Gamma National Sorority 78
Sigma Nu fraternity 143
Sigma Phi Epsilon 103
Silveira, J. M. 20, 44–45, 47
Sipple, J. W. 54, 116
social conformity, hazing obedience and 113
Sorin, Edward 41
sororities 52–61; Black 53; case studies 59–61; challenges in 58–59; diversification of 53–54; exclusivity in 55; group member transition phases

171

INDEX

55; hazing as ongoing issue in 54–55; hazing/tradition connections 56; history of 52; moral disengagement, hazing and 56–57; multicultural 53–54; opportunities in 59; organizational practices in 90; overview of 52; Peterson on 77–78; tradition in 55–56; trends in 57–58
Sosis, R. 68
South Carolina 86, 88
South Dakota, 86, 102
Spencer, D. 144
state definitions of hazing 86–87
Stirling, S. 28–29
St. John's University ROTC hazing case 69
St. Olaf College 30–31
StopHazing.org 47
student accountability 105–106
student-athletes, hazing prevention role of 34–35
student demographics 140–141
Substance Abuse and Mental Health Services Administration (SAMHSA) 116, 119
Sutters, P. 70
Sweet, S. 146

Tau Beta Sigma 43
Tau Kappa Epsilon 103
team building *vs.* hazing **127**, 129
Tennessee 89
Texas 87, 90, 92
Texas A&M University ROTC hazing case 69
Texas Senate Bill 87
Texas State University 102
Thayer, R. 146
Thoma, S. 113
Title IX legislation 138
toxic masculinity 139–140
traditions: defined 4; in fraternities/sororities 55–56; hazing and 3–4, 56

trauma: defined 116; treatment 119
traumatic hazing 116
Turner, T. 55

Ukura, K. 29–30
Union College 52
University of Florida 34
University of Iowa 8, 78
University of Kentucky 91
University of Louisville 91
University of Massachusetts Amherst (UMass) 102
University of Michigan 102
University of Minnesota 29–30
University of New Hampshire ROTC hazing case 70
University of Northern Colorado 29
University of Notre Dame 41
University of Texas System 106–107
University of Vermont 30
University of West Virginia 91
U.S. Department of Defense 66–67, 90
Utah 86, 93

Van Raalte, J. L. 128
Vermont 90, 92
Virginia Military Institute hazing case 70

Wade, George, Jr. 70
Waldron, J. J. 28
warning signs, recognizing 141–142
Washington 89
Wesleyan University 58
West Virginia 86
Wheaton College 31
Wilhem, Keiffer 89
Williams College 58
Wisconsin 86–87
women fraternities 53
Wyoming 86, 102

Yale Hazing Prevention Task Force 105–106
Young Harris College 103–104